Winning the
High Tech Sales Game

Winning the High Tech Sales Game

James T. Healy

With A Foreword by Jim Holden

Reston Publishing Company, Inc.
A Prentice-Hall Company
Reston, Virginia

Library of Congress Cataloging in Publication Data

Healy, James Thomas
  Winning the high tech sales game.

  Bibliography: p.
  Includes index.
  1. Selling—High technology. I. Title.
  HF5439.H54H43   1985   621.381'7'0688   84-15114
  ISBN 0-8359-8700-0

To my wife, Hwa-Cha, for her understanding and support

Contents

○ ## PART 1: The Person and the Tools

PART 2: The Customer and the Competitor

PART 3: The Manager and the Territory

Foreword

Being involved in sales, you have no doubt both won and lost orders. But, have you ever seriously thought about why you have won or lost? How many people would say, "I won because I had the best product," or, "I lost because of delivery"? Certainly these responses may reflect legitimate issues, but they do not address the fundamental reason for winning or losing—the existence of *sales control*. Control is setting the pace for the competition where they are competing with you versus you competing with them. It's not only getting the order, but getting the order in a timely manner and keeping the sales cycle as short as possible (See Figure 1).

Control in a sales situation is a function of organization. Organization, especially strategic organization of the selling process results in efficiency in terms of exposure to prospects and effectiveness in terms of hit rate or the number of prospects who become your customers, rather than the competitor's customers.

In a fast-paced competitive selling situation, the competition can be full of surprises. The question becomes, how do you handle them and inflict a few potent surprises of your own? More importantly, how do you achieve and maintain control of the selling situation and keep the competition at bay?

Suppose, for example, that as the customer is about to choose between your office automation system and a competitor's, your adversary suddenly offers a free-installation-and-trial period or cuts the price, both strong concessions leading to a close which your company cannot match. Do you simply slink sideways out the door? Or have you planned for such contingencies in a way that makes those competitive moves less harmful or even advantageous to you?

Or suppose the prospect is scheduled to visit your plant one day and the competition's plant the next. Usually it is very difficult to close the sale on the first day of the tour but you fear the competition might be able to close on the second day. Rearranging the dates is impossible, so now what do you do?

The basic question is: How do you develop the psychological side of the selling–buying relationship to your advantage? How do you take control?

Control is what *Winning the High Tech Sales Game* is all about. But it's not just a book cataloging a range of sales principles and techniques. It is a road map to becoming a strategic thinker.

Strategy stems from the Greek word *strategos*, which means the art of the generals, not the foot soldiers. Strategy is more than an approach to accomplishing a sales objective; it is a way of thinking.

To cite a simple example, suppose a salesperson is involved in a sales situation where the product being sold is red and the competition's is blue. Furthermore, the competition, making an important gain in controlling the selling situation, has demonstrated the value of having a blue product, which the customer now agrees is important.

The salesperson hears an objection: "We like your product, but wish you had it in blue." A foot soldier reacts by rushing to the hardware store for a can of blue paint or calling the factory and saying, "If we don't paint our product blue, we'll lose the order."

The strategist asks, "Why is blue important?" The strategist searches for the underlying concern which precipitates the objection. Perhaps the concern is over appearance. The strategist tries to show the customer how a red product, along with other minor changes, can act as an accent, thus enhancing the area's appearance. The strategist addresses the real concern and neutralizes the objection.

The strategist recognizes the essential components of a sound plan that is fit for a selling "general."

If maximizing control of a competitive sales situation is important, so too is the ability to think strategically. Control is a leadership quality that resides within the strategist, not the tactician or foot soldier. Clearly, salespeople must act as foot soldiers in day-to-day selling; the key, however, is not to think like one.

JIM HOLDEN

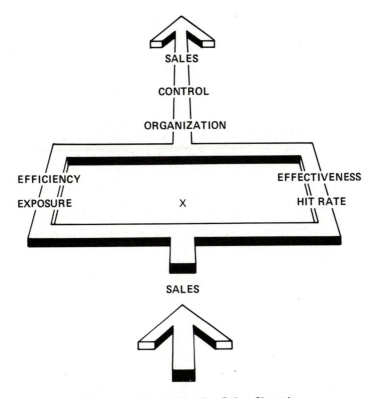

Figure 1: Control in the Sales Situation

Acknowledgments

This book intends to fill the need for a comprehensive, unified, and practical approach to selling high technology products and services. It is the product of 15 years of experience in high technology sales and sales management. I have drawn on this experience, and the expertise and works of many other people in developing this text. To these people I wish to express my sincerest gratitude.

This book would not have been possible without Jim Holden. His contribution in the areas of strategic planning and power selling is the keystone of this text. Jim, president of the Holden Corporation, a sales productivity company, is also a friend. Jim says, "A sales strategy or plan which is devoid of the politics involved is nothing more than a product plan. A sales strategy must incorporate both a product and a political component." Jim has provided me with information from his training courses, which will whet the reader's appetite for more. In sales training, it is not the written word but active participation and interaction that enhances sales skills.

Dr. Gunther Klaus, author of the sales training book, *Sell 'Em*, a fascinating and exciting lecturer on management by objectives and marketing by objectives, a professor at the University of California, a member of the Board of Directors of many companies (four of which he founded), and my former employer, was a strength for me in writing this book. Every time I had a mental block, listening to his tapes would relax me and I would be back on track. He has graciously permitted me to quote him liberally in this text.

For the psychological aspects of selling, particularly the verbal and non-verbal skills, I relied upon the writings of Allen

E. Ivey and Lynn Simex-Downing, specifically their textbook, *Counseling with Psychotherapy: Skills, Theories and Practice.*

For much of the motivational and political theory in this book, I referred to Harold J. Leavitt's excellent concise fourth edition of *Managerial Psychological.* His book helped me gain a better understanding of things I knew intuitively.

I have also referred to information contained in The Alexander Hamilton Institute's Modern Business Reports: *The Marketing Newsletter.* These letters outline pragmatic approaches to the many problems salespeople face.

I would specifically like to thank Frank J. Burge, the man who convinced me to become a salesperson and who provided me with my first sales training through a series of newsletters based on the ideas of the old masters of sales training, Zenn Kaufman, Morris Pickens, Red Motley, and J. Douglas Edwards.

Strictly speaking, customers are those who customarily buy from you. Otherwise, they are prospects. I have avoided the cold words "prospect" and "vendor" in favor of the warmer words "customer" and "supplier." I have also used the words "customer," "buyer," and "user" interchangeably, depending on the focus I was trying to achieve.

Finally, I wish to offer my sincerest gratitude to Suzanne Nobel, Sunny Merik, and to all the other people (too many to mention) for helping me achieve my goal.

Introduction

High technology selling is neither an art nor a science: it is a game. The selling game is not a typical game where two opponents compete by a set of predetermined rules, nor is it a game of alliances where one group engages another in battling for a specific prize.

Selling is a multifaceted game of elimination, without rules, among several contenders, with the customer as the prize. Often, it isn't until the prize is won that the real game, to keep the prize, begins.

The selling game is a game of strategy, maneuvers, and patterns. A strategy is developed to position and present the solution being sold in terms of both the customer's needs and the political environment. Maneuvering misleads and deludes the competitor, while pattern recognition compensates for the lack of rules.

The buyer and competitor do not play by a set of rules, or if they do, the rules are ambiguous and neither fully accepted nor fully known. Therefore, what passes for rules in the sales game are actually patterns. Just as there is a pattern to a typical negotiator's conduct, so competitors and buyers follow certain distinguishable patterns.

When playing the sales game, it is vital to discern the business and political patterns of the customers and the strategic and tactical patterns of the competitors, then use this knowledge to gain an advantage. It is these patterns that give relevance to how the high technology sales game is played.

Over the centuries, selling has remained essentially unchanged, although the emphasis and focus has shifted from time to time. Salespeople in high technology must acquire the qualities of ego-drive and empathy, and develop customer and product knowledge. In addition, they should think strategically. Thinking strategically means looking beyond the obvious and understanding the big picture. High technology salespeople, in fact all professional salespeople, have to augment conventional selling habits and attitudes with strategy to win in today's business environment.

If the strategy focuses the many skills required in playing the sales game on a business-solution in terms of the political environment, the salespeople will gain control of the sales situation. They will diminish the competitor's influence while advancing their own position. They will win consistently.

Control in this sense means the ability to simultaneously exercise self restraint and influence others. It is the means by which the sales process is regulated. In fact, control is the process, the mechanism or technique, for achieving the result.

A salesperson in control does not react when the competitor acts; does not say "How high?" when the customer says "Jump!"; is not surprised when the customer places the order, and does not sink into the depths of depression when the factory slips the delivery.

Control means being prepared for a competitive attack or counterattack, means ensuring that the customer understands the value of the offer, means influencing the timing of the purchase by collapsing or extending the time frame as required, and means that contingencies are in place for dealing with the fact that the product and the factory cannot perform perfectly all the time.

In this book, various aspects of gaining control when selling high technology products are addressed, including personal selling skills, strategic competitive focus, and political customer orientation. Additionally, selling tools such as proposals, demonstrations, and presentations are described in detail. Finally, the organizational and environmental issues surrounding a high technology sales force are reviewed.

This book was written to provide salespeople with alternative courses of action so that they can gain and maintain control of the selling situation.

Winning the
High Tech Sales Game

PART

1

The Person and the Tools

CHAPTER

$$1$$

The salesperson makes the difference

No profession includes as many hacks as sales. The sales profession has a low status image and unfortunately a large number of salespeople cannot sell.

The Ancient Image: In the past, the sales profession has been looked down on almost universally

Since ancient times, sales has been considered a less than honored profession. In general, salespeople were thought to be dishonest and lacking in integrity. Merchants and tradesmen of both East and West were beneath the contempt of the nobility. In Japan, the merchants were forced to crawl before the Samurai.

The ancient Romans had a legal maxim: "Let the buyer beware."[1] Shakespeare said, "Let me have no lying; it becomes none but a salesman."[2] "If fools went not to market, bad wares would not be sold," is an old Spanish proverb.[3]

Probably the most notorious salespeople were the Russian "Kit Kitych" popularized by Ostrovskii in his comedies. The Kit Kitych never looked beyond the immediate product they were selling. They thought only of kopeks and the present, rather than the rubles and the future. The stereotypical Kit Kitych wanted to get more for his product than its worth, and dreamed of declaring fraudulent bankruptcies to cheat his creditors.[4]

Throughout the world, the nobility often depended upon these merchants and tradespeople for their lifestyle if not their very livelihood. Yet these early salespeople were still held in low esteem. Even the rare marriages between merchant and royalty were morganatic. Successful merchants were never fully accepted socially by the patriciate.

In more modern times, salespeople have been called everything from snake oil artists and blue suede shoe characters to peddlers, hucksters, and hacks. To a certain extent this is still true in Europe. As late as the spring of 1981, an American writer attributed Britain's sorry economic state to the fact that a stigma was still attached to people in the sales trade.[5]

McMurry, in his book, *Mystique of Super Salesmanship*, described a person with a successful sales personality as "....a habitual 'woer', an individual who has a compulsive need to win and hold the affection of others....his wooing, however, is not based on a sincere desire for love because, in my opinion, he is convinced at heart that no one will ever love him. Therefore, his wooing is primarily exploitative....his relationships tend to be transient, superficial, and evanescent."[6]

McMurry's disingenuous personality evaluation of a successful salesperson is not very flattering. Possibly this charac-

[1]Bergen Evan, ED., *Dictionary of Quotations*, (New York, NY: Avenel Books, 1978), p. 83.

[2]Ibid., p. 703.

[3]Ibid., p. 430.

[4]W. Bruce Lincoln, *In War's Dark Shadow*, (New York, NY: The Dial Press, 1983, p. 72.

[5]William Manchester, *The Last Lion*, (Boston, MA: Little Brown and Company, 1983), p. 64.

[6]Philip Kitler, *Marketing Management* Fourth Edition, (Englewood Cliffs, NJ: Prentice-Hall, Inc., 1980), p. 553.

terization of the salesperson, and the fact that even at the best universities the professors are often not aware of the sophistication of sales, are the reasons only one in twenty college students show an interest in selling as a profession.[7] Universities and business schools rarely encourage students to make sales a career and they do little research into sales training methods. Consequently sales is still a very misunderstood profession.

◯ *The Modern Image: In modern times, the beauty as well as the utility of sales is being recognized*

Students and educators might do well to ponder the fact that one-quarter of the presidents of large U.S. corporations started out in marketing and sales. For example, at IBM, both the president, Frank Cary, and the founder, Thomas Watson, Sr., were salesmen. In fact, most IBM executives have been salespeople during their careers. IBM's sales orientation has been a main ingredient of its success.

Until recently, society has not understood that sales is what makes it all happen. People do not appreciate the difficulty of selling and few comprehend what it takes to be a salesperson. They have no realization of what it is like to have to go into the trenches day after day and be pummeled day after day. The daily psychological beating a salesperson takes is often brutal. In spite of a predetermined resolution to the contrary, emotions will creep in and at times it becomes difficult to survive.

Mayer and Greenberg, in a Harvard Business Review article, "What Makes a Good Salesman?", concluded that a good salesperson had two basic qualities: empathy—the ability to feel as the customer feels, and ego-drive—a strong personal need to make the sale, to win.[8]

In high technology, the salesperson must also have product and customer knowledge. Selling sophisticated high technology products and systems requires an unusual combination of skills, including engineering skills to understand the cus-

---

[7] Alexander Hamilton Institute, Inc. Modern Business Reports, *"The Marketing Letter"*, (The Alexander Hamilton Institute, Inc., 1633 Broadway, New York, NY 10019) Vol. 2, No. 5, August, 1975, p. 3.

[8] Kotler, *Marketing Management*, p. 554.

tomer's applications and selling skills to persuasively present the product value.

There are many engineers who possess the necessary technical skills but lack the empathy to understand the customer or the drive to plan effective sales campaigns.

On the other hand, there are many experienced salespeople who lack the technical ability to understand the customer's application and effectively communicate product benefits. Consequently, the successful high technology salesperson is rare and in demand. In today's high technology industry, the sales force is often the driving force within the company that makes the product successful. The importance of the salesperson was recognized by Sinclair Lewis in *Babbit* when he wrote, "....the romantic hero is no longer the knight, the wandering poet, the cowpuncher, the aviator, nor the brave young district attorney, but the great salesperson."[9]

○ ***High Technology Products: Selling high technology products requires education to understand the technology and skill in helping others understand***

High technology products have created a need for a new breed of salespeople. High technology products may be defined as any product, system, or service designed to process information or enhance automation, leading to improved productivity. A high technology product may be a custom integrated circuit, a complex computational system, a software program, or a consulting service.

People and businesses want to improve their productivity but do not wish to expend too much effort to learn how. People want user-friendly products, that is, things that are easy to use. Businesses are no different. They continually try to improve productivity by automating and by meaningful processing of the mass of data and information collected. Integrating the many information processing and automation systems is the superordinate objective of the high technology industry.

Professional electronic workstations that give engineers and other professionals direct control of their work, and instant

[9]Henry Davidoff, ED., *The Pocket Book of Quotations,* (New York, NY: Pocket Books, 1942), p. 325.

feedback of the results, is an example of information process-ing. When these workstations are integrated into a network so that others can share the ideas, automation is occurring.[10]

Selling this information and automation is the charter of the high technology salesperson. This person must have the ability to clearly understand the customer's needs or problems and provide an environment for the customer conducive to understanding the solutions. In selling concepts and solutions, it is the salesperson, not the product, that makes the difference.

[10]Diebold Group, Inc., *Strategies for Growth,* Special Advertising Supplement, *Newsweek,* Oct. 1983, (Referenced).

CHAPTER

(2)

Know your product but know your customer first

If a salesperson can accurately sense and understand the world of the customer, the possibility of making the sale is greatly increased. Grasping the customer's world requires mastering the concept of empathy.

○ *Empathy: A salesperson must develop the ability to empathize*

The psychologist Carl Rogers once defined empathy as the ability "to sense the client's private world as if it were your own, but without losing the 'as if' quality."[1]

---

[1]Allen E. Ivey with Lynn Simex-Downing, *Counseling and Psychotherapy: Skills, Theories and Practice,* (Englewood Cliffs, NJ: Prentice-Hall Inc., 1980), pp. 92, 175, 260, 395 and 420.

Empathy comes from the German word "einfuhling" and means "feeling into."[2] Empathy exists when you recognize the customer's feelings as being the customer's feelings and not your own, and are then able to communicate back to the customer the same feeling so the customer can recognize its similarity to the one expressed.

In communicating empathy, although nonverbal behavior is more important than verbal messages, caution must be exercised since empathy is different among different cultures. In some cultures, for example, the United States, you are expected to be specific and direct, while in others, like Japan, ambiguity, circumlocution, and indirectness are considered the correct approach.

It is not necessary to feel exactly what the customer feels, but it is necessary to make them aware that you understand their thoughts and feelings. If your tone is in accord with the customer's, and you pace yourself carefully, always in harmony with the customer, you will communicate with empathy.

Dwight David Eisenhower was a master of empathic communication as well as diplomacy. One example is his ten minute D-Day speech given during World War II to the King of England, Churchill, the Allied Generals and some diplomats.

The sense of possible failure was all pervasive and the tension was high.

Ike sensed this and used his ten minutes to champion interallied cooperation. Ike knew those present were clearly aware and feeling the gravity of the situation. Ike participated in their feelings and was sensitive to them.

His smile, his warmth, his confidence, his peace of mind and his feeling for those present was communicated to them. Doubt dissolved, the tension disappeared, and the gathering was sold.

Ike knew he was not perceived as a master strategist like Montgomery, nor a blustering, swaggering "Give 'em Hell" leader like Patton, so he approached the group with genuineness true to his relationship with them.

He did not analyze the facts, for that would have created additional doubts. The facts were based on tenuous assumptions at best. A fighting speech would have served to increase tension as most felt the complexity of the operation was such that only Divine Guidance could make it succeed.

[2]Bruce Shertzer and Shelley C. Stone, *Fundamentals of Counseling*, (Boston, MA: Houghton Mifflin Company, 1974), p. 265.

Instead, he employed non-verbal means to express caring. His smile was especially effective in projecting warmth. He was specific about the risks, yet used this concreteness to take pressure off the group by accepting the burden of responsibility. He drew out the positive aspects of the Allied relationship. In essence, he maintained the delicate balance between the needs of those before him and his own knowledge and expertise. Hence he won the sale.[3]

○   Balanced Approach: There is a happy medium between pushing too hard and being too diffident

Sales are often lost because the salesperson pushed too hard or didn't push hard enough. A delicate balance is necessary. Empathy helps achieve the required balance.

To develop this balance, first develop a relationship with the customer. The customer needs or wants something, has a problem that must be solved, or is open to better ways of accomplishing his or her objectives. You as a salesperson authentically wish to help the customer through your product or service. This forms the basis of the relationship.

In a truly empathic relationship, the customer is open to suggestions. People want to be told what to do; they want to be led. Therefore, both your verbal and nonverbal behavior should say, "I understand the way you feel." Your objective is to establish a rapport with the customers that will result in their heightened awareness of you and what you can do for them, intensifying to the point where you will be able to influence or persuade them to buy.

Once you determine where the customer wants to go, if necessary, discard previously thought-out tactics in favor of ones in concert with your customer's needs. There is no hurry to talk directly about your product. Listen first, then refer to it indirectly. Later, after you have put the customer in a receptive frame of mind, you can directly influence the customer and refer to the product. Whenever you talk about the product, your objective is always to close. To close, your customer must be in a receptive state.

[3]Omar N. Bradley and Clay Blair, *A General's Life,* (New York, N.Y.: Simon and Schuster, 1983), p. 240-241.

○ *Receptive State: People will not listen to you if you put them on the defensive*

A receptive state cannot be facilitated if you contradict the customer verbally or nonverbally. If the customer takes a strong position, agree with him or her and then go on to point out an advantage that meets or dispells the concern or objection.

Never unnecessarily take a strong position. If forced into a situation where you are expected to take a position that might harm your credibility, reply with an appropriate joke or anecdote. Be deferential, be agreeable, stay ahead of the customer.

In other words, if you can sense the point the customer is about to make or the conclusion he or she is about to draw, and if you suggest it first, you will be perceived by the customer to be in synchronization with his or her beliefs. Then by associating your product or solution with the point made or conclusion reached, you in effect set the stage for the customer to accept your conclusion.

Your objective is not educational nor evangelistic; it is to get the sale. As long as the problem can be solved by your product which implies integrity and proper account qualification, there is no need to expound philosophy, principles, ideas or ideals which are not in concert with your customer's thoughts. You should facilitate discussions about the value of your solution. You should avoid issues which can create doubts about what you are offering.

According to Tommy Corcoran, a Washington observer, Lyndon Johnson was a master at this. Corcoran said, "No matter what someone thought, Lyndon would agree with him—would be there ahead of him, in fact. He could follow someone's mind around—and figure out where it was going and beat it there...." Lyndon Johnson had mastered the skill of empathy.[4]

Empathy can be mastered through training, example, modeling, and role playing. After extensive research, psychologists have concluded that empathy is a trait that is measurable, is found in varying degrees, and can be improved through training and practice.

Ideally, you want to see as the customers see, hear as the customers hear, feel as the customers feel, and communicate this similarity back to the customers. If the customers accept

---

[4]Robert A. Caro, *The Path to Power,* (New York, NY: Alfred A. Knopf, Inc., 1982), p. 256.

that you understand the same way they understand, you can lead them to your conclusion and the customer will be pleased.

○ *Ego-Drive: The ability to believe in what you are selling and the ability to express and share that belief are also necessary to sales*

Believing in what you are selling and enthusiastically conveying that belief to the customer exemplifies the second characteristic a salesperson must possess or master to be successful: ego-drive. Ego-drive focuses a salesperson's energy on making the sale, on winning. Ego-drive is a function of motivation, which causes a person to act, and enthusiasm, an intense, inspired, ardent interest or zeal to accomplish an objective. Motivation and enthusiasm, in turn, are functions of both the external environment and the internal mind.

External factors such as money, recognition, and business perks are extrinsic environmental motivators. Self-actualization, satisfaction, and winning the sale are intrinsic motivators or generators of enthusiasm.

Although enthusiasm is stimulated by success, whether this success is real or imagined is immaterial. If you visualize yourself as a successful person or if you visualize yourself in a successful situation, you will rouse enthusiasm. Therefore, enthusiasm is a function of your personality which is controlled by the brain.

The brain is not deterministic. It controls, through chemical processes, your mental processes. These processes are not uniform, are often unconscious, are not predictable, and are difficult to control from the environment, from without.

You perceive reality as a function of your emotions. If you believe it is real, if you feel it is real, your mind will process it as real and you will become enthusiastic. Then your ego will drive you to act, to seek out your objective.

If you like seeking the objective, if the act of doing is itself rewarding, if you are doing something for its own sake, motivation is intrinsic. You are said to be self-motivated.

Your personality, far from reacting to instinctual urges or external stimuli, to a large extent drives itself. Your mind in essence, maintains its own information system and uses this data base to actually urge you to seek out your objective.

O   ## *Objectives and Goals: A salesperson needs an objective to work toward in steps called goals*

Therefore, to generate motivation and arouse enthusiasm, you need an objective and a goal. An objective is a general aim with a basic direction and ultimate destination. It is simple, logical, and easy to communicate. Typical objectives might be to become the highest performing salesperson of the year within your company, to capture an account that has eluded you or your company for years, or to have a good family life.

The goal is the quantification of the objective. It is expressed in numbers and is specifically tied to time. In terms of the objectives, the goal might be to book ten percent more than any other salesperson in your company within the next twelve months, to sell your product to an unfriendly account within six months, or to spend eight hours a week of dedicated quality time with your family.

Goals should be realistic and attainable. Disproportion between effort and possible gain should be avoided.

Simply setting goals, however, will not produce results. It is what you do with them, how you program your mind, that determines achievement. Visualize attainment of your goals daily. Allow your goals to direct your behavior, and like them, so that they will motivate you with enthusiasm.

For example, if your goal is to capture that elusive account, visualize yourself closing on the reluctant potential user of your product. Rehearse what you will say, then say it aloud. Since achieving this goal will require much time with an unfriendly account, set a series of short-term objectives to be accomplished with each visit and look for positive signs. Each accomplishment or positive sign is a small reward which will help you like what you are doing through satisfaction in achievement. Each morning when you awake, imagine what it will be like when the purchasing agent shakes your hand and hands you the purchase order. Then imagine what your management will say when you bring it home. Visualize each step in the process and how you will deal with it.

Eventually, belief in your product or in your solution, coupled with the motivation to win, and fueled with enthusiasm, will be evident to those around you as well as to your customer. This in turn will not only get you the order but will provide you with the opportunity to grow, to excel, and to become what you are capable of becoming.

Most successful salespeople, at least in high technology sales, make a reasonable living. A few make a fortune. For those who are fantasy-oriented, whose motivation lies in the future, for those who are driven by the dream, remember that as you strive to reach the top of that mountain, have fun on the slopes.

○ Product Knowledge: Salespeople must understand how to use the products

Empathy and ego drive aside, it is difficult if not impossible for the salesperson to establish credibility in the eyes of the customer if the salesperson does not know the customer, the product and its application. Customers want a valid and rational reason to invest in the solution to their need, desire or problem. This means the salesperson must be capable of clearly and succinctly communicating the solution the product offers in terms of the customer application and the customer's own technical or intellectual level. If the quality or value of the solution is communicated from the customer's point of view, the customer will more readily respond and relate to it. There is no innate, intrinsic, or fundamental product value. Value exists only as a customer perceives it. Therefore, extensive research into the product application and experience in meeting diverse customer needs is necessary to successfully position the solution.

With product knowledge, the salesperson is able to communicate those solutions to which the customer can relate. The salesperson can also focus on specific values the product represents to the customer. To do this effectively, it is necessary to have customer knowledge to focus the product features on how they provide the solution. Buzz words alone are not enough to communicate value. Product knowledge used at the proper time and in the proper sequence is what leads to the sale.

When selling high technology products to a group or committee, the various members may have different wants, needs, and problems. Although they are buying a promise of a result, they do not necessarily each want or need the same result. Consequently, the solution the product offers to the primary user should be supplemented with other solutions to satisfy the wants and needs of other members. In this case, both customer and product knowledge are used to determine in advance all the probable solutions that can be realized through the use of the product, so the salesperson can select the solutions that meet the needs of the committee or group in question. How the solution is then realized is explained sometimes informally without going into excessive technical detail.

○ The Sales Team: If the salespeople don't fully understand their products, engineers should be on hand to answer technical questions

Since many high technology products are extremely complex, requiring indepth understanding of complex engineering functions and product circuitry, many companies employ a sales team approach to sell them. A sales team consists of the salesperson backed by technical personnel and sometimes a financial analyst. The team follows the lead of the salesperson, who orchestrates the sales process. The team may include an application person to work directly with the customer demonstrating exactly how the product will provide a solution and meet the requirement.

A product specialist may be called upon to work with the technical management sometimes, in a more theoretical capacity, answering "what if" and "how" questions about current and future applications.

The financial analyst is required to develop financial models such as return on investment, and other analyses, such as cost of ownership, for justifying the purchase.

Product knowledge is important even for the good capital equipment salesperson who is a master at arranging or leading a sales team effort. He or she should still learn at least enough about the product to give a credible technical presentation. This knowledge is required to gain the confidence of the customer.

If the salesperson is unable to give a credible technical presentation, the customer will circumvent the salesperson and deal with people who understand her or him. The salesperson will lose control of the account in the process. Eventually, the salesperson will become known as Peter the Greeter, good at arranging meetings and paying for dinners, but unable to carry on an intelligent conversation about the product with the customer.

In summary, as illustrated in Figure 2, sales ability is a function of certain personality traits. The set of traits most conducive to excellence in sales is product knowledge, ego-drive and empathy.

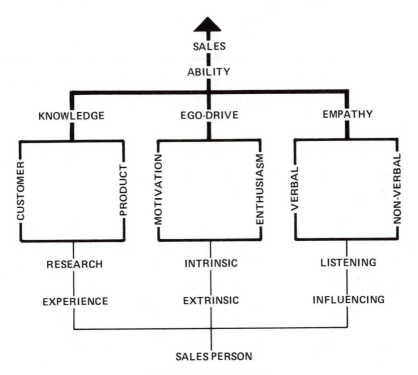

Figure 2: Sales Traits

CHAPTER

3

Promise less than you can deliver

In selling high technology products or services, the higher the technology involved, the greater the tendency to use more product knowledge than is needed to close the sale. Although you can never know too much about your product, you can certainly talk too much about it.

○ *Single Value Focus: It is best to be sensitive to the customer's need and show how your product can meet that need*

It is best to translate product knowledge into values with which the customer can identify. Values may be product, political, or business oriented and presented as solutions. In other words, your objective is to show the customer the value in owning your product.

Often, in an attempt to cover all the bases, a salesperson takes a shotgun approach and overwhelms the customer with technical details and feature-benefit presentations. In a panic to ensure that the customer hears everything about the product, the salesperson gushes forward with a myriad of specifications. The customer, faced with data considered unnecessary, unintelligible, or unmeaningful, becomes bored or confused. This is not the desired response.

C: *"Is the computer over there portable?"*

S: *"Yes it is and it has a built-in battery, 256K of memory, is powered by an 80C86 chip, is 16 bits wide, is IBM® and Apple® compatible, runs Lotus™ software, has a built-in modem and two dual discs!"*

C: *"Wow. I'll bet the battery won't last long with all those features. I am only interested in keeping my budgeting up to date."*

RESULT: Likely lost sale.

C: *"Is that computer over there portable?"*

S: *"Yes it is. In fact, it will fit right into that airline bag you are carrying."*

C: *"How long does the battery last?"*

S: *"Depending on the options you select, 24 to 48 hours."*

C: *"What options do you offer?"*

S: *"Well, in addition to an extended life battery and a high-speed battery charger, we offer most standard computer features. What are you particularly interested in?"*

RESULT: Likely sale.

To paraphrase Chip Thayer, Jr., product manager of Teradyne, the desired response is not, "What do you mean by that?" or "Wow, I don't need all that!" It should be more along the lines of, "Gee, how do you do that?" or "I see, that is exactly what I want." The shotgun, multiple benefit approach stems from a fear on the salesperson's part that the customer will infer that embracing one benefit means others will be sacrificed.[1] In fact, multiple benefit positioning loses impact and focus, may confuse the customer, and can play directly into the hands of a wily competitor who knows what the customer really wants. Unless your objective is to educate the customer, you only want the customer to buy your product. Therefore, let your competitor do the front-end missionary training work. It is not necessary to tell the customer everything about your product. Eventually the customer will tell you what she or he wants. It is better to focus on a single value, one that is specific and quantifiable.

Quantification does not mean detailed specifications committed under pain of death and signed in blood by your management. Quantification means examples, such as a ten percent increase in throughput, a twenty percent reduction in data entry time, enhanced accuracy due to the specification of one or two nanoseconds instead of the normal three or four, a savings of ten thousand dollars per month, or a similar illustration.

These quantifications must be presented from the customer's point of view and labeled "typical in the industry" or "in similar applications." In the early stages of the sales process, you do not want to be tied down to detailed specifications.

Simplify Technical Details: Don't make your customer feel uneducated

Technical details should be simplified; in fact, they should be over-simplified if they are to have the desired effect. Excessive technical detail and extraneous information should be ruthlessly pared from presentations. Technical terms and jargon should only be used judiciously.

It is not necessary to prove yourself or be a technical guru. As a sales process moves forward, you will find that the customer does not expect you to know everything. For nitty-gritty details, a customer expects you to provide back up material or rely on your design, product, or application engineers.

If you are a brilliant technical salesperson, never play the role of a brilliant technical salesperson. And above all, avoid

---

[1]C.B. (Chip) Thayer Jr., *"Industrial High Tech Positioning"*, (Industrial Marketing, June 1982), (Article).

upstaging the customer or showing off your depth of technical knowledge.

Bernie Cornfield advised, "Put your ego in your pocket." Unfortunately, he also said, "Write the business first and fix the sweat later."[2]

His last statement is dangerous counsel. Although your benefit claim or solution may address over-simplified issues, your over-simplification must bear up when the issues are scrutinized. This does not imply you should make a weak value statement. The more powerfully stated solution is more likely to lead to success.[3]

O
Promise Less Than You Can Deliver: Leave room for positive discoveries

In high technology sales, there are by necessity many engineering compromises. If you pick the right set of compromises in terms of what is valuable to the customer, you will establish a ground on which the competitive battle will be fought. If the competitor got there first and the battleground is already established, you must secure a favorable position until you can change the battleground.

When you are in an unfavorable position, your immediate tendency is to compare products. But avoid at all costs a comparison contest, even if you have product superiority. Wily or entrenched competitors can manipulate product comparison evaluations simply by ensuring that their oranges are compared to your apples in terms of their oranges. Through the weighting process, the outcome of competitive product analysis can be made to say whatever an originator wishes it to say. There is simply no objective analytical approach to decide which to buy. Therefore, it is best to stay with your solution, your value, focusing on what is important to the customer. Align your value or product with your customer criteria for buying. When you focus on a specific value or solution, your customer will also focus on it. Then, when you deliver your product, your customer will expect you to come through with it. Therefore,

[2]From *Do You Sincerely Want to be Rich*, Charles Row, Bruce Page, and Godfrey Hodgson, Copyright © 1971 by Times Newspaper Ltd. Reprinted by permission of Viking Penguin Inc.

[3]Thayer Jr., *"Industrial High Tech Positioning"*.

leave lies to your competitors and hyperbole to your marketing department, and stay with the fundamental believable truth.[4]

A lie is a false statement, truth is in accordance with the facts, and hyperbole is an exaggeration made for effect and is not meant to be taken literally.

The difference between a lie and the truth is usually distinct. But the difference between hyperbole and the truth may be indistinct. Deciding what to say and what not to say requires sensitive judgment. To be unnecessarily direct and delve into minute detail is not always safe or necessary. It may only serve to confuse the customer.

Abdul Aziz, the first ruler of modern Arabia, was less impressed with the technological wonders that the British staged for his amazement in 1916 than he was with British honesty. Later, in 1933, when his court supported the American offer for Arabia's oil rights because in their words, "...we all felt the British, although honest, were still tainted by colonialism. If they came for our oil, we could never be sure to what extent they would come to influence our government as well." The Americans, on the other hand, were also honest, but they would simply be after the money, a motive which the Arabs as born traders could readily appreciate and approve. Still, Abdul Aziz tried to push the deal Britain's way. It wasn't until Britain told him to accept the American offer that he did and America got the lucrative Saudi oil rights. The British honestly thought there was no significant amount of oil in Saudi Arabia.[5] So they urged the Arabs to sell it to the Americans.

Honesty is the best policy, but often those who expound this policy are less than honest themselves. In such cases, honesty is certainly the best propaganda.

Since your company or your product may not perform perfectly all the time, always promise less than you can deliver, no matter what the factory says. If you inadvertently over-commit, and if your company's attitude is dedicated to making things work and not to making excuses or disclaimers, the customer will notice and be satisfied.[6] Absolute truth is difficult to determine, so as a rule of thumb, it is best to say no more than is required, without misleading customers or allowing customers to mislead themselves. What you do not say is as

[4]Ibid.

[5]Robert Lacey, *The Kingdom*, (New York, NY: Harcourt, Brace, Jovanovich, Publishers, 1981), pp. 234-236.

[6]Thayer, Jr., *"Industrial High Tech Positioning"*.

important as what you say. Remember the words of Calvin Coolidge, "You don't have to explain something you haven't said."[7]

⭕ *Word-of-Mouth Advertising: The best advertising is word-of-mouth*

Propaganda is a method of creating a positive attitude about your product or service by influencing opinion. Propaganda is not necessarily a dirty word. Less-than-honest, radical political zealots have tarnished the word in recent times. As a result, propaganda is often associated with lies.

When Harry Truman said the Marine Corps had a "...propaganda machine that is almost equal to Stalin's," he was immediately proven right by the furor that led to his apology. Public opinion had been influenced by the Marine Corps' propaganda machine.[8]

Propaganda can be positive or passive. A word-of-mouth advertising campaign is an example of positive propaganda at work.

More business decisions are made over lunch or dinner than at any other time. Often these decisions rely on word-of-mouth advertising. Word-of-mouth advertising makes use of people relationships. Before selecting a high technology product, engineers and managers will often ask for references to contact or sites to visit that use the product.

Word-of-mouth advertising takes place when people talk about your product and its value at trade shows, in technical articles, textbooks, and training programs, and when customers—especially first-time users—promote or recommend it to others.

Word-of-mouth advertising tends to be more credible since it emanates from a human being and is tuned to the listener by the teller. Most people make up their own minds and then search for facts to substantiate their thinking. If a nearby "expert" verifies their position, they need look no further. More facts are unnecessary because "they" say it is so. Experts can participate with recommendations without being compromised. Word-of-mouth is efficient since, although it takes longer

---

[7]Robert A. Caro, *The Path to Power,* p. 319.

[8]Evans, *Dictionary of Quotations,* p. 559.

to disseminate, it is delivered directly to those who need the information. Feedback is also instantaneous.

HOW TO USE IT: You can start a word-of-mouth advertising campaign

Advertising by word of mouth is used to communicate intangible values such as credibility, efficiency, quality, reliability, ease of use, low cost of ownership, adaptability and support. A word-of-mouth campaign usually starts with personnel in your company, such as product marketing, then moves through sales management out to the field. It is then picked up by salespeople, distributors, and service engineers, until the customer finally hears it. It then flows from customer to customer. Eventually it becomes your rallying cry.

Regis McKenna, the president of Regis McKenna, a large public relations firm in California, says, "....people may know what to sell, how much it costs, and even when to sell, but the enthusiasm, the rallying behind, the commitment, the picture of the future, and the character of the management and the company all come through word of mouth."[9]

One way to effectively use word-of-mouth advertising is to select a satisfied customer to talk with the prospect to whom you are trying to sell. If the prospect is ready to buy but skeptical, have the prospect talk to your satisfied customer. Needless to say, this must be carefully planned. Make certain your satisfied customer is aware of the call and the questions likely to be asked.

After coaching, advise your satisfied customer approximately when the call will be made. Set up the call for your client, then leave the room while they talk. As your product gains acceptance, customers will begin talking to prospective customers without your involvement. That is when you realize the real benefit of word-of-mouth advertising.

HOW TO START: The first step is to develop your message

To consciously start a word-of-mouth campaign, suggest your management enlist the services of a professional public relations firm. The firm will develop and analyze an appropriate catchy or dithryambic message, made from the customers'

[9]Regis McKenna, *Word of Mouth* pamphlet (Palto Alto, CA: Regis McKenna, Inc., 1982).

perspective, segment the word-of-mouth network into managable pieces, determine how information passes through each segment, how the segments are linked, and who the influential people in each segment are. Finally, targets will be identified. Credible managers in your organization and possibly customers will be chosen to deliver the clear, simple, differentiating messages to the selected market segments. With a little patience, relationships will build and your word-of-mouth campaign will be off and running. People hearing it will take it as a given, assumed and unquestioned.

CHAPTER

4

Sell solutions, not products

Selling solutions demands an abstract approach to the selling process. The product is thought of as the facilitator of the solution, not the solution. Solutions fulfill needs, satisfy desires, and solve problems. In other words, they represent value to the investor. Solutions are also invisible to the task.

○ ### *Products Facilitate Solutions: Look at your product as a means to solve a customer's problem*

Assume a company has a problem in typing, editing, and retyping technical manuals. Since the changes are manifold and continual, the manuals are never current, and the customers always complain. The solution to this problem is text automation through the purchase of a word processor. This will allow timely manual updates, enhancing the company's ability to keep the technical manuals relatively current and solving the customer-complaint problem. The solution can be facilitated by a word processor.

The company then decides to do an objective in-depth evaluation of all word processors on the market, and finds fifteen vendors that can solve the problem. In addition to solving the problem, the company requires a vendor who can provide reliable equipment over time at multiple locations. The need for reliability in the product, producibility of the product in the quantities and time frame required, and support for the product once installed, are next evaluated. The list of qualified vendors quickly drops to three.

The next evaluation criteria is the desire for a cost-effective solution. One vendor is considerably more expensive than the other two, but cannot justify the incremental value the company will realize and is eliminated. A second vendor is considerably less expensive than the other two but cannot justify how or why they are willing to accept below-standard margins. They are also eliminated. The last vendor charges a fair price and will make a fair profit in the eyes of the customer, fulfilling the desire for a short-term cost-effective solution along with security for future product updates and products.

○ ### Characterization of a Solution: Know that your product is only part of the solution

In this evaluation, the product itself is only one-third of the overall solution. The Holden solution model has three characteristics: the quality of the solution, the resources required to support the solution, and the financial parameters surrounding the solution.

The quality of the solution is a function of the technical capability—can it do the job—and reliability—can it do the job all the time over time.

The resource parameter is a function of producibility: has the supplier the capacity to produce a product in the needed quantity in a timely manner over time? and support: once installed, can a supplier support it to the required level?

Financial considerations surrounding the solution include cost effectiveness in terms of return on investment, and cost of ownership: when do I realize a payback and how much will it really cost me to own it? Another important financial parameter, especially for capital equipment, is whether the supplier will realize a fair profit on the sale. A willingness on the part of the supplier to sell the product at a low margin or below cost may mean the product is or soon will be obsolete, the supplier is having financial or business difficulties, or the supplier is attempting to buy their way into the business. This could mean hidden costs or higher prices after the customer commits, or may simply indicate poor business judgment on the part of the supplier.

⃝ *Selling Solutions: Successful solutions require mutual commitment*

Salespeople who sell a product and who focus on product features and benefits without seeing the big picture, or the overall solution the product facilitates, are vulnerable to strategically thinking competitors. Strategic thinkers look beyond the obvious and project results. Strategic thinkers deal with probabilities and concepts. They sell solutions.

To sell solutions, salespeople must first understand the customer's requirement. Second, a mutual commitment to the solution on the part of both of the customer and the supplier must be obtained. Finally, the supplier must have the ability to implement the solution and the customer must have the ability and commit to support the implementation.

To understand the customers, the salespeople must know what is driving the customer to make the purchase. The driving mechanism is usually time-related. It also involves how the product provides product, business, and political values.

Commitment to a successful installation implies that effort and desire as well as the capability and willingness to use the product are present. Many installations, especially capital equipment installations, have proved costly due to the lack of a firm commitment on the part of the customer or the supplier. Although it is possible for the customer to take responsibility for the installation and make it successful, it is never possible for the supplier to make an installation successful if the environment is hostile or the customer is not committed. Mutual commitment is often a function of philosophical compatibility between supplier and customer.

Implementation ability is the last parameter of successful solution selling. The installation must not destabilize the environment. In fact, the solution should, for all intents and purposes, be invisible to the task. A person experienced in using a typewriter to type a report is not aware of the typewriter as the task is accomplished. In essence, a typewriter is invisible to the task.

If a word processor is installed, a new or different method must be employed to accomplish the same task. Manuals must be studied, the keyboard function keys must be understood, and associated software packages must be mastered. The word processor suddenly becomes very visible. Automation is not free; therefore, the ability to implement a solution unobtrusively is an important sales tool. In other words, the solution should be invisible to the task.

CHAPTER

5

Differentiate your position

When selling a concept such as a solution, it is important to answer these questions.

- "To whom am I selling?"
- "Why are they buying?"
- "What am I selling?"

The answers are not as obvious as they may first appear. By responding in clearly defined but somewhat abstract terms, the responses may be categorized, and generalizations may be made. From these generalizations, standard approaches to the selling process that will hold true most of the time can be developed. Once the approach is defined, concepts ancillary to the solution will also manifest themselves.

Three Categories of Customers: Customers fit into three different categories; your approach to each category should be different

The answer to the first question falls into one of three categories: committed customers, uncommitted prospects, and unconventional suspects.

The committed customer represents the installed base of customers who have already purchased your product in the past. In dealing with the committed, the selling mode is mainte-nance-oriented. The objective is to keep the customer com-mitted and to obtain follow-on business.

In a competitively charged environment, you will find your-self locked in battle with your competitors for uncommitted prospects. Your product may not be the prospect's first choice. It may be more expensive. It may be perceived as too new or too old, or it may actually be inferior to the competitive offering. In each of these cases, you must find a reason for the uncommitted prospect to buy your product. If, by chance, your product is clearly in the lead, you must ensure that the uncommitted prospect does not find a reason to buy from your competitor. In a competitive selling mode, focus on your solution as superior to the competitor's product or solution.

Unconventional suspects are potential new product ap-plications in non-traditional industries or accounts. The com-petition, if any, may be in-house manufactured items or other suppliers with whom you normally do not compete. Selling to the unconventional suspect requires innovation.

The suspects may not know they need your product or may not know how to apply it in a particular circumstance. Con-sequently, you must identify a need, create a desire, or find an application, and then convince the suspect to buy. In the case of the uncommitted suspect, your solution should focus on the application.

Growth beyond the business forecast and beating the sales quota is often dependent on sales resulting from innovative rather than maintenance or competitive selling. By finding new applications for your product and by increasing the number of people who want or need it, sales will increase incrementally because sales forecasts and business plans are normally based upon repeat business from existing accounts, and new business from identified competitive accounts.

There may be other account categories, such as committed prospects or uncommitted customers, but these tend to be exceptions.

○ Product Focus: Once you have shown how your product can solve a customer's problem, show how it keeps solving it

People do not buy shoes because they want a shoe. They buy protection, support, or style. People do not buy watches just to tell time, otherwise Texas Instruments would be the leader in the watch business, and we would all be wearing $2.98 TI® watches. Assuming your product will do the job it was designed and built to do, and that you have qualified both the account and the application and offer a proper solution, then the customer will buy for reasons not directly related to your product.

The committed customer may be purchasing additional capacity in the case of capital equipment, or incremental supplies in the case of inventory. If the customer buys from the original supplier, issues associated with compatibility, service, and the like will be knowns. The product will have been qualified and the risk will be predictable. If the committed customers were to purchase from the competitor, change would be necessary, harmony might be disrupted, and certain risks would increase. The committed customer who buys your product again is actually buying stability. To sell stability, it is necessary to focus your sales strategy on the product first. The existing product must be supported and perceived as solving the customer's current and future needs through expansion options or new compatible products. Product value is what is important to the committed. If the installation or product has been successful, then the political value to those in power and the business value to the company of continuing to purchase your product will be reinforced and obvious.

○ Political Focus: Those who buy your product may do so for political reasons

In a highly competitive sales situation, the environment is politically charged. The uncommitted prospect's company, department, or individual objectives are of utmost importance. For this reason, addressing the political component of the sales strategy is critical to success. The business value offered is of secondary importance, and the product itself, if it will do the job, is of tertiary importance.

The personal agendas of the individuals in power must be ascertained and satisfied through the purchase of your product. Personal agendas include advancement of a particular individual as a result of the purchase. A stable political environment for the individual making the decision is an objective of a person seeking not advancement but longevity and security in his or her current position. Ego satisfaction resulting from owning the *latest and greatest* is another possible personal goal. All of these agendas have one underlying theme: gain. Advancement of personal objectives represents attainment in one form or another for the people making the decision or associated with the decision to purchase. In effect, they are buying advancement of their personal agendas; in other words, gain.

To win in the competitive selling mode, it is necessary to first focus on the competitor's strategy. Once the strategy is understood, it can be countered in terms of the personal agendas of the decision-makers. For example, if the competitor is selling product superiority and the decision-maker wants political stability and security in his or her current position, then by selling a field-proven, highly reliable, cost-effective solution, you can counter the competitive strategy of product superiority. Field-proven reliability is in concert with the personal objective of the decision-maker.

○ *Business Focus: Can your product do something a new and better way?*

Doing something that has never been done before is creative. Doing something different is innovative. Finding new applications for your product is inventive. Unconventional suspects should be approached, from a salesperson's perspective, in a creative, innovative, or inventive selling mode. The application becomes a primary strategic focus, with emphasis on the business value to the account. The decision to purchase a product for a newly identified need or newly created desire is driven by the business value of the product. The business value must be substantial enough to motivate the suspect to alter the traditional methods or implement a new method. In either case, the suspect is buying change. The product is of secondary importance, although it must be perceived as the agent of change and be fully capable of doing the job. Since the traditional competitors are most likely not aware of your attempted penetration of the unconventional account or application, the political component of the sales strategy is of less importance. This answers the second question.

The answer to the question "What are you selling?" should now be obvious. Although you are selling a solution and the customer is buying a solution, the committed customer is also buying stability. The uncommitted prospect is also buying gain, and the unconventional suspect is also buying change. You are selling the concepts of stability, gain, and change facilitated by your product.

Your solution must maintain stability with the committed customer, must offer value for the uncommitted prospect, and must promote change with the unconventional suspect. Jim Holden says, "As you contact each account, it is helpful in developing your sales strategy to categorize the customers in terms of *who they are* and generalize your approach based on these categories until you can ascertain the right approach."

The following matrix (Figure 3) categorizes the approach to be taken with each type of account. These approaches will be further developed in subsequent chapters.

SALES MATRIX

TYPE OF ACCOUNT	SELLING MODE	FOCUS	STRATEGIC VALUE			ANCILLARY CONCEPT
			PRIMARY	SECONDARY	TERTIARY	
COMMITTED CUSTOMERS	MAINTENANCE	CUSTOMER	PRODUCT	POLITICAL	BUSINESS	STABILITY
UNCOMMITTED PROSPECTS	COMPETITIVE	COMPETITOR	POLITICAL	BUSINESS	PRODUCT	GAIN
UNCONVENTIONAL SUSPECTS	INVENTIVE	APPLICATION	BUSINESS	PRODUCT	POLITICAL	CHANGE

Figure 3: Sales Matrix

CHAPTER

6

Develop strategy around the customer's objectives

Due to the nature of high technology products and systems, the customer often makes the initial sales contact. This is especially true for expensive capital equipment with a long sales cycle.

Generally the customer needs a certain type of equipment, and contacts various suppliers. Sometimes the customer has already decided to purchase from one supplier but contacts a second and third to obtain competitive bids. The contact may be by telephone, telex, or letter. Often it comes in the form of a Request For a Quote (RFQ).

○ *Background Data: Salespeople need information about their customers to develop their strategy*

In any event, after the first contact you will have the name of the person requesting information about your product. At

37

this point you probably do not know if the person who contacted you is the head of a committee with the task of deciding which product to purchase, a technical support person, the true decision-maker, the purchasing agent, or a clerk with no significant power. Consequently, your response should be carefully planned to collect data.

Assume that the decision to buy will be made by a group or committee, since this is true in most companies buying industrial and capital equipment.

Telephone the person who contacted you and do an initial qualification. Does your product fit the need? Can they afford it? Are delivery expectations reasonable? How will the decision be made? Who is the competition? If the decision will be made by a committee or group, find out this person's relationship to it, then set up a meeting with the person to collect data and develop background information about the customer.

The initial sales interview is critical to your sales strategy. This is the data-gathering phase of the sales process. Do not agree to give a product presentation on your first sales interview, unless you are sure you can close the sale. Until you understand the customer and have a strategy, you should keep all discussions about your product general.

During the sales interview, your objective is to obtain clear, concise answers to your questions. Fortunately, the customer is probably not going to fill out a form. If he or she did, you would be off to a bad start, because you would have no idea how the customer feels. The content of the answers to the questions you ask will give you the cognitive data you require. How they are answered will give you insight into the customer's feelings, and may surface hidden agendas, unvoiced needs, or competitive positioning.

○   *Questions to Ask: Background data should answer certain questions*

The questions that should be answered first are:

- What are customers' objectives?
- What is their need?
- What is their problem?
- What is their desired solution?
- How do they feel about it?

This information is critical in formulating your strategy. Their replies will give you information on how to present your product, what to stress, what to avoid, and help develop a financial justification.

Next find the answers to these questions:

- When can they place the orders?

- What are their terms and conditions of purchase?

- What is their budget?

- How long is the purchase requisition cycle?

- When must they have delivery?

- Who is the competition?

- What equipment do they currently use?

- How do they feel about it?

This information will help you develop your tactics to deal with price and delivery issues, the competition, and the installed base. It is important to obtain this information from their point of view.

Next get the name, title, and position in the organization of each person involved in the decision. Also determine the technical and managerial level of those most likely to attend the presentation you will eventually give.

Through careful questioning you should be able to start locating the group or committee leader and the real decision-maker. Often they are not the same. If you can identify the personal interest of each member, you will have a significant advantage when you develop your sales strategy. People not directly involved in the decision should not be forgotten; they may become your saviors if things go wrong.

Data to Research: Information on the customer's needs is necessary

The following information should be acquired next:

- The company's long-term plans and direction,

- The organization chart for the company,

- Information about the company (annual report, product brochures, market data, competition, and customers),

- Information on the company's goals, philosophy, and policy,

- Information on key individuals in the company (the founders and the president),

- Other data, such as community issues, labor issues, past dealings with your company, and past dealings with your competitors, is also useful.

This information may be obtained from a variety of sources. The best is the company's public relations department. Next try the customers of the company, the public library, or the city or state offices where the company is registered. These sources can provide a wealth of information. Other sources include stock brokers, suppliers doing business with the company, and trade journals.

Have no qualms about asking for this information. Usually the customer will give it to you gladly because it shows you care enough about their needs to be sure you provide a proper presentation and proposal. It also indicates you do not intend to waste their time.

During the data-gathering phase, show both understanding for their objectives and concern for their problems. Above all take copious notes, as much for their benefit as yours.

Obtaining this information may seem like an overkill, but it is better to have too much data than not enough. As Hy Kaplan, a professional salesman and author, says, "The error of commission or omission is unpardonable. Any part of the information may provide you with the secret needed to get the buy decision."[1]

Many salespeople do a good job of preparing their product sales presentation but fail to collect or use this background information about the account to gain a competitive advantage. After obtaining the background information, prepare a dossier or account profile. Do this to the best of your knowledge at that point in time. These data are likely to change as you develop your sales strategy and continue profiling the account.

[1]Hy Kaplan, *"Selling Effectively to Committees"* (Unpublished Article).

○ **The Account Profile: From the background data and information collected, select what may affect your sales approach**

Categorize the data collected as follows:

- Customer application
- Your proposed product
- Your proposed solution
- Customer philosophy
- Objectives
- Major products, markets, and customers
- Annual sales and market share
- Competition
- Location of installations
- Draw a map to their facility
- Draw an organizational chart and identify:
  — Decision-makers
  — Influencers
  — Supporters
  — Non-supporters
  — Evaluators
  — Approvals
- List the installed base of products similar to the one you are selling.
- List of strengths and weaknesses of the installed base of both you and your competitor.
- Prepare a general key point competitive analysis for the product you are offering versus that of your competitors. Include specifications, price, delivery, and strengths and weaknesses.

- Concerning the customer, determine:
  - — When they need delivery
  - — Why they need it then
  - — Alternative to the delivery
  - — What their exact application is
  - — What their exact product needs are
  - — Alternative to the product needs
  - — Funding source
  - — Budget amount
  - — Financial condition
  - — Competency in using your product
  - — Competency related to the application
  - — Business potential, short-term
  - — Repeat business potential, long-term
- List each contact with the customer. Include visits, telephone calls, and correspondence, and state what transpired.
- List all commitments, actual, implied, or imagined, on the part of both parties.[2]

Other data about the customer, such as community, business, labor relations, or their competitive issues, may also be catalogued. This information is useful for understanding pertinent issues relating to this buy. It also puts you at the same knowledge level as the company's management, who are normally concerned about these issues.

[2]Jim Holden, *Vanguard,* Training Course, (Schaumburg, IL: Holden Corporation, 1982).
*Holden has an "Account Control System" form which aids salespeople in organizing their thoughts. They can be obtained by writing directly to the Holden Corporation, 150 N. Martingale, Suite 838, Schaumberg, IL 60194.

○ ### *Using the Account Profile: Your account profile should give you guidelines for a specific sales approach*

The sales process really starts by collecting company background information, then generating an account profile. Profiling is not an event, but a process that occurs over time. It keeps you abreast of all pertinent sales data and provides you with useful customer-related information.

From the profile, you will derive four important advantages. First, you can use the data to qualify the account.

- Do you want to do business with them?

- What chance will the installation have of being successful?

- How much of your time will it take to get the sale?

- Will it be worth it?

- Does the account qualify? If not, do not waste your time.

Next, you can determine the customer's objectives and present your product in concert with them. Never present your product unless you clearly understand the customer's objectives.

The third advantage relates to your strategy. By finding out what the customer thinks is feasible, by getting customer input, by canvassing the total organization using their words and numbers, the assimilated data can be fed back to the customer as your strategy.

Finally, the data can be used to develop your sales message. The sales message, the value the customer can expect from purchasing your product, will be repeated over and over again until you close the order.

CHAPTER

7

Selling is changing the customer's behavior

Simply stated, selling is convincing or influencing someone to buy. Influence is the power to affect or alter someone by indirect or intangible means. When you affect someone, you stir their emotions. If you affect them in the way you wish, their behavior will change the way you wish it to change and they will buy. Therefore, selling involves behavior change.

If you are not intimately aware of the political climate, the environment, the customer's objectives, and your position relative to the competition, you will not be able to affect behavior change when you present your product, system, or service to a group or committee.

Additionally, if you have not presold at least some of the key members of the committee, you may be in for a rough ride. Your objective is to develop an intimate account relationship. To do this you must establish both a technical and a personal relationship with as many people in the account as possible. This should be started prior to any group presentation.

◯ ### *Establish Individual Relationships: There is no successful selling without interpersonal involvement*

Never present your product until you have talked individually with key members of the group, and clearly understand all their objectives.

Ideally, in terms of closing the sale, the sales presentation is nothing more than a group approval of your product, a confirmation of a decision to buy that has already been made during the various individual meetings. At each individual meeting, present your product informally, as you intend to present it formally to the committee.

Study the person's reaction and listen to what he or she says. Use the information you obtain from each individual meeting to link to the next. Your strategy is to divide and conquer.

As you sell to each individual, look for anything that might negatively affect your presentation. Be especially alert for conflicts of interest that might surface during the group presentation.

Since you never have a second chance to make a first impression, if your initial contact with a customer has created a bad or less-than-perfect impression, emphasize the good parts of the relationship.

The good parts must be exaggerated. Don't exaggerate the benefits of the product, but exaggerate or emphasize the good information that will repair the poor first contact. Talk about what is of most interest to the customer—their interest, not yours—or concentrate on a people-to-people relationship that will improve the first impression.

An item with no bearing on the product but of strong interest to the customer can act as a common ground of agreement, which will help repair the bad first impression, or breach, in the relationship.

If you drop the ball or otherwise get into trouble, allow the customer to forgive you rather than dwelling on an apology. Do not draw negative attention to yourself. Keep apologies out of your conversation except to the extent necessary to express sorrow for any inconvenience. Do not reinforce the negative.

C: *"We traveled to your factory last month and the demonstration was a disaster. Now you want us to go back again!"*

Reinforcing the Negative:

S: *"I am really sorry about the poor demonstration. Every-*
     body makes mistakes. We had a power outage the night
     before which caused some unexpected problems. Please
     give us a second chance. After all, it wasn't our fault."

Reinforcing the Positive:

S: *I am truly sorry about the inconvenience the power*
     outage caused. Still, we did get to check most of the items
     on your list, and you did have an opportunity, albeit
     unexpected, to meet with those potential customers for
     your new product. In any event, another visit would be
     beneficial since we can spend more time concentrating
     on the items most important to you. I can arrange the
     demonstration for Monday or Friday, which day do you
     prefer?"

It is important to convince some of the individuals to endorse your product privately. Endorsements by users to their managers or the decision-makers are helpful in promoting your product, especially if the user wants it and his manager favors the competitor or is undecided. Usually the decision-maker will listen to the user, if the user expresses a definitive reason to purchase.

Non-endorsements, that is, criticism, may come from people in your competitor's pocket or people trying to impress their managers at your expense.

It is risky to let a factory person, plant engineer, applications engineer, or anyone else give customer presentations without your presence. Managers should not make impromptu visits or calls without your involvement. They are unlikely to be in tune with your strategy and methodology and can disrupt any relationship you may have built.

Never assume the customer will understand if you are not present for a meeting after arranging it, especially if it is in your name. Customer-salesperson relationships are fragile and can be broken easily.

Entertainment is a tool that may be used to establish a relationship with individuals prior to a group meeting.

Customer entertainment, from simple lunches to sightseeing tours such as flights over the Grand Canyon, is an important selling tool. During excursions you will have a better opportunity to relate to the customer. All other things being equal, people like to do business with people they like.

Although these business relationships are personal in nature, they are not necessarily long-range and must be treated as a mutual means to an end. The customers want to know if they can trust you so they can decide whether to buy from you or not. You want to learn how to better understand the customers so you can sell to them.

In a way you are selling to each other. The customers are selling you on supporting them. You are selling the customers on buying from you.

When working with each group member individually, ask for a favor, not just any favor, but a favor that will allow the customer to feel good. Ask for something that has to do with the customers skills, knowledge, hobbies, or something you know they would like to do. Sometimes just asking for advice is enough. The objective is to develop a closer relationship with the customer.

Also, do a favor for the customer. Small favors go a long way in developing genuine and continuing human relationships.

Preselling is an iterative process. You can try something, observe the reaction, and adjust accordingly. This constant adaptation to the person and the situation allows you to find the right path to changing behaviors.

○ *Change is Emotional: Your customer must feel emotionally comfortable as well as rationally satisfied*

Since change is a highly emotional process, treat logic as a useful but limited tool. The process of selling is more an emotional than an intellectual task. To paraphrase the authors of *Do You Sincerely Want To Be Rich*, by Row, Page, and Hodeson, sales is a process of unrelenting emotional control in which every nuance of human intercourse is directed toward persuading someone to buy.[1]

Although persuading a customer to buy is facilitated by the satisfaction of a need, by a solution to a problem, or by the fulfillment of a desire, careful observation of the selling process indicates that reason or logic is only a small component of the persuasion. Customers will change their behavior—will buy—more in response to feelings than to facts.

[1]Row, et al., *Do You Sincerely Want to be Rich*, p. 75.

When you sell high technology products, more often than not the sale is being made to a group or committee rather than a single individual. The group must be sold just like the individual. The facts for an individual become the task for the group. The group task may be to decide which of several competing products to purchase.

To complete this task the group will deal with the facts. In dealing with the facts, the group will go through a process. The individual group members must communicate with one another, evaluate data, and make decisions. The way the individual group members go about their task is called group process. The task is deciding which product to purchase and is talked about in the formal meetings. Process, the emotions around the decision to be made, is observable outside the formal meetings.[2]

Individual group members, in addition to selecting a product, are also trying to advance their own personal agendas. In addition to promotion, stability and ego-satisfaction previously mentioned, a member may be interested in getting more power or a bigger piece of the action. If the individual personal agendas are in concert with the goals and objectives of the company, then the group can collectively bring more information and viewpoints to bear on a situation than an individual can. They can critically analyze information better and they can generate commitment by their members.

○ Adapt to the Group: Establish the position you want within the group pecking order

When you deal with a group, it is important to promote communications, to get the group members to express their personal feelings and needs.

Involve each member. Switch periodically from discussing the product to reviewing the process. This will help you better understand the group's emotions.[3]

In a group situation, adapting to the group is not easy. You must appeal to the group consciousness yet address each

---

[2]Harold J. Leavitt, *Managerial Psychology*, Fourth Edition, (Chicago, IL: Chicago University Press, 1978), pp. 197-213.

[3]Ibid.

person individually. This can be done more effectively if you have previously cultivated personal relationships with the important people and if you have presold the key thought leaders and decision makers.

Groups tend to be judgmental by their nature. If the group is solid, with its members reinforcing each other in favor of the competition, making the sale will be difficult. If, on the other hand, the group is weak, the chance of influencing them is much greater.[4]

In summary, when you sell to a group or committee, the attitudes of the group must be changed. First identify the specific interests, prejudices and personal agendas of each member and work with them individually through one-on-one meetings. Then, during group meetings, address the interests, prejudices, and agendas of the various individuals through the orientation and structure of the presentation. The group behavior is changed through the individual members.

[4]Ibid.

CHAPTER

8

Close before answering all the customer's questions

The sale of high technology products and systems, especially high-ticket items costing hundreds of thousands of dollars, requires repeated sales calls before a buy decision is made. High technology products are rarely sold in a single call. It is not uncommon for the sales cycle to take six months, a year, or even three years before the customer releases the purchase order.

○ *Regular Exposure: Keep in contact with your customers*

The users of high technology products, and sometimes even the purchasing agents, are experts, often knowing more about the product than the salesperson. Consequently, they like to buy rather than be sold. They are not impressed with the old high-pressure sales techniques, lavish presentations, jokes, or excessive flattery.

Rhetoric is not enough with these buyers. Promises must be kept, schedules must be met, and committed follow-up must be put into effect. The key to selling these buyers is exposure. Through regular exposure they will get to know you, begin to believe in you, and see the value you can provide.

Another reason for regular exposure is so you do not miss an opportunity. Things move very fast in high technology companies. Decisions to spend millions of dollars are sometimes made in days. On the other hand, future requirements are sometimes known internally months in advance of when a request for quote is made. Through regular exposure, you can become aware of them before they are known outside the company and get a head start on your competitors.

Continually develop good reasons to return and talk to the customer. The members in an evaluation team or committee are likely to have different reasons to buy. Through multiple meetings, you'll be able to ferret out these motives. As you understand them more clearly, you'll be better able to sell your solution.

Regular exposure will also help you measure your progress, continually assess the situation, monitor the competition, and uncover new objections. Even more important, regular exposure will help you better serve the customer.

○ Customer Meetings: Make sure they're useful, frequent enough, and timely

Just after you have made a formal presentation is an excellent time to call again on the customer. Set up an appointment with at least one member of the group or committee. If you have left certain items out of your presentation, things that you could not have covered properly anyway, at least not in the time allotted, you will have reasons to return to the account. When you return, provide these items and amplify other information about the material previously presented.

If specific information has been requested, it is important that you respond as quickly as possible with it. Ensure that the data is accurate, as this will help develop your credibility and enhance your image, and the image of your company.

When you develop a credit rating, you must borrow to owe something so you can pay it off over time. Likewise, if you provide your customer with accurate information regularly and on time, you'll develop a great credibility record.

Never mail or ship anything to a customer if it is practical to deliver it by hand. This will give you more face-to-face contact and provide you with an advantage over the competitor who uses the mail.

A summary of reasons to return include:

- To provide items not included in your presentation.

- To address any outstanding issues.

- To provide more technical information.

- To discuss in further detail the application or problem.

- To deliver and explain the proposal.

- To discuss the terms and conditions of purchase.

- To discuss installation logistics.

- To discuss training and post-installation service of the product or system.

- To arrange a factory tour.

- To arrange a product demonstration.

- To provide financial information.

- To arrange an upper-management meeting.

- To meet with the corporate strategic planner to discuss future plans and directions.

- To obtain some information about something relevant.

- To develop a mutually beneficial rapport with the customer through social contact, such as lunch.

These meetings should be planned as part of the overall account sales strategy. The more sales calls you make, the greater the probability of obtaining the order, if the calls are planned quality calls. Another excellent reason to return is to help the customer prepare the purchasing specification. This call should be made prior to making a presentation or submitting a proposal.

○ ## Call Objective: Never call on a customer without a sales reason

Why am I making this call? Ask yourself this question and answer it before you take up a customer's time. Every time you make a call on any customer you should have a clearly defined objective. Determine what it is you want the customer to accept, decide, or do, before you make the call.

If your objective is to gather facts, ensure that during the fact-finding call you link to the next call. Never call a customer just to ask for the order. Make sure that prior to asking you provide some useful or informative data.

If you know it is time to call on the customer but you have nothing to say, you've got a problem. A salesperson with nothing to say is like an Apple without bytes. It indicates you have not done a proper job of researching the customer or you have answered all the customers questions without closing the order.

○ ## The RFQ: The buyer's Request For Quote should be written to describe your product

The buyer usually purchases to a specification, often in the form of an RFQ. Your objective is to help the buyer write the RFQ. After the initial contact, ferret out the people responsible for writing the specification for the RFQ and help them. Sometimes these people are knowledgeable enough to write it, but too busy or not inclined to do the paperwork. They will welcome the help you offer.

At other times, they are not knowledgeable, or lack confidence, and will be forever grateful for your assistance. Others simply do not wish to be bothered and will delegate it to anyone; you can be that anyone.

Ideally, the RFQ ends up being a copy of your product specification. If this is not possible, work to include the features exclusive to your product or specifications that only your product can fully meet. Also include items with which your competitors will have difficulty complying, or which will discourage them.

If you are successful, your product will become the reference against which your competitor's product will be compared. If your product is superior to the competitor's, they will not bid, propose a reduced specification, or try to sell around the RFQ.

Conversely, if your competitor's products are superior to yours, you will have neutralized their advantages by having the RFQ written with a specification in terms of your product. The competitive product may now be viewed as an overkill—more than what is required to do the job.

○ *Long Sales Cycle Problems: The long sales cycle for high technology products has attendant problems*

During the lengthy sales cycle, other problems will confront you. The buying committee will probably be dynamic, changing over time, through personnel promotions, resignations, or reassignments. Sometimes, just as you have cultivated a committee member, he or she will leave and you must start all over again.

The customer's product requirements or even your product may change before the sale is made. The product you were selling initially may not even resemble what they finally buy months or years later. Prices and competitive pressures will also change. New safety factors may appear. A new product from your competitor may be announced. Elaborate handling or financing may evolve from a simple agreement. Decisions and needs will be revisited and revisited and revisited.

The longer it takes for the order to be placed, the more chances you have of changing places with the leader, if you are not the customer's first choice. On the other hand, if you are the customer's first choice, the longer it takes for the order to be let, the more vulnerable you are to the competition.

It is not uncommon for the salesperson who lived and bled with the account for months or years, who spent time and money educating the customer, to lose the sale in the eleventh hour due to the actions of the competitor, due to a last minute change in the requirement, or due to a change in personnel assigned to make the decision.

For example, after a salesperson spends months educating a potential customer to the features of the software, the competitor swoops in just as the order is about to be placed and working on the customer's fears, sells the customer on a low risk hardware alternative. (After all, you can see and feel hardware;

software is sort of mystical and esoteric.) The salesperson is then left wondering what happened. Had the customer been presold on the value of the solution as well as educated to the benefits of software, the outcome might have been different.

In the second example, after the salesperson convinces the customer the product she or he is selling is the only one that can do it "this" way, everybody wants to buy it. Unfortunately the budget is delayed and delayed. Finally, just as the budget is about to be approved the company changes direction and wants to do it "that" way. Now the competitor wonders what happened as he or she picks up the order.

In the last example, the salesperson focuses on one individual to the exclusion of everyone else; after all, this individual is the decision maker. Then, just before the order is placed, the decision maker is promoted into a different department and the new decision maker who wants to make his or her own mark buys from the competition.

Hy Kaplan says, "The burden of customer penetration, development and control lies heavy on the salesperson when the elapsed time to make a sale is lengthy."[1] Always have a reason to return until after the close.

---

[1]Kaplan, *Selling Effectively to Committees.*

CHAPTER

9

Present your solution early

High technology sales often call for two or more presentations before the order is placed. These presentations have two purposes; a technical purpose where the product and benefits are presented, and a business purpose where solutions are proposed.

Depending on the product's complexity, multiple technical presentations may be made prior to the proposal presentation. During the presentations, as the product and solution are presented, look for objections to overcome, problems to solve, and conditions that might stop or delay a buy decision. It is your objective during the presentations to differentiate your solution from the competitor's while reaching mutual concurrence with the customer on all major points.

After you have addressed all major objections satisfactorily and if the customer is ready to buy, the timing is appropriate to make your proposal presentation. The objective of the proposal presentation is to close.

○   ### *Conducting the Presentation: Product presentations have characteristically effective times and methods*

Formal product presentations to a group or committee, especially for capital equipment and systems, can be as short as 20 minutes or as long as a full day. Unlike mystery plays or jokes, the *denouement* or punchline must be delivered early within the first 18 minutes of the presentation, even though multiple product presentations will be made before a sale is closed. Everything after the first 18 minutes is reinforcement to expand or complement the solution you offer.

There are several reasons to conduct a presentation in this manner. First, since retention of critical items is limited by time, you must earn the customer's attention early and deliver the solution clearly and succinctly.

Second, key individuals and top managers may only be willing to devote a short period of time to your presentation, usually at the beginning.

Since there will often be a mix of financial, technical, and management people at the presentation, to reach this diverse group your presentation must be carefully planned. Present a general overview and your solution, emphasizing the key benefits or values in laymen's terms. Your objective is to create interest and explain your solution.

After the overview, present major aspects of the product and supporting data, always focusing on your solution. Never introduce new solutions after the first 18 minutes.

Make your key presentation interesting, exciting, and enthusiastic. Know your material cold but do not be overbearing or too assertive. Take an indirect approach. During your presentation, talk with, rather than at, the audience. Be prepared to deviate from your planned presentation if you are not getting through.

The degree of formality is a function of the composition of the audience. Normally it is better not to be too formal, except when presenting to top management or an executive committee. Then assume a high degree of formality until a familiar atmosphere is set by the audience. Be prompt but do not become perturbed if you must wait for people to show up. Delay enhances the power of the host. If you are late, do not rush in. Take a few moments to compose yourself. You want to look in control at all times. Always finish on time, even if delayed,

unless an extension is granted. Take blame for all misunder-
standings, but do not grovel. Look out for your own interests. Be
firm yet diplomatically flexible. Be honest and avoid statements of exaggeration.

Reiterate and summarize often. Draw the audience into
your presentation, tell them what they want to hear, then sell
them. Then tell the audience what you want them to hear, then
sell them again. Show them what they want is what you offer.
Repeat your sales message again and again. You can't make
your point too often.

If you know and understand the competition, then you can
combat them by thoroughly differentiating and selling both
your company and your product. Weave your competitive
strengths and advantages throughout your presentation. Point
out what to look for in the kind of product you are selling. These
points should be your competitor's weaknesses.

Compare your methodology to other competitive techniques and clearly show your superiority. Differentiate your
product or service in at least two areas, one product-related
and one market-related. Diifferentiating your product and company will bias the customer's choice because the customer is
likely to remember you. For high technology products, differentiating or positioning requires rigorous and continuous competitive customer, product, and market-needs analysis.

If the top managers do not show up during the first 18
minutes but drop in later, and if you have already made your
major point or points, other members of the group, if suitably
impressed, will ask you to review the key portions. They will do
this for their manager's benefit as well as their own. This is
especially true if members of the group support your product,
and are intent on convincing their managers that your product
is the right way to go.

If they do not ask you to review, repeat yourself by making
the same point or points again without interrupting the natural
flow of your presentation, keep your format flexible.

The ability to be quick on your feet can be decisive during a
presentation. Winston Churchill was a master presenter. He
spoke frequently with both wit and ease. He sold others on his
politics and ideas. He ralled the country in dark times. He was
a polished performer, a natural speaker. "No member could be
quicker on his feet than Winston."

Yet this eloquence and quickness required intense preparation. "Few knew....of the exhausting rehearsals....the infinite pains that went into each polished performance."

Winston also "….followed every important speech delivered by the oposition with alertness, and mental agility."[1] Winston was a great *salesman*, strategist, and presenter because he knew his competitor and he practiced.

Always dry-run your presentation with your peers, sales colleagues, or spouse. If no one else will listen, do it alone in front of a mirror or with audio/visual (A/V) equipment and be your own audience. Rehearse and practice. Master the art of presenting to groups and you will have a clear advantage.

○ Controlling the Presentation: The salesperson should maintain control of the presentation

To maintain control over the audience, employ the standard methods of making eye contact with each person, acknowledging each person, and using personal names.

During your presentation, all major points must come across clearly and succinctly. Make the fullest possible use of questions to stimulate desire and lead the thinking. Ask the audience to express their views and reactions periodically. Listen, stop, clarify, and verify as required; manage the presentation to maintain control of the conversation.

Control means not allowing digression or deviation from the direction you wish to take the audience, unless you perceive it will benefit your cause. This doesn't mean you should in any way limit interaction with the audience. In fact, if the customer is not asking questions and directly participating, you're probably not reaching them.

○ Audience Participation: Give the audience something specific to do

Audience participation does not mean audience control. Establish the ground rules and entertain comments and questions during the presentation if the presentation is short and simple. If it is long and involved, it is better to hold or delay discussions until the formal part of the presentation has been completed, but not at the expense of participation.

[1]Manchester, *"The Last Lion"*, p. 344.

In other words, avoid being sidetracked, and avoid digression, but always recognize interruptions. Acknowledge the interrupters, compliment him or her, restate the interruption in your own words for purposes of clarification, and so the others will understand your answer. If you cannot answer it, field it to another member of your group who has the answer or put it on hold until the end of the presentation.

It is mandatory to involve the customer if you are to have a successful presentation. If you have done a thorough job of gathering information on the background of the company, the people, and their needs and problems, you should have no trouble orchestrating a participatory presentation.

Only through interacting with your audience will you be able to determine the impression the audience is forming. Through involvement you will be able to ascertain the thoughts and, more important, the feelings of the customer. Too often presentations are so formal, so structured or *canned* that the customer feedback is very limited.

If the product is not portable or if you wish to avoid a full demonstration, using physical objects such as a short computer printout, a printed circuit board, a gear, or a connector is an excellent way to involve a customer. Also, induce some of the audience to get up and write on the flip chart or white board to explain or clarify a point.

Getting the customer to feel things, help you, hold charts or papers, move around a little, and explain how something works or should be done is a powerful psychological reinforcer for the message you are trying to communicate.

If the audience does not appear to be responding properly, if they're unresponsive or communicating negative messages, change subjects, ask for a break, or change physical positions in the room. such tactics will relax the environment and the people and help get you back on track.

It is important to know what you don't know. Don't ever try to explain a complicated graph, chart, or concept unless you totally and thoroughly understand it. If you do get confused, your customer will become irritated.

If you find yourself in such an embarrassing position, stop, look your customer in the eyes, smile, and say, "I am sorry but I guess I really don't understand myself."

Continue with, "I will be back with the correct explanation."

However, if your customer says, "Let's see if we can figure it out together," take the opportunity to build a closer bond, through shared exploration. Interest, togetherness, and people-to-people contact will result in success.

Although it is important to involve the customer, it is a mistake to distribute copies of your presentation, manuals, proposals, specifications, or anything else that will tempt the customer to look ahead, or read at the expense of your presentation.

Material or objects distributed should be meaningful and relevant, but not distracting. You should not pass out anything that will compete with your presentation.

In the final analysis, it is not the objective of the presentation to present the product or educate the customer, your objective is to close the sale by communicating your solution.

○ *Critiquing the Presentation: Learn from the presentation by discussing it afterward*

After your presentation, critique it with your sales team, or if alone, with yourself.

- Was it worth the time and effort?
- Did you achieve your planned results?
- Was the audience prepared for you or did you surprise them?
- If they were surprised, was it because you introduced new information, or because you did not effectively presell them?
- Did you differentiate your product?
- Did you anticipate the objections?
- Were there too many objections?
- If there were too many objections, was it because your presentation was premature?
- What can you improve upon in your next presentation?
- Were you in control?
- In your estimation, did you neutralize or eliminate the competition?

CHAPTER

(10)

Use showmanship judiciously

To make a results-oriented presentation, know your target. Make the presentation in terms of your audience. Organize your presentation to be specific enough to illustrate but general enough to captivate. This is accomplished by developing several concepts while focusing on one main theme or idea.

○ *The Opening: The beginning of your presentation should make it memorable*

Open your presentation in a meaningful, interesting, and exciting way. But don't start your presentation with a joke and don't say, "I am going to talk about...". Start with a question and attention getter or anecdote that is appropriate.

"The semiconductor industry tests too much. (pause) This is due to its lack of knowledge about the semiconductor manufacturing process."

"Everything I am going to present to you today is already obsolete."

"Information is an asset. (pause) Just like capital."

"What do you think is the greatest cause of inefficiency in your manufacturing process?"

"Did you hear what AMD's president, Jerry Saunders, said about success after their stock rose three hundred percent in just three months?"

The Delivery: You won't sell your product on dry facts

The best presentations, even presentations for highly technical products and systems, should have action, life, and human interest. You are not selling to a computer; you are selling to fellow, often busy, bored, human beings. Enthusiasm is essential.

Vary laughter and seriousness. Balance general statements with specific experiences. If you are the best or No. 1 in the industry do not tout this, for you may appear insecure—or your criteria for being No. 1 might be different than the customer's criteria. It is better to enhance your position in the customer's mind. Be clear about why your solution is best and support advantages with fact. Remember, you should be presenting a solution that has already been agreed upon by many of the key participants. Also remember not to assume those committed to your solution will support you during your presentation. The committed ones may wish to stay low key, may not wish to publicly declare themselves, may prefer to play the devil's advocate, or may simply be shy.

Professionalism breeds confidence. How you look, how you act, and the props you use are important. Dress impeccably but appropriately for the environment. A three-piece Brooks Brothers suit may not go over well in El Paso, Texas. Do not smoke during the presentation. If you do smoke later, ask permission first.

As you get into your presentation, talk to each customer individually. Never try to address the group en masse. Stand straight and move about. Be demonstrative. Talk fast, slow, loud, or soft as appropriate to maintain attention, but don't race. Pronounce your words clearly and keep your voice pitched low, but project it.

○ The Props: Visual or audible aids can help customers remember the information you give them

Although looks, behavior, and props will not close the sale for you, they can facilitate a deciding notion in the minds of many of the participants, especially key upper managers.

Some common props are flip charts, or viewgraphs, (opaque transparencies with a projector), 35 mm color slides, video tapes, and if appropriate, product mock-ups, parts of the product, or the product itself. Avoid movies; they often present set-up difficulties and are noisy and distracting.

If you use slides or viewgraphs, do not darken the room completely. Leave enough light to see the faces of your audience. To use visual aids effectively requires practice and preplanning. It is important to use your audience's sense of sight and hearing when you drive a point home.

Writing on blank viewgraphs or flip charts will hold the attention of the audience better than prepared media. Blank props provide showmanship possibilities. You can write a large sized word for emphasis, tear off or throw away for effect, or underline to stress a point. These props also provide you with the ability to develop your ideas as you go along.

Partially prepared charts or transparencies with single titles or words allow you to make points around what is written. Conversely, fully prepared media has the advantage of efficiency. It is not necessary to write as you talk.

Practice your presentation and know exactly what you are going to write. With flip charts, pencil in notes that the audience can't see. When you do write, keep talking or you will lose or bore your audience. Do not write in script. It is difficult for some to read and has less impact. Print large enough so that everyone can see it. Always stand sideways when you are writing; never turn your back on the audience. If you write in response to an unanticipated question, pause, think carefully, get clarification, and respond briefly.

With transparencies and flip charts or white boards, use colored pens. Be generous with underlines, circles, asterisks, arrows, and other symbols. Eye-catching forms, catchy phrases, and originality, as well as some humor, can be used for emphasis. In the case of prepared media, use color and keep things simple, uncluttered, and specific—one idea to a page or slide. Ensure that attention is focused on the main point. Some humor can be effective if carefully prepared and appropriate. Always remember, thought organization is more important than art.

In the case of projected visuals, set everything up prior to the presentation. Check that the projection bulb is not burned out, that the power cord reaches the wall outlet, and that the control cord for the slide projector is long enough. A remote control unit is best.

Follow these rules with visuals: know the sequence, have a theme that ties everything together for continuity, tailor and personalize your show to the company or situation, use duplicate charts or slides to repeat key points, never say, "This slide just means....", never flip back and forth, and do not overwhelm your audience with too many pages or slides. A rule of thumb is a maximum of one slide or page per two minutes.

Cover each page or slide in its entirety or your audience will read it and ask questions, or become confused, or wonder why you did not cover it all. Restate the main theme of each visual before going to the next. In the case of video tape, after showing it, turn it off and repeat the main points.

At the end of your presentation, summarize verbally or use a close chart or slide.

◯ Showmanship: Use showmanship judiciously

Don't avoid showmanship. Showmanship helps people remember what you said and makes your presentation fun to see and hear. On the other hand, showmanship must not be used in an attempt to cover up a poor presenter or presentation.

Some showmanship ideas include mystery, realism, and contrast. Covering something until you are ready to unveil it is a mystery. A display of static electric when you are talking about antistatic products is realistic. Comparing the size of a vacuum tube to a microcomputer chip is contrast.

Use showmanship in your presentation, but use it judiciously, and you, your product, and your solution will be remembered.[1]

[1]Alexander Hamilton Institute, Inc. Modern Business Reports, *"The Marketing Letter"*, (The Alexander Hamilton Institute, Inc., 1633 Broadway, New York, NY 10019) Vol 1, No. 11, February 1975 through Vol. 4, No. 11, February, 1978 were referenced in this book. For this chapter refer to Vol. 3, No. 7, Oct. 1976, p. 3 and Vol. 3, No. 9, Dec. 1976, p. 3.

CHAPTER

(11)

Demonstrations are risky

Often, a factory demonstration of your product is required to provide convincing proof of its operation and to overcome buyer reluctance, fear, and lack of confidence. The extent of the demonstration depends on the reputation of your product or company, your experience with the application, and how new your product or technology is. A nationally recognized company or product will require less assurance through a demonstration than a small, relatively unknown company or a new product.

Sometimes a demonstration is a mere formality or a justification for a visit to your factory. Whatever the reason, demonstrations are risky. There are just too many things that can go wrong. Worse yet, the customer may see something he or she doesn't like. In competitive situations, beware of demonstrations where the competition has set you up by informing the customer of all the *negative* features of your product. In this case, the customer's intention in asking for a demonstration may be to confirm them and disqualify you.

On the other hand, a carefully planned positive demonstration can win you the order. A successful demonstration is a result of preparation. Everything and everybody must be prepared in advance. An in-depth dry run of the demonstration must be made.

The purpose of the demonstration is not to show off the features of your equipment, but to reinforce in the customer's mind the decision to buy. Demonstrations to prove operation, confirm specifications or develop credibility are risky if the buy decision has not yet been made. The demonstration should not be used to develop interest or save a sale. Interest should be developed early in the sales process, and demonstrations rarely save lost sales. The steps required to have a successful demonstration follow.

○ *Preparation: Demonstrations require careful preparation*

- If required, meet the customer at the airport, make hotel accommodations, arrange tours, send a basket of fruit, wine or cheese to their room if this is not against their company's policy, and otherwise treat them as royalty. As far as you are concerned, they are.

- If the customer comes the day before or stays the night of the demonstration or if they are local, take them to dinner and have a top manager present. Depending on the situation, take them to lunch or have lunch catered. Do not use the company cafeteria unless you have access to an executive or customer area. Out-of-context statements or emotional conversations overheard in the company cafeteria could cost you the sale since they may be misunderstood by the customer. Have refreshments available during the demonstration.

- When the customer arrives at your facility, have badges with their names prepared for them in advance. Better yet, deliver them to their company or hotel the night before, along with an agenda.

- Make sure you are present. Never let the customer attend a first time or critical demonstration without you being present. Remember Murphy's law. Sales are sometimes lost after an unsatisfactory factory demonstration. You might have been able to save it.

• If the demonstration is complex and takes place at a trade show or a customer site, make sure your demonstration team is there the day before to ensure everything is in order even if the customer will actually conduct the demonstration. They will need your support.

• Dry run the demonstration first, even if you have to do it at midnight. Then forbid anyone to touch the equipment.

• If a benchmark, that is, a verification of the performance of your product under defined and controlled conditions, is involved, make sure all details are known well in advance of the dry run. Do your utmost to avoid or head off surprise requests by the customer. Do not attempt bench marks at trade shows or exhibitions. The chance of something going wrong is an order of magnitude greater than it would be at your factory.

• Prepare and clean up the demonstration room or area. This is not as obvious as it sounds. It is usually overlooked.

• Is the room is noisy, use a microphone. If most of the action takes place on a video display terminal, have a large remote display available.

Conducting: Conduct demonstrations as carefully as you prepare for them

• Use block diagrams or flow charts during the demonstration. Prepare them on flip charts or a graphics computer terminal. These explain what is happening internal to the system or equipment if a complex interaction is taking place.

• Prepare a demonstration kit for the customer which explains the demonstration and provides such things as computer print-outs, benchmark data, or photographs as appropriate. These data should be thoroughly screened for errors, proprietary information, and relevancy to the sales situation. Use the customer's name and logo wherever possible in this kit.

- Ensure that the person performing the demonstration is not a droner but can articulate with conviction. If the person performing the demonstration is not capable of detailing the benefits to the customer, have the salesperson or a marketer talk as the demonstrator performs.

- Make a presentation about the equipment prior to the demonstration. Cover what the customer will see in detail so that the customer knows what is happening.

- Set the customer's expectations low. Promise less than you can demonstrate.

- Ensure the demonstration shows the system or equipment at its optimum performance. Demonstrate only what works well and is impressive.

- Clearly point out where you are different from the competition. Explain why you are different, and the benefit to the customer, but do not mention the competition by name.

- Clearly point out the competitor's weaknesses, again without mentioning the competitor by name, but by showing the customer what to look for during a demonstration. The look fors should be your strengths.

- Show how you designed for quality and built for reliability. This is a golden opportunity to show off your workmanship.

- Get the customer involved. Let them push switches, play with the keyboard, adjust the oscilloscope, hold things, review the print-outs, and give feedback.

- If the demonstration takes place in your facility, have the highest level manager stop by to shake hands and say hello, even if the visitors are technicians. It only takes 2–3 minutes of the manager's time and it will be remembered.

- If the demonstration is over 30 minutes and highly technical, and if non-technical people as well as technical people attend, find something to interest the non-technical people if they are lost or start getting bored. A talk with their counterpart in your company is a useful and informative activity.

- If the demonstration takes place at your facility, be sure to give the customer a plant tour and show off your technology. Don't overlook the quality, manufacturing, engineering, and finance departments. Find something to say about each department or area which explains how the customer will benefit from your organization, policy, and procedures. Plan and dry run the tour inadvance.

○ ## Critique: Talk over the demonstration with your customer

- Meet with the customer right after the demonstration. Critique all results and record action items. Explain away any problems which may have been encountered. Link to the next step in the sales process or close the order.

- Never assume you can overcome poor performance with your fantastic personality, charm, wit, friendship, or a great dinner. Those attributes and sales condiments are used to soften a customer but will rarely result in a sale. Only hard work and professional performance will succeed.

Some of the above steps may be modified or eliminated depending upon the type and price of the equipment, the size or potential size of the order, and the status of the visitors. Use your judgment but go first class and like the Boy Scouts—be prepared.

CHAPTER

(12)

Respond rapidly and personally

A sales letter is a genius in minor art form. Sales letters may be grouped into five categories: introductory, follow-up, transmittal, thank you, and response. Each letter has one fundamental aim: sales impact. Each letter has one fundamental characteristic: clarity. Each letter begets one fundamental result: immediate attention.

○ The Sales Letter: Sell in the first sentence

Sales impact means communicating a valid and convincing argument. Punch lines and surprise endings do not work in business. It is best to get to your point quickly; in fact, it is better to start with your point and be specific.[1]

[1]Alexander Hamilton Institute, *The Marketing Letter,* Vol. 4, No. 7, Oct. 1977, p. 1.

Use exact words and numbers whenever possible. Tell exactly what value you are offering, how they can save money, or increase production, or whatever it is about your product that will make the customer want to buy.

Avoid extravagant claims. You may not be believed even if it is true. Give the reader a solid, credible reason to buy.

If you are offering something special, say so in the first sentence. Many business executives never read beyond the first sentence. Otherwise ensure the first sentence attracts the attention of the reader.

In any letter, use simple words and phrases to communicate your product's value. Always be sure to differentiate yourself from the competitor in some way. If you "me too" them, you will not have the effect you seek.

Clarity cannot be emphasized too strongly. Too often we write too much about something when a clear, simple message is more effective. Keep sentences short, never over fifteen words. Use transitional phrases to link your messages, and show your direction.

"In contrast to," "on the other hand," and "therefore" are useful phrases that help bring clarity. Good writing per se is not the objective. You may have to sacrifice good writing for a blunt sales approach and clarity, but this is not a license to break the rules of grammar.

Errors in punctuation or spelling are *verboten*. No letter should ever leave your office unless it is letter perfect. Reread and retype or edit as many times as necessary until you are satisfied it says exactly what you want it to say and is grammatically free of errors.

If there is a verb for it, use it. Use verbs instead of nouns whenever possible, and do not make nouns out of verbs.

Eliminate big or uncommon words, needless phrases, and redundant sentences. Keep your letter to one page. That's right, one page. Use clear logic, no shoddy thinking, and communicate both reliability and accountability. Use attachments for any information that must be presented and does not fit on a page.

A spare prose style encourages direct action. For example, newspaper-style writing inspires action.

On the other hand, if you are trying to project a certain formality, you may wish to write in the passive voice. This appeals to certain readers.

Study the little book *The Elements of Style* by Strunk and White; in fact, master it. Remember that short sentences and common words achieve clarity and inspire action.

How would you react to the following two sentences:

1. "Concentrate on obtaining a commitment from the customer by converging on that predilection as your
cynosure, ensuring all your actions and thoughts are
centripetal to it."

2. "Believe in nothing, nothing except getting the sale.
Everything you do, everything, must be what you need to
do to get this sale."

Write the letter from the customer's viewpoint. The readers
will want to know what is in it for them. Form letters are
anathema. Personalize your letter. Because a typical executive
receives so many letters and proposals, the personal touch may
facilitate immediate action.

Introductory Letter or Telephone Call: Give them a reason and a desire to consider you and your product

An introductory letter introduces you, your company, and
your product. It gives the reader a reason to agree to meet with
you. An introductory letter should contain a powerful sales
argument and should clearly communicate value.

The introductory letter is also used to blaze the trail for the
telephone call you will make to qualify the account and arrange
an appointment.

A telephone call can also be made in place of the introductory letter, in which case the same message that would have
been delivered in the introductory letter is delivered verbally.

Some pitfalls of telephone conversations include being too
technical or referring to the competitor, verbosity and using
superfluous adjectives or overfamiliarity, talking too fast, being
unprepared or tentative, and being presumptuous or asking
permission. When you talk to the customer, especially if it is a
cold call and if the contact is a high level manager, remember
these three rules:

1. Just communicate the value you offer. You are not expected to make lapidary statements. Management should
not be expected to break out the chisel and cut your
profound words into granite.

2. It is o.k. to say, "I don't know." No one expects you to know all the answers, just where to get them.

3. Don't forget the purpose of the call. If your objective is to set up a meeting, do not let the thrill of talking to a high level manager, or a pleasant and delightful conversation, divert you from your purpose. You will feel like a fool if you hang up with a warm glow and then realize you forgot to arrange the meeting.

The content of the following sample introductory letter could have just as easily been communicated in a telephone conversation.

Dear Mr. Customer:

As a corporate executive, over half of your working time is spent reading, analyzing, and producing documents.

For the past twelve years, our Corporation (company name) has been in the business of automating these aspects of the executive office. Yet, in spite of advances in information processing, studies show that more than 50% of all documents are still created on a typewriter.

As the Account Representative in your area, I would like an opportunity to demonstrate how we can help you save time. I will contact you next week to arrange an appointment.

Sincerely,

The first paragraph generates immediate attention. In the second paragraph, both the company and the problem are identified. The final paragraph communicates the value and sets the stage for a meeting. The letter is short, concise, and clear.

○ Follow-Up Letter: Use follow-up letters to document the results of a meeting or telephone call

The second type of letter, the follow-up letter, is sent after a meeting or important telephone conversation and is used to continue the selling motion by confirmation. This is important for high technology products where the sales cycle is long. Always confirm any agreements or commitments, and link to the next meeting. The follow-up letter is also used to make assurances to the customer.

○ *Transmittal Letter: Use transmittal letters to stimulate interest*

The transmittal letter is the introduction to the quotation or proposal. It should be imaginative and stimulate interest. It should recognize the joint efforts of your company and the customer in making the proposal possible. It should show how your product will improve their operations, and should conclude with a request for action. Sometimes, especially if your objective is to attract attention, telex the introductory letter along with the quotation or an abridged version of the proposal. If a manager receives a two- or three-foot telex or TWX it will attract attention.

○ *Thank You Letter: Use thank you letters to tidy up any loose ends*

The thank you letter thanks the customer for the order, commits the delivery, and requests an appointment to develop an implementation program. This letter is the start of your keep-the-customer-happy strategy.

○ *Response Letter: Use response letters to let your customer know you're on top of things*

The response letter must be sent within 24 hours of a customer's request, even if the customer did not ask for a response. It is vital that you respond quickly. If the response must come from higher management, write it for them and have it signed by them. If the specific manager isn't there, write, "In the manager's absence I am advising you...." If the manager does not wish to become personally involved, write, "In talking with Mr. Manager...." or "Mr. Manager has agreed...."

In any event, answer every letter or telephone call personally and answer it within 24 hours. Even minor requests should be answered immediately. If you are waiting for a response from another department which is due the next day, a short delay in replying is acceptable. If the response may take a week or more, reply immediately and inform the customer when you will have the answer. Then make sure you meet that commitment. Remember what somebody who must have been famous once said, "Writing maketh the exact person."

CHAPTER

(13)

The proposal is your signature

A written proposal supports and follows your presentation to facilitate group approval of your solution. You close with the proposal. The proposal is the grand finale, the culmination of a well-conducted sales campaign. Therefore, a poorly written proposal is a recipe for account salmonella.

○ *Definition of a Proposal: The key is careful planning*

The proposal is a previously discussed and agreed-to plan. It is reviewed by upper management, finance, purchasing, and associated departments and personnel. It confirms what you have already told others during your presentation and one-on-one meetings, and it informs those who have not participated in meetings with you.

The proposal provides the mechanism by which the customer analyzes your offer and clearly sees the course of future action. It supports internal discussions about your product or service, and it acts as the basis for future negotiations.

It also justifies the time and money the customer must invest to acquire your product.

Finally, a proposal is a legally binding offer to sell, so you must be willing and able to follow through with your commitments.

The proposal is designed to advance your position in the sales process. It must be interesting, factual, easy to read, and easy to understand. Both content and form are important.

The proposal is designed to confirm the customer's belief that the decision is the right one.

The proposal is short yet complete, having all the necessary information. As a minimum, it contains a list of advantages, a list of financial considerations, and an implementation plan.

A proposal should not contain irrelevant or tangential material. It should not use strong, emotional, promotional, or exaggerated language. Above all it should contain no surprises.

A surprise will reopen negotiations and delay the close. It is never acceptable to introduce a surprise unless you are losing the sale or have lost it.

If you feel you are losing or have lost, inform the supportive key individuals of what is coming, so they can prepare themselves and their management. Then introduce your surprise, based on some *new* information as an addendum or revision to your original proposal. If carefully planned, a loss can be turned into a win through the proposal.

◯ Contents of a Proposal: Summary, scope, benefits, implementation, contracts, and financial analysis

An effective proposal is made when concurrence has been reached between you and your customer on all important points. The proposal starts with a transmittal letter directed to the individual responsible for the purchase, and the purchasing agent.

An *executive summary* that ties your proposal to key individuals in the account, and restates past agreements, follows the transmittal letter. This summary references the customer's selection criteria, lists the major reasons to buy, and asks for the order.

The executive summary is an important part of the proposal because it will be read by the most people. It should never exceed two pages and should consist of short paragraphs and be easy to read, with major benefits highlighted. This is the section that will sell the proposal.

A *scope section* follows the executive summary and states the objectives of the customer and the nature of their needs.

A *benefit section* catalogs the advantages you provide. These advantages are written to present you as the clear-cut winner. The benefits should be indexed to detailed proof in other sections of the proposal.

The *implementation plan* is the most important part of the proposal and details your responsibilities and the customer's responsibilities. The plan shows the customer how you will help meet the objectives and contains a time line or a Gant chart that lists the major events on the vertical axis, and the time when they will occur on the horizontal axis. This chart is extremely helpful to the customer in fully understanding your proposal. It also lets other departments such as facilities, personnel, and finance know when they are expected to perform some action.

A *contracts* or *quotation section* includes the configuration of your product or the details of your service, the price, the delivery, and the terms and conditions of the sale. Terms include method of payment, discount conditions, if any, warranties, guarantees, services, and other contractual details. The terms and conditions should include a disclaimer. A disclaimer avoids providing a guarantee of expected performances. This will ensure that any estimates of performance or cost savings are just that, estimates, and will not be regarded as expressed or implied warranties.

The disclaimer should not be a separate section, but included somewhere where it will not draw special attention to itself.

A true contract cannot exist unless there is a complete understanding, by both the buyer and seller, of all elements of the offering. It is incumbent upon you to ensure the buyer understands all these elements. Do not avoid these details, even if it raises objections.

The contract should also include a place for signature so that everything is ready and the stage is set if the customer agrees to buy when you present the proposal.

It is unlikely the customer will sign your contract. Purchasing agents usually generate their own contracts, patterned after yours if you have done your job right, for you and your company to approve and sign.

A *financial consideration section* manifests the cost justification in your favor. It may include a return-on-investment and cost-of-ownership analysis, and any improvement factors over the way the customer is currently accomplishing the task involved.

O   *Financial Justification: You must show how much your product will save*

Proposal selling focuses heavily on value such as hard financial analysis data and cost justifications. The major thrust of proposal selling is to project your product or service as a profit improving method. The proposal is made in concert with the customer's profit-making objectives. It economically justifies your company's method over the customer's current way of operating. It is also designed to project your degree of excellence.

Central to the proposal is incremental investment return, reduction in operating costs, or the avoidance of a unique loss. The payout on the investment in your product should be realized within a reasonable period. Ideally the payout is measurable in terms of the customer's incremental net profits. The proposal should focus on a project that uses your product or service and links to additional projects and products over time.

Finally, the proposal suggests a partnership where both you and the customer share in the risks and the rewards. This results in a mutually beneficial customer-supplier alliance in which the customer consumes your product or service, and you assist the customer in achieving their profit goals.

If satisfied, the customer will operate over a longer time with you and will be less sensitive to your competition.

To develop a financial justification using the customer profile data, ascertain the goals and objectives of the customer. Follow this with an in-depth needs assessment and analysis. It should then be possible to generate a detailed requirements definition. With this data you will know what is necessary to increase the customer's return on investment, or decrease the cost of ownership.

Next, perform an analysis of his existing capability. Review the costs of the required application, software, preparation of facilities, installation costs and write-offs of obsolete products. These are normally one-time costs. Recurring costs include personnel, supplies, maintenance, and other logistics such as training and utilities. From this data, the customers will gain an understanding of the initial investment, entry cost, cost of ownership, which is their on-going investment, and the investment return that will result if they form a partnership with your company.

Another approach to pursue in proposal selling is a systematic study of the relationship between the performance of your product or service and your customer's operational costs versus their current method and competitive methods. The objective is to show how you optimize the relationship between cost and performance to increment value. If performance increases or cost decreases, value will increase. This shows that lower prices are not the only way to enhance value. By improving the customer's operation with a product that has better performance, or by providing a more useful service, you will both justify the customer's investment in your solution and offer a better hard-core investment return.

○ *Completing the Proposal: The sales proposal should be reviewed by everyone who might be accountable for it*

The completed proposal, before being presented to the customer, is normally reviewed and approved by technical, financial, and higher management people in your company. This requires a proposal review meeting where the proposal originators and reviewers discuss it and attempt to achieve understanding and agreement on the various issues.

Often you must work just as hard to sell your company on making the proposal as you will work to sell the customer on accepting it.

In summary, when you write the proposal, select and organize the following sections to suit your purposes. Invent new ones if you need them.

    I   Letter of transmittal

    II   Table of contents

    III   Executive summary

    IV   Scope of proposal

    V   Benefits

    VI   Implementation plan

    VII   Contract and quotation

    VIII   Financial considerations

    IX   Appendices

        Installation

        Training

        Service and support

Package the proposal in a binder or have it bound with the customer's name and logo. Some salespeople are content to provide the customer with a quotation and a cover letter, avoiding a formal proposal. Sometimes this is adequate and justified but in a highly competitive situation involving the customer's top management or multiple divisions or departments, the potential supplier with the formal proposal has a decided advantage. Before you present the proposal to the customer, make sure the customer is ready to buy. If you have not properly conditioned the customer to agree on what you are proposing, your chances of success are low, no matter how well the proposal is prepared.

If the customer is not ready to buy, the proposal is premature and your timing is wrong. You may win the Pulitzer Prize for the best proposal, yet lose the sale.

CHAPTER

(14)

Charge for everything

Customers are not necessarily loyal. They will buy from the most convenient source. A buyer's axiom might be "to buy acceptable products from convenient sources."

In his *Marketing by Objective* tapes Gunther Klaus says, "It often appears a buyer feels he is in business to put you out of business. Buyers want something for nothing."[1]

Recently, especially in high technology, the trend has been toward developing better and longer term relationships between the buyer and the seller. Changing suppliers in high technology brings with it high risk. Unless the buyer–seller relationship becomes strained, or prices increase substantially compared to the competition, buyers will seldom switch vendors. In other words, the relationship is not very price sensitive.

---

[1]Dr. Gunther Klaus, audio cassettes on *Marketing by Objectives* (I.A.P. and Associates, 256 South La Cienega Boulevard, Beverly Hills, CA 90211), Referenced in this and subsequent chapters as noted.

Consequently, a competitor with an installed base and a reasonable relationship with the customer is difficult to unseat.

High Technology Pricing: Your strategy depends on many factors

High technology pricing is usually set at whatever the market will bear, and the market is not always elastic, especially with capital equipment. Since there is no fundamental relationship between the cost and the selling price, except that the selling price is usually higher than the cost, pricing is either based on some targeted return on investment, or set intuitively. Prices tend to stabilize in each segment of the industry. This stability is upset when a company has a technology break-through, and unwisely lowers prices, or when a new company aggressively prices their product to enter the market and gain share.

Stability may also be disrupted if a company selectively drops prices to break into a key account owned by a competitor.

Aggressive pricing, planned strategically for finite periods of time, to enter a new market or get a foothold in a key account, is acceptable and workable. Indiscriminate price cutting is a poor strategic move. It essentially says your sales plan is a failure. It labels your company as a schlock house.[2] It reduces your profits. Finally, at least in high technology, it will not necessarily get you the business nor the relationship with the customer that you need if you are to win over the long term. This is especially true if the price cut is made at the eleventh hour in a desperate attempt to secure the order that is being lost.

Legally, the same product must be sold at the same price to all customers. This law is often circumvented in many, sometimes ingenious, ways. Except for some market leaders, discounts are a way of life in high technology. Therefore it is important to understand the pricing game.

Although there are many pricing schemes, retail, wholesale, distributor, representative, and Original Equipment Manufacturer (OEM), the most common method employed to discount high technology products is the quantity discount agreement. The OEM purchaser purchases equipment not to stand alone but to be used in the final product being manufac-

---

[2]Ibid.

tured and resold as part of that product. A customer signs an agreement to purchase a specific number of units over a specified period. Each unit carries a discount. Usually the discount percentage increases with the number of units actually purchased. Non OEM customers also obtain discounts.

A customer may contract to purchase ten systems over one year where the first system carries a 1% discount, the second 2%, the third 3%, increasing to 10% for the tenth system. If all ten systems are purchased, the total discount will be 5.5%. Since the customer *intends* to purchase ten systems, the buyer may request 5.5% on each system. It is understood that, should they not purchase all ten, they will be billed for the difference between what they earned through actual purchases versus what they would have earned had they purchased all ten systems. In other words, the discount calculations are based upon the volume of business the customer will eventually buy during the life of the contract. The customer then purchases one system at 5.5% discount, never buys a second system, and the supplier never bills for the difference.

Demonstration products or products that were used by your company allow legitimate discounting when they are sold to a customer. If sold strategically, they can be used to gain entry into a new account or to match a competitive price cutting thrust elsewhere.

○ ## High Technology Costs: It is useless to sell a product without proper support

With high technology products, support costs are often greater than the costs of producing the product. Support for software-intensive products may exceed the hardware costs by several orders of magnitude.

Some buyers purchase products without support. OEM agreements result in a substantially lower product selling price, sometimes by as much as 30% and, when tied to very high volume, as much as 50%. With an OEM customer, the supplier is not responsible for supporting the equipment once it transfers to the buyer. The buyer incorporates the seller's equipment into his own product, and then warrants and supports the total final product or system in the field.

Because of this and other service related issues, buyers seek and sellers grant substantial price differentials on volume and support. This practice is probably in keeping with the spirit, if not the letter of the Fair Trade Commission's interpretation of the law.

Two other costs that result in price differentials are location and transaction costs. It costs more to obtain an export license and ship, install, and support a product in, say, Poland than it does for the product shipped next door. Obviously, expenses associated with the direct cost incurred are passed on to the customer, but indirect costs such as maintaining a remote service center, flying people to a foreign country during a service warranty period, and other costs associated with doing business internationally, means the international customer must pay more for the same product purchased locally. The differential is anywhere from six percent to twenty percent, depending on the product, support requirements, and location.

Other transaction costs that enter into the equation are selling time and effect, cost of collecting receivables and inventory float, the time a part, spares, or a portion of a system is in transit or consigned to a customer or territory. For these reasons, some manufacturers refuse international business. They also avoid doing business with customers who demand excessive support, or purchase only one unit or system and are not sophisticated enough to use it even with proper training. This can result in excessive support costs and negative reflections on the product itself.

For these reasons it is important to price everything in the proposal and charge for it. The equipment should have a base or entry price for specific or standard configurations. Standard, custom, and special options, accessories, and services should each carry a specific price.

Some companies, which maintain a low price on the base product, make up for low margins on the options, accessories, spare parts, and follow-on services. On the other hand, if these options do not result in real value for the customer, the customer may not purchase them.

In the final analysis, you get what you pay for. In high technology, the application of some of the product features may not be clear when designed, may be designed for one purpose but found useful for another, or may be ahead of their time, a feature waiting for the benefit.

A company over time should put every optional feature possible into the product. Customers will find needs for them and sales people will always find problems to solve with them.

CHAPTER

(15)

You have two ears and one mouth. Nature's message is: Listen twice as much as you talk

Anyone not deaf can hear; the trick is to listen. Hearing is the act or process of perceiving sound. Listening is the accurate empathic understanding of what the customer intended when he or she made the sounds.

○ ### The Listening Skills: Listen with your mind as well as your ears

Accurate understanding involves both meaning and feeling. If you master listening skills you'll learn more about the customer in less time. By truly listening, you'll put customers at ease, which facilitates receptiveness on their part and you'll reduce the chance of frustrating them because they will know they're being heard. Finally, if you listen to your customers, they'll probably listen to you.

Many salespeople fail because they fail to listen.

Listening involves concentration. If you think about something else or about what you are going to say next, while your customer is talking, you're not listening. If you try to talk while the customer is talking, you're not listening. If your body language is not in concert with what the customer is saying (unless done for effect) you're not listening. Inattention is communicated through your body. The customer will tell you if you're not listening by repeating what was said.

To master the art of listening, ask questions. Questions encourage the customer to talk so you can listen. Then be quiet; you can't listen if you are talking. Put the customer at ease by looking and acting interested and by doing nothing distracting. The customer needs your full attention.

As you listen, try to understand the customer's point of view and allow them to express themselves. If an objection surfaces, let the customer talk it out. Occasionally, the objection will resolve itself during the course of the conversation.

When you listen, you are an observer. Although observing, you are active. In other words, you are participating but not directing. Your objective is to collect accurate data.

Active listening helps you move forward quickly in the selling process. It is necessary to know the customer's objectives and concerns in detail to develop your sales strategy.

The four listening skills are questioning, paraphrasing, aligning, and summarizing.[1]

○ Questioning: Use questions to get the customer talking

Questioning starts the customer talking so you can listen. Open-ended questions solicit information. Open-ended questions begin with words such as *what, why, could, how,* and *would.* They facilitate the discussion and the customer's exploration of issues. Closed questions, which can be answered with *yes* or *no,* are generally not helpful.

---

[1]Allen E. Ivey with Lynn Simex-Downing, *Counseling and Psychotherapy: Skills, Theories and Practice,* (Englewood Cliffs, NJ: Prentice-Hall, Inc., 1980), pp. 51-116.
*The work of A. Ivey especially in the area of micro counseling was adapted for chapters 15, 16, 17 and 18 and referenced as noted.

Open questions are used to secure examples, induce elaboration, and motivate the customer to focus on a particular issue. While you listen, nonverbal encouragers such as nods or leaning forward, and verbal encouragers such as *so, and, then* and *oh* urge the customer to continue expressing thoughts or feelings.

The open question is best for establishing two-way communication because it solicits a response. People like to respond. When asked a question a person automatically searches for an answer. Even people who overheard the question but were not directly asked will think of a reply. It's difficult to resist answering a question.

On the other hand, care must be taken not to allow questioning to deteriorate into an interrogation. Customers don't like to be cornered, or asked questions they can't answer.

Use questioning to your advantage. Use it freely. It takes confidence to encourage two-way conversation. Your knowledge may be incomplete and you may not know the answer to a particular question, but don't let that stop you. If you don't know the answer, admit it, commit to getting the answer, set a specific time when the customer will have it, and follow through. The customer does not expect you to know all the answers. In fact, it is better not to know all the answers. You don't want to appear smarter than the customer.

- *"Could you give me an example?"* results in an example.

- *"Why do you say that?"* induces elaboration.

- *"How do you feel about this method?"* focuses on a particular issue.

- *"What would you suggest?"* helps you obtain information, and develops customer involvement and interest.

Open questions can also be used to place your product in a positive light in spite of what the competitor may have said.

C: *"Your competitor has quite a few advantages."*

S: *"What advantages do you see in my product?"*

The response will solicit a positive reply concerning your product and provide data on what is important to that customer. The customer may then go on to say....

C: *"....But your competitor can do it better...."*

You have two ways to go. If you know a disadvantage in the competitor's method you can respond with....

S: *"Aren't there some disadvantages in that method?"*

The customer will look for them and you can tactfully help him find them. The second way to respond is....

S: *"I understand exactly what you are saying. May I explain how we do it and why we chose a different method?"*

You now focus on your strengths and counter the competitor without negative selling.

Encouragers are used to urge the customer to continue. In addition to those mentioned, if you react to a key part of the customer's statement and show surprise, it encourages further explanation from the customer.

C: *"Your price is too high."*

S: *"Too high?"*

C: *"Your service is lousy."*

S: *"Lousy?"*

In both cases the customer will be forced to elaborate while you listen then formulate your response.

Paraphrasing: Paraphrase what you heard the customer say, to check your understanding

The second listening skill, paraphrasing, conveys to your customers that you hear what they say. It also makes what you heard more precise and provides a check for the accuracy of your understanding. Paraphrasing is neither a restatement of what the customer said nor an interpretation. It is the essence of what the customer said. It gets into the customer's frame of reference. It shows that you truly understand.

By paraphrasing the buyer's statement in a question, you can effect an interim close, or link to the next step in the sales process.

S: *"In other words, the ability to test different device types at different test stations as offered is the final consideration in your evaluation?"*

S: *"Do I understand it right: by February 15th you will have generated a preliminary specification and when I visit on February 16th we will review the specification together. Is that correct?"*

S: *"Then we agree that by Monday I will see if we can provide a bare bones capability. Meanwhile you will see if you can get an additional $27,000 approved. Is that correct?"*

⭕ *Aligning: Respond to the customer's feelings*

Whereas paraphrasing is concerned with the cognitive content of listening, alignment, the third listening skill, is focused on the emotions within the customer. When aligning you are trying to understand the customer's feelings and align yourself with them. A clear understanding of the customer's feelings provides the basis for understanding the customer's attitudes, thoughts, and prejudices.

S: *"I can appreciate that. If it were important to me I would feel the same way. Tell me, why is that so important to you?"*

S: *"I understand how necessary that is for you. I was in a similar situation once when....Have you considered other solutions?"*

Focus on the feelings behind the words. If the customer is upset about something, words, if not actions, will reveal it. The emotional words a customer uses are clues to what that customer is feeling. The words often tell you more about the customer than about the subject of the conversation. By noticing and attending to the emotional content of what customers say, you will learn much about their attitudes toward the subject at hand.

C: *"I find your software weak."*

Focus on "weak." Is the customer unfamiliar with your software, unable to see the value in it, weak in using it? "Weak" is the key to this customer's attitude. Align yourself with the customer's feelings behind the word "weak."

S: *"You feel the software is weak. I felt the same way until I discovered how much power it really has. What is it in particular that appears weak?"* Or the customer may say:

C: *"The fact that you have it and your competitor doesn't is trivial."*

Focus on "trivial." Is this customer unwilling to admit it is important because he or she is sold on the competitor, or does the customer mean that your product is trivial?

S: *"I gather that particular feature is not important to you. I thought it was trivial myself until one of my customers told me what he accomplished with it. Why do you feel it is trivial?"*

Words like *weak* and *trivial* are laden with emotion. They reveal vital information about the customer's underlying attitudes and feelings toward your product. It is helpful to pay close attention to emotional words used by the customer.

○ Summarizing: Summarize to make sure the conversation is understood

Summarizing, the last listening skill, is a resume of the meeting which occurs at the end, or at well-defined break points. Summarizing helps you and the customer pull all the loose ends together. It also confirms that you are not distorting or misinterpreting what you heard.

Both content and feelings should be summarized. This gives your customer a chance to reflect on the progress made. It focuses the interview and helps promote further discussion.

During the interchange of ideas, information about the customer's problems or about the competitor's position may have surfaced. Some of the objections you will face will have been mentioned. Therefore, it is important to feed back the key points for agreement, so that you can proceed with the confidence that you understand the issues.

S: *"To summarize, we both agreed this capability is an absolute requirement, and my product more than does the job, right? Secondly, we agree...."*

Active listening is necessary to obtain information and develop a relationship with the customer.

CHAPTER

(16)

Kindness is a powerful sales device

Influencing takes place after listening and facilitates behavioral change. Listening and influencing occur in tandem, repeating until the sale is closed.

When you listen, you are trying to closely understand the customer's situation as it is, so you can develop a strategy to deal with any objections.

○ *The Influencing Skills: After you have listened, it's your turn to speak sensitively*

When influencing, you take active control of the selling process. Now your objective is to influence the process of change. When you were listening, the customer was in the spotlight. Now you are on center stage. You must both lead the customer and share.

The sales motion now becomes a process of interpersonal influence. The influencing dimension is directive. In the case of an objection, if you have listened effectively, the customer will have experienced emotional release and will now be receptive to your ideas.

The influencing dimension encompasses four specific skills: leading, interpreting, expressing, and self-disclosing.[1]

◯ *Leading: Phrase your questions to get the answers you want*

Leading guides the customer toward your objective with questions and directives. By using questions adroitly, you can conduct the buyer's thinking along a predetermined path to a buy decision, and at the same time monitor how you are faring in the sales situation. By being explicit and directing the customer to take a specific action, you can close.

S: *"So you agree this computer will solve the problem?"*

C: *"Yes, it looks that way."*

S: *"It looks like the software library more than meets your requirements, doesn't it?"*

C: *"We can live with it."*

S: *"As I understand it, the computer is within your budget."*

C: *"With the quantity purchasing agreement, it is."*

S: *"Good, then I can ship the first one in 30 days if I have the purchase order today. Can you have Purchasing generate one right away?"*

C: *"I guess so."*

In this instance, a problem had been defined and the circumstances surrounding the problem were understood. The computer was found to be a solution. The salesperson had to influence the customer to buy. The salesperson used questions

[1]Ivey, *Counseling and Psychotherapy*, pp. 51-116.

to lead the way and search for any latent objections, then used a directive to close. A directive is often the most effective close in this situation.

"If I have the purchase order today" may not look like a directive, but it can be defined as one since it directs the customer to buy, or by implication, lose the delivery. If, in fact, the 30-day delivery is not contingent upon an immediate purchase order, the salesperson was being manipulative.

Note that the salesperson was not sidetracked by the customer's lukewarm response to the software library question. If the customer had not agreed to place the order, the salesperson might have gone back and probed the lukewarm response to the library.

Once in Purchasing, the salesperson may have to settle for a letter of intent, a purchase order number, or a verbal commitment, but in any event the salesperson closed.

Examples of other directives are:

C: *"I have to talk it over with my boss."*

S: *"Ok, let's go see him together."*

C: *"I'll have to think about it."*

S: *"If you buy now, you'll save 10%. Our prices increase 10% next week."*

C: *"It is difficult to decide. Both you and your competitor look equal in most respects."*

S: *"You've been evaluating suppliers for six months. You really should decide something. Decide now and go with us; our support will overcome any difficulties that may worry you."*

With an indecisive customer a paradoxical instruction from a salesperson sometimes works.

S: *"It's a tough decision. I understand why you've been wrestling with it so long. Don't make a decision right now. Sleep on it and I'll be back the first thing in the morning."*

The customer may be motivated by the words, *don't make a decision* to decide immediately. If they don't, but agree to meet with you the next morning, they know you'll expect a decision.

If a customer is anxious about making a decision, telling him or her not to make a decision in a way that deliberately creates a situation that encourages a decision may immediately change the customer's behavior. This is a sophisticated technique and is not recommended for a beginner.

Leading is, in essence, telling the customer what to do and providing a direction for action.

○ *Interpreting: Reinterpret the customer's needs in terms your product can solve*

Renaming and relabeling the customer's thoughts and feelings is the second listening skill, an interpretation skill. Interpreting sometimes includes a value judgment.

Meaningful interpretations agree with the customer's way of thinking, but from a different viewpoint, so the customer can think about it differently. Through interpretation you can gently move the customer toward the buy decision.

C: *"I can't possibly give up the software investment I have in your competitor's product....even though I need the new technology you offer."*

S: *"It appears you have a real dilemma. You want to stay with the old technology to protect your software investment, yet you need the new technology."*

C: *"That's right. But my investment is so high I can't afford to change. I'll just have to find a way to make the competitor's product last longer."*

S: *"It almost sounds as if the diminishing return of your software investment is more important than keeping pace with technology and your competitors. What do you think?"*

The salesperson is giving his interpretation of events in an attempt to help the customer see it from a different viewpoint; the diminishing return of the software compatibility versus the looming threat of new technology in his competitor's hands. The customer may now interpret the issues in the salesperson's favor. *"What do you think?"* forces the customer to rethink his or her position.

Leads such as *"You've been talking about the importance of this software investment, but how about technology? How do you compare the importance of each?"* or *"Is this what you meant by....?"* facilitate the customer interpreting her or his position and finding new views of old situations. The customer's insight into the situation can be very helpful to you.

⭕ *Expression: You'll need to express your own opinion at some point*

The third influencing skill, expression, is giving your opinion of how you see or hear the particular sales situation. During this process you express both content, such as giving advice, sharing information, making suggestions, providing reassurance or customer feedback; and feeling where you share your emotions and attitudes.

Expressing is communicating facts and distinguishing them from emotions. Expressing is also used to encourage the customer to take a particular course of action and to reassure the customer that it is the correct course. A salesperson might say,

> *"When someone sells me something, I expect the performance promised, but if it doesn't meet the specifications, he gets it right back in his lap."*

The salesperson is focusing on effect, and is feeding back to the customer personal feelings about sales promises and what he or she does about them if they're broken. The salesperson is providing the customer with a model for a particular course of action and is attempting to establish credibility.

⭕ *Self Disclosing: Don't be afraid to touch on problems with a view to solving them*

To win the trust of the customer, you must make your intentions known. Self-disclosure or the sharing of your true thoughts and feelings with the customer facilitates the development of a deep trusting relationship. This is the fourth influencing skill. Mutual sharing is often demonstrated by the use of the pronoun "I", by including a related experience, and by speaking in the present tense.

Through self-disclosure, a customer-to-salesperson rapport will build. A quality of friendship will develop followed by openness, trust, and a closer interpersonal relationship.

> **S:**   *"Our system has performed in many similar installations, but I really do not understand your full application. Could you help me by explaining in more detail how you...."*

> **S:**   *"I know we shipped you an unreliable system once and then failed to support it. Since then we have doubled our service force, and burn in all our components for reliability. Also, our new systems are three times as fast and 20% lower in cost. The reason I asked to see you is that I think you will be very satisfied with this new system and our new support policy. Maybe, after a thorough evaluation, you would be willing to do business with us again. How do you feel about your progress?"*

With these statements, salespeople are on their way to a deeper customer-salesperson rapport. Honest salespeople who make their intentions clear, who really tell it the way it is, make their customers feel comfortable.

These statements are models of interpersonal openness, and serve to facilitate customer self-disclosure and sharing.

Although it is appropriate to ask for help, self-disclosure does not mean begging for an order, or using problems you or your company are experiencing as a reason for the customer to buy. Such tactics are inappropriate. Your problems are not your customer's concern.

If your customer wants a "return with no obligation clause" in the contract, your company may not be willing to offer it because they need the revenue that month. Such a contingency would preclude revenue since the transfer of title would not have taken place. This is your problem. Crying to the customer about your company's revenue issue is not good salesmanship even if it works. It is not the intent of self-disclosure. You are better off finding another, more creative way around the problem.

Self-disclosure also involves very personalized, direct, and mutual communication.

S: *"Marvin, I sense you have an extremely difficult decision to make. You seem to be moving toward a conclusion that means I will be your new supplier, and you know this will require a lot of explaining to your management. Believe me, I feel almost as perplexed as you."*

"I want this order, you know that, but it is also important to me that this installation be a success. I am convinced it will be, and I am willing to do whatever is necessary to help you and your management feel the same way."

"Marvin, we have not known each other very long, but I sense we communicate. What do you think? How can I help you?"

Personal names and pronouns are used extensively and sharing takes place in the here and now. This kind of communication normally occurs close to the final decision. If you are winning, it helps reassure the customer, and motivates him or her to continue moving in your direction.

If you are losing, it will arouse second thoughts and may move the customer back to your side. It only works if it is genuine.

If you are honest in your disclosure, you will not present mixed messages. You will integrate your verbal and nonverbal behavior. Authenticity and spontaneity are characteristic of genuineness. Extreme care must be exercised in attempting to self disclose. Self disclosure is a highly professional technique, learned through experience.

In many sales situations, although you should be genuine, complete openness may not be appropriate. A more distant professional relationship may be expected. But if you are genuinely humble and kind, and if you share your thoughts and feelings in a very real and personal manner, your customer is likely to follow your lead and respond in like manner.

Affecting a humility akin to Dicken's Uriah Heep or similar to Robert Caro's description of Lyndon Johnson, who wrote letters to various powerful officials telling each that it was he alone who made such and such possible and thanking each profusely, is not genuine humility, but groveling humility or raw flattery. There is no place for this behavior in high technology sales. The customer doesn't have time for it.

On the other hand, you can be modest and humble in a professional sense without compromising your pride. Being humble will help you cultivate professional kindness. Professional kindness means being kind to a person even if you do not particularly like the person. Kindness is a valuable part of business life, and a most powerful sales tool, for kindness is disarming and begets kindness which begets buy decisions.

You will have your repertoire of responses, benefits, solutions, experiences, insights, and perceptions. It is through this repertoire that you will make the sale.

By mastering the listening skills, you'll truly understand the customer. By mastering the influencing skills, you'll have several alternative routes to obtain the buy decision. By sharing with the customer through self-disclosure, you utilize interpersonal influence to develop a long-term and trusting relationship.

CHAPTER

(17)

You don't have to talk to communicate

Through analysis of body language and words, a skilled salesperson can identify specific nonverbal and verbal behaviors of the customer. A salesperson's attitudes and feelings are also transmitted to the customer through nonverbal behavior. With body language and words, the skilled salesperson can wilfully communicate interest, assurance, and confidence.

Using what psychologists Allen E. Ivey and Lynn Simek-Downing call the microskill approach, the complex interaction of the sales process may be divided into managable, learnable dimensions. The verbal and nonverbal dimensions of a sales situation involve eye contact, body positioning, verbal synchronization through vocal tone and speech rate, and a combination of the listening and influencing skills.[1]

[1]Ivey, *Counseling and Psychotherapy*, pp. 51-116.

○ Nonverbal Activity: Salespeople should be in control of their nonverbal activity

The salesperson's nonverbal behavior is extremely important in establishing and maintaining a relationship with the customer. It is also a powerful tool for changing the customer's thinking and behavior.

Salespeople attempting to communicate the value of their product to the customers are obviously biased in favor of their product, which their nonverbal activity reveals. Every effort is made to lead the customer through nonverbal behavior to a mutually satisfactory conclusion—the sale. Although the best nonverbal behavior is the salesperson's own natural and comfortable style, nonverbal behavior will vary among cultures and is different for men and women.

When attempting to influence North American customers nonverbally, execute a firm handshake and make sure your head is erect. This communicates self-esteem and confidence. Smile when appropriate and maintain steady eye contact, but do not carry it to an extreme. Direct eye contact is appropriate when listening, but while talking, eye contact should be less frequent.

A customer who frequently breaks eye contact is often uncomfortable. If eye contact is broken consistently on certain subjects, take heed: important or difficult issues may be involved. It is vital to be aware of such behavior, to discern more precisely what is happening in the sales situation.

○ Verbal Activity: Be aware of the timing of both speech and thought

Make silence an ally. When responding to the customer, allow the customer time to listen, reflect, then talk. High pressure sales techniques rarely work in high technology sales due to the length of the sales cycle and the sophistication of the high technology buyer. Give the customer time to explore ideas or solutions. Also make sure your responses are clearly parallel and related to what the customer is saying.

Interventions should be kept brief and to-the-point. This allows the customer time to reflect, agree or disagree. Do not jump topics, talk about irrelevant issues, interrupt, or forget what the customer has already said.

Vary your vocal tone through inflection, emphasizing key points, but keep your speech rate moderate. As you talk, slowly match the speech rate, volume, tone, and rhythm of the customer's voice. Mirror your customers so they feel you are like they are. Pace your customers so they will feel you are in coincidence with them. Use the same kind of words they use. Sense their mood and put yourself in the same mood. If they're depressed and you are happy-go-lucky, you lose.

C: *"Every time I buy a piece of equipment it breaks down. (pause) It's terrible!"*

S: *"I know what you mean....(pause)....I bought a new car last week, it broke down and is still in the garage."*

C: *"Did you see our stock jump? At this rate I'm going to make a bundle with my option."*

S: *"Boy, your stock sure did jump and I am really glad I bought some last month."*

C: *"The economic climate appears to be improving. The book-to-bill ratio for our industry is on the rise."*

S: *"That is true, and with interest rates on the decline, and the Federal Reserve Board raising the limit on the money supply growth for the year, the market for your product should improve substantially."*

During the interchange lean slightly forward if seated. This indicates attention and confidence in your point of view. Facing the customer in an open position communicates openness to disagreements or alternative viewpoints.[2]

○ *Body Movement and Positioning: Maintain a confident, relaxed position*

The quality of your motion is important. Fidgeting, folding arms, and abortive and jerky movements should be avoided. Subdued, halting, or cataleptic behavior is disastrous. These activities convey nervousness, disinterest, or insecurity.

[2]Shertzer and Stone, *Fundamentals of Counseling*, pp. 300-305.
*Shertzer gives another perspective on nonverbal meaning which is a result of Dr. Kagan's research at Michigan University.

Controlled, relaxed, and planned movements communicate best. Look for customers who lean away or shift around on certain topics. This may indicate they are uncomfortable with what is being said. Watch also for tenseness, rigidity, and slouching. These are warnings that something is not right.

If you are relaxed, the customer will probably relax. To relax tense customers, get them to change their position by responding positively to you through activity, or through reacting to something you say, such as an attention-getting statement. Often it is necessary to change both your verbal directions and body position to get the customer to change theirs. If this happens, it is likely the customer's thinking and attitude toward you will also change.

You can use your body motion to communicate a negative position as well. Since you do not wish to argue or contradict the customer, taking a defensive posture such as firmly crossing your arms or making a suspicious gesture (such as placing your index finger alongside your nose) at the appropriate time, will get your message across.

Awareness of the customer's physical space requirements is important. Cultural and individual boundaries are determining factors. Some people prefer to remain apart, while others like to be close. Consequently, it is difficult to determine the exact position to take.

Often the closer you can get to the customer, the closer you are to making the sale.

The most common method of using nonverbal behavior to your advantage is to involve the customer in physical activity. Don't just stand or sit back and talk. Your objective is to get the customer into a friendly receptive mood.

○ ### Suggestions: Suggest to customers that they are ready to buy

Once you are in synchronization with the customer in mood, thought, verbal following, and nonverbal positioning, you are ready to close. Suggest that the customer buy by leading the customer to desire your product.

S: *"You are thinking how nice it would be if you could buy a materials control system to keep your inventory in check."*

S: *"You would like to make that trip to Mexico, wouldn't you! And a materials control system that you could rely on would free up some of your time, especially if it is user friendly. What you need is a user friendly materials control system."*

When attempting to close, what you say is not as important as how you say it. Emotion, not logic, is the *force majeure* behind behavioral change even for hard-nosed engineers, sophisticated doctors, and pragmatic businessmen and women.

When you influence, maintain eye contact, lean forward, and use gestures of direction and suggestion. Synchronize verbally with your customer.

Speak slowly with conviction, and look directly at the customer. Use personal pronouns and first names if appropriate. Emphasize your solution or value. Stress the key words or phrases that will make the customer want to buy.

S: *"Try picturing this test system on your production floor. You know and I know it will test all your products the way you want to test them. George, if you will invest in this test system, you'll solve the quality problems. Imagine what both your customers and your management are going to say when the quality problems disappear. George, you want this system, buy it."*

Here the salesperson creates a word picture so the customer can visualize the event. The salesperson reiterated the benefit, stressed the solution to a problem, emphasized the personal value to the customer, suggested that the customer wanted the product, and then asked for the order.

If properly qualified, if the customer believes in the salesperson and what the salesperson is saying, and if the salesperson has verbally and nonverbally communicated the sales message (both consciously and subliminally), the customer will buy.

To learn and understand nonverbal selling skills, months of formal training are required and available at sales training institutes. Some universities also specialize in teaching nonverbal skills.

After proper training, practice in front of the mirror. You will be in good company. Winston Churchill became a great parliamentarian and political salesman, "....by practicing endlessly in front of mirrors, fashioning ripostes to this or that parry."[3]

Since ripostes are retaliatory verbal sallies, why did he use a mirror? Churchill understood the importance of nonverbal language. To be an effective, conscious, and wilfull practitioner of nonverbal skills requires training, commitment, and practice.

○ *Nonverbal Messages: Be aware of nonverbal disagreement*

If your customers say they like your product and at the same time tightly cross their arms, you may be getting a double message (unless the room temperature is exceptionally low). Most salespeople intuitively interpret nonverbal behavior. Unfortunately, nonverbal language varies so greatly between individuals and cultures that generalizations are dangerous. Nevertheless, there are certain general behaviors that may provide insight into what the customer is really thinking.

Norman Kagan of Michigan State University is referenced in Shertzer and Stone's book, *Fundamentals of Counseling*, as having identified sets of categories of nonverbal behavior that are useful to understand and are helpful in sales situations.[4]

In the first set, the customers are unaware of their behavior. They will make short forceful gestures for emphasis, and attempt to facilitate the discussion to increase clarity by using their arms or hands to help accentuate key points or draw out certain words. These are usually unconscious body motions related to feelings, and are useful expressions for a salesperson to learn and discern.

In the next set, customers may or may not be aware of their actions, but if they were aware they would probably not alter them. A salesperson or buyer, for example, strives to show agreement and interest through body positions, verbal tone, and facial expressions. This direct form of nonverbal communication is called *portrayal* and is an easily understood, frequently used, and normally conscious gesture.

Unconscious tension-motivated behavior where customers are usually unaware of their actions is another category and the

---

[3]Manchester, *The Last Lion*, p. 33.

[4]Shertzer, *Fundamentals of Counseling*, pp. 300-305.

most important nonverbal behavior to understand in sales. This behavior is often exhibited when the sales situation is peaking, that is, during a close.

Tension-motivated gestures originate from feelings and, if negative, could indicate a major deep-seated objection.

This last category of nonverbal behavior, conscious tension-motivated behavior, involves awareness on the part of the customer, and is often manipulative. These behaviors are fully intended. They are tension associated, such as key jingling or leg swinging, and are used in an attempt to annoy or distract the salesperson. They are deliberate ploys on the part of buyers to demonstrate their feelings nonverbally.

The dilemma a salesperson faces is determining whether the various behaviors exhibit the buyer's true feelings, or are attempts to intimidate or manipulate. Is the buyer communicating a strong message, or acting?

○ ## Interpreting Nonverbal Behavior: Be careful not to misinterpret nonverbal behavior

Although it is important to understand nonverbal behavior, because of the lack of commonality among individuals, caution must be exercised in interpreting it. Yet salespeople must develop a sensitivity to these signals to enhance their closing skills.

Opening and studying a brochure or specification could be a buying signal. If followed by an artificial cough, the customer may be indicating doubt or criticism.

Finger or knuckle-cracking is a sign of frustration, aggression, or hostility. Leaning forward and being attentive, relaxed, and open reveal true interest.

Playing with an object could be a release of tension, an indication of conflict, or a result of a decision having been made. If it is your product or prop, and if handled with care, awe, interest, or desire, a subtle buying signal is present.

Customers who rub thumb and middle finger may be searching for a solution. Putting the index finger alongside the nose indicates disbelief, yet simply touching the nose may be a manifestation of anxiety.

A general increase in the level of nonverbal activity, such as a reaction to visual materials or the presentation and the taking of notes, indicates either an increase in the customer's stress, or positive emotional involvement.

People often react physically before they speak, so changes of nonverbal activity will signal what is actually going on in the customer's mind before it is verbalized. Since verbal messages are often different from nonverbal ones, discrepancies must be observed and interpreted.

A revealing clue to these discrepancies and what the customer is thinking is how the customer follows your lead. For example, if you are saying something positive, slowly move your head up and down. If the customer's head moves up and down, they are probably in agreement with you. If on the other hand, their heads move back and forth, unless they are from India, they are probably in disagreement with you.

If your body motion and language are in concert with your speech, the customer's body will also move in concert with your speech if they are in agreement with you. On the other hand, unsuitable or inappropriate body movement on the part of the customer when compared to your movement or speech indicates dissonance.

Identification of incongruence between movements and speech is an excellent source of information in a sales situation.

CHAPTER

(18)

Be vague to get clarity

Customers often have difficulty expressing themselves clearly and directly. Sometimes they prefer not to be concrete concerning the sales situation, and avoid a direct response to a question. To clarify facts and feelings, to motivate the customer to be specific, and to uncover objections, use vague statements to facilitate concrete discussions.

○ ## *Word Usage: Be sensitive to word usage*

C: *"We will most likely purchase a new computer from your competitor."*

(Clear—*"most likely"* means the decision may not have been made).

S: *"Could you tell me why you are leaning toward my competitor?"*

(Clear—*"leaning"* implies no decision).

C: *"Well, their price looks good."*
(Clear).

S: *"We can probably take care of the price issue."*
(Vague—left open for discussion after finding out if there are other objections).

S: *"Is there anything else still at issue?"*
(Clear—Is there a real quantifiable objection other than price?)

Vague modifiers such as *perhaps, probably, kind of, rarely, seldom, maybe, most likely,* and *sometimes,* plus a host more, are ways both you and your customer can keep from being clear and direct. Watch for vague or ambiguous language and deal with it first.[1]

To have immediately dealt with the price issue would have been a mistake. Using vague language "... probably take care of...." about the price issues was appropriate since all the objections may not be on the table.

It is important to clarify the issues. If price really is the issue it will surface thrugh judicious questioning. If not, the real objection will become clear.

There are other ways to use words in your favor. Competitive products are cheaper; yours are less expensive. They offer deals; you offer opportunity. The customer pays for the competition's product; and invests in yours. The competitor makes pitches; you make presentations. The customer buys the competitor's product; but owns yours.

> **S:**   *"I can appreciate your comments. The competition's product may appear a little cheaper and they are offering you a rather interesting deal...."*

Weak words such as *little, rather* or *very* are not used except in conjunction with the competitor. The statement made by the salesperson about his or her product should be clear, direct and confident.

> **S:**   *"Let's review what makes up the true cost of ownership."*

[1]Ivey, *Counseling and Psychology,* pp. 51-185.

The salesperson with concrete examples explains why the product is less expensive over the long term and that the opportunity to invest in the product will result in the protection of the customer's investment for years to come.

If the salesperson's statements are made with confidence and authority, they will usually not be questioned. The way the answer is made means as much as what is said. How something is said is also important. A "yes" can be read as a "no" if it is said unsurely.

The customer will react to the words you use and the way you use them. Positive statements made with authority instill confidence.

○ Project Confidence: If you aren't sold on what you're doing, you won't be able to sell to anyone else

If you feel inferior, doubt your company or product, or are self-conscious, it will be perceived by your customer. Confidence rests within yourself, not outside.

Sometimes a customer's need or confidence in your product or company will overcome a lack of faith or trust in you, especially in the high technology marketplace, but this is not the norm. Normally, the customer will not buy if he or she does not have confidence in you.

A customer will not automatically trust you. You must develop the buyer's confidence in you. It is most effective to start the development effort in an informal environment or atmosphere such as a restaurant or one-on-one in the customer's office. Once the newness in the relationship wears off and the customer feels comfortable with you the stage is set. It is now time to act as the customer expects you to act, to demonstrate that you are capable of understanding their problem and articulating a solution, and to prove that you are trustworthy. The customer should be convinced that if this sale is not in the best interest for both of you, you will walk away from it.

As the customer develops trust in you the customer will talk more openly, confide in you, discuss important issues with you and nonverbally say, "I believe you can help me and I think I can trust you."

If you fail to build confidence in your customers, they may suspect you have embellished the truth, or not told them everything. How many times have you heard a customer say, *"He's a good salesman....Too good!"*

Customers need to feel that the decision they're about to make is good for their company and themselves. They must believe in you to believe in your price, product, support, quality, reliability, dependability, performance, or commitments. You are the representative of your company and your product.

○   ## *Working Through: Don't let hints slip by*

Incongruous and inconsistent words, phrases, or sentences often warn of double messages, hidden agendas, and unclear objections. Working through these incongruities in a nonhostile manner is one way to help the customer see things differently. When working through the issues it is essential not to arouse hostility or defensiveness and not to negotiate.

Working through is necessary when a customer is either avoiding an issue or is unaware of the consequences of his or her belief. In the latter case, confronting the issue and working it through is sometimes the only way a salesperson can point out differences, incongruities, and discrepancies.

Often the customer and sometimes the salesperson will deliberately seek to avoid discussing crucial objections or issues.[2] They may see the truth but fail to act with reference to it. They may follow a line of thought that, no matter how wrong, no matter how many times they may have failed in the past because of it, still goes unquestioned. Nothing will shake their belief in the essential excellence of their position. When working through the issues the salesperson must not take a position no matter how right she or he might be. Working through is a discussion around the differences. Care must be taken not to allow the discussion to deteriorate into antipathy over issues or between people.

A customer may make the following statements:

C: *"I really would like to purchase your product, but I feel it doesn't meet my requirements."*

[2]Ibid.

C: *"I want to buy your system. It will certainly do my job better than any other, but I don't have a large enough budget and I can't go back to management for more funds."*

C: *"You work for a good company and you have an excellent product, but I am afraid your company will not provide adequate support."*

Each of these statements is inconsistent and disharmonious, and gives double messages. Mixed thoughts and feelings about the sale are stated. The inconsistencies about the issues in question must be worked through directly if the objections are to be overcome. Why would the first person wish to purchase the product if he feels it doesn't meet his requirements? If the system is exactly what the second person needs, why is she unable or unwilling to ask her management for additional funding? In the third case, how can the company be "good" if he thinks they will not provide adequate support?

These words are symptomatic of a more fundamental problem. There is probably a hidden agenda which has nothing to do with the statements made. You must facilitate the customer's understanding of what they are saying versus what they really mean, or what they may do compared to what they are saying. If there is an underlying objection it must be uncovered.

S: *"What is it about my product that makes you want to purchase it?"*

Working through focuses on the feelings and thoughts concerning the desire to buy instead of the issue of not meeting the requirements. This may force the real objection to surface, giving you an opportunity to use the customer's motivation to buy your product to answer it, or to subtly point out the discrepancy in his statement.

S: *"How do you feel it would do your job better?"* After she tells you, say, *"Well if you feel that way, wouldn't your management expect you to at least bring it to their attention?"*

Here working through concentrates on the ambivalent statements *"I want to buy...."* and *"I can not go back...."* The reply forces the customer to deal with the ambivalence, after confirming her reasons for wanting to buy.

S: *"Why do you feel a good company with an excellent product would not totally support the product?"*

The incongruity of *good* and *excellent* versus *not....provide* is faced. Working through focuses on the inconsistency in an attempt to either uncover the real objection, or address the illogic of the customer's statement.

The resolution or synthesis of these incongruities is essential if the sale is to be made. This can best be accomplished by working through the inconsistencies through discussion around the issue with consistent focus on the incongruities in thinking and logic.

○ ### Warmth and Respect: Don't hide any warmth and respect you feel in the name of being businesslike

Some purchasing agents have difficulty respecting others or offering enhancing statements. Often this is a ploy, although it could be a result of a lack of self-respect. Other buyers may be cold and distant, feeling this is a professional characteristic, or because they cannot differentiate warmth from a company policy of not fraternizing with suppliers. Still others use warmth and kindness to their advantage in an attempt to exercise control over people. Kindness is a powerful mechanism for control.

When any of these characteristics are observed or encountered, communicate warmth and respect through your response, facial expression, and tone of voice.

Warmth, a positive attitude toward the buyer, will strengthen your positive message relating to the observation.

To project warmth you must share your feelings and accept the associated vulnerability. It's risky business, but if you want to help the buyer over his or her frustrations, and win the sale, you must deepen the relationship and develop mutual trust. Every effort must be made to communicate that you are acting out of concern for the relationship between your two companies, if not between yourselves.[3]

Smiling is an especially effective way to communicate warmth and respect. When objections are encountered, deal

[3]Ibid.

with them openly and honestly. Tolerate differences and focus on the underlying concern. Use respect, warmth, and kindness to your advantage.

If the difference of opinion, or disagreement, results in frustration, invariably negative feelings will follow. Sometimes the buyer will focus these negative feelings on you and refer to them as anger, disappointment, or displeasure. Often these feelings are based on false perceptions.

Show respect for what the buyer said with statements like

> *"You expressed your opinion well,"*
> *"That shows good insight,"*
> *"I have always thought that too,"*
> *"I never thought about it that way before."*

If the statement is so different that agreeing would damage your position, credibility, or integrity, show respect with statements like,

> *"I can imagine why you feel that way, but may I mention another point of view...."*
> *"If I were in your position I would feel the same way. Now what we have done about that...."*
> *"What we believe about that...."*

then support your belief with facts and data.

There is nothing wrong with having a difference of opinion with the buyer. In such cases, frank discussions of the differences in a respectful and warm manner will facilitate resolutions.

You may find out after listening to the customer for a while that you are wrong or are taking a wrong approach. Timing is important in sales but the perfect time never comes. It is usually best to deal with these problems immediately, in the here and now. When dealing with this conflict or these negative feelings, change them into behaviors that help the relationship and lead to the sale. Don't assume the other person knows what you know or knows why you may be saying what you are saying. Draw the person out by questioning and listening.

When listening, watch for misperceptions on the part of the buyer. Be honest with yourself if you find you are part of the problem. Don't label or evaluate, and be sensitive to the buyer's needs and feelings, but remember the buyer may not be as fragile as you think. Buyers who are incongruous and inconsistent are also often pedantically formal, professionally cold, intellectually distant, or captiously minatory like a shrew.

They are also insecure in some respect. When dealing with them, maintain a professional formality and an aura of intelligence, be vague, use circumlocution if you must, but avoid being cold or distant. Cold and distant people convey a lack of power and conviction.

CHAPTER

People do things for their own reasons

Selling is a personal experience. Successful selling means the salesperson has considered the customer first. People new to sales often concentrate on the product, and fail to work *with* the customer. Working with the customer means understanding the motivations of the individuals who must be sold. It means synchronizing with their mood. It means overcoming hostilities. It means dealing with inane objections. It means understanding that in a dark room, the customer will probably not know the difference among competing products since most likely they will all do the job. Hence the buy decision is likely to be an emotional one. This does not mean to imply that the salesperson should avoid selling benefits or providing solutions. It does mean the salesperson must first and foremost focus on the interpersonal component of selling.

If the product the salesperson is selling is clearly superior and required by the customer, the personal component is less important. But in competitive sales situations, understanding the motives of the key individuals in the company is vital to success. What are they thinking? What are they feeling? What are their personal agendas? These questions must be answered.

○ ### *Freudian Slips: Word changes can tell you what to expect*

You can learn a lot about a customer's thinking, feelings, or assertions from slips of the tongue called Freudian slips. Errors in speech are often clues to unconscious motivations or conscious attempts to mislead.

S: *"When do you expect to give us confirmation of the order?*

C: *"I expect the 'confrontation' in a few days."*

Be prepared for a tough negotiation.

S: *"When do you expect Purchasing to issue the order?"*

C: *"You are a little ahead of yourself. We have not even decided on your product, let along written the purchase order."*

Later in the discussion:

S: *"When will you require the new high speed option?"*

C: *"Immediately. It is already on the purchase order."*

Your position may be stronger than the buyer wants you to know.

C: *"I am doing the evaluation and will make the decision. So there is no need for you to call on anyone above me."*

Later in the discussion:

C: *"I will have to get approval for that."*

If you haven't penetrated upper management you could be in big trouble.

Hostile Buyers: You must convince a buyer to want to listen before you can sell

A customer who forgets appointments, allows meetings to be interrupted needlessly or regularly, does things to distract you from your purpose in being there, and then repeats this behavior unnecessarily, is exhibiting hostile conduct that can be revealing. The forgetting, interruptions, or other frustrating actions may mean the customer is extremely busy or disorganized, but it could also mean he or she is paying you lip service and is really not interested in you or your product.

A customer who has bought from your competitor and does not wish to take a risk and change suppliers may take the path of least resistance and forget your benefits, fail to hear what you say, or simply fail to acknowledge your solutions. In this case, solutions and benefits won't get you the sale. You must first deal with the repressed desire not to take risk or make the change. You must show the customer that the reward that will result from the risk-taking is worth the risk. How does the customer win with your proposal? How does your customer benefit from a business relationship with your company? These are the questions to be answered.

If a customer has a proposal from the competitor that is feasible to implement, but has very high risk associated with it, the customer may deny the risk or fail to recognize the reality of the situation. This customer cannot be sold with benefits and solutions. You must find out why the customer is willing to take such an obvious risk.

If the existence of the risk is denied, find out why. Unless he or she is deranged, the buyer perceives a reward worthy of the high risk. The reward could be anything from advancing his or her political position within the company to repaying a favor to your competitor. If he or she honestly does not realize the risk being taken, you must make it clear without negative selling.

A buyer may transfer to you feelings he or she has about another supplier blaming you or your company for something for which you are not responsible.

C: *"The last time we did business with a small company, they did not follow through with their committed support."*

Here the customer is transferring past problems with a previous supplier to you. In effect, the customer has projected the behavior of another small company to your company, over-generalizing the situation. In this case a direct response to the commitment issue may be the best approach but will require assurances.

A customer may take an immediate dislike to you—or may project to you a behavior in himself or herself. This may not be apparent until after several meetings.

After going over the proposal several times you find the customer continually asking for different quotations and configurations. You always respond to these requests in a timely manner. Then one day the customer accuses *you* of being confused. When faced with projections that deny the reality of the situation, an immediate response might be:

S: *"Sounds like I am in trouble. How do you think we can resolve this problem?"*

Hopefully this will get you from a disastrous situation to one that is simply unpalatable.

Next, ask a question that will invoke a response and give you insight into the thinking or feeling behind the customer's projection so you can deal with the behavior as it is exhibited.

A longer term approach may be to attempt to circumvent these behaviors by building credibility with the customer, and providing value in some way. In these situations, the customer could have had a bad day and be treating you badly to displace pent-up anger or frustration. In this case, at your next meeting you may find the customer especially preferential or open.

Sometimes, especially in a negotiation, the buyers may, with biting wit, behave as they think you expect tough buyers to behave. They may try to provoke you in hopes you will lose control, or otherwise resist you as a negotiating ploy, hoping to reduce your responses to pitiless philippics or a tirade. Always follow the sales principle "Nothing a customer can say to me will make me take offense." Never react. Identify and label the situations for what they are; then develop a plan to deal with the customer's thoughts, feelings, or ploys in terms of the exhibited behavior.

In dealing with these and many similar behaviors, a psychologist will use the technique of free association where the client will associate the exhibited behavior with past experience or feeling. Through this association the psychologist will help the client understand himself or herself better and develop the ability to deal with the behavior or overcome it.

A salesperson is not a therapist. Any attempt to interpret or alter what is behind a customer's behavior should be avoided. A salesperson must learn to deal with the customer in terms of these behaviors. Therapeutic interpretive skills require years of study and supervision. Generalizations of behaviors are risky. Your only objective is to convince the customer to buy your product.

Awareness of these behaviors will help you understand why people do certain things and better understand the customer so you can uncover underlying objections. It will also help you discern the customers' personal needs so you can better serve them.

PART

2

The Customer and the Competitor

CHAPTER

20

Know where you're going or you'll end up somewhere else

When you sell high technology products, you assume people have problems and need help solving them. Customers listen to you because they have been led to believe you can help solve their problems. Your objective is to find problems in the customer's operation that your product will solve in a manner superior to present methods, or to your competitor's methods. This, in effect, will set the pace for the competition.

○ *Sales Leadership: To outsell, you must be willing to take the lead*

Setting the pace for the competition requires leadership ability. Leaders influence others to follow. Leadership in sales is not necessarily dependent upon a person's individual character or traits but rather on the person's perceived role behavior relative to problem solving. If a person's role behavior appears to unite others behind him or her and to stimulate them to purchase a particular product, that person may be classified as a sales thought leader.

Effective role behavior encompasses technical, interpersonal, and conceptual skills. Technical skills operate on things and include knowledge of both the selling process and the product. Interpersonal skills are required to work with people through effective human interaction. Conceptual skills deal with ideas. Conceptual skills are extremely important because they enable the salesperson to deal with intellectualizations and abstractions and use them to find customer problems, then devise plans to have the solution accepted. These skills will help the salesperson take control and be perceived as a thought leader.

Sales leadership includes problem solving, but it also encompasses problem finding. As a thought leader, you must find the right problem, then stimulate the customer to accept it as valuable. This requires planning.

The problem most salespeople have is finding time to plan. If Gresham had a law of planning, it would be: *"Programmed work drives out unprogrammed work."* We tend to do programmed work, our normal daily activities, at the expense of unprogrammed work, the things we do once in a while—like planning.

◯ *Planning: Plan sales calls carefully*

Planning plays a major role in the selling process. A salesperson who blunders into a sales call will sell less than a salesperson who carefully plans each call.

When developing a sales campaign for a product, territory, or account, plan it. The plan is a vehicle designed to achieve a particular objective. Planning benefits you in three ways. It provides thought organization, problem examination, and a course of action.

Once the plan is completed, for all intents and purposes it can be thrown away. It is not in the plan, per se, but in the planning process that you derive value. The planning process disciplines your thinking and puts you in control.

The plan must be dynamic because the conditions on which the plan is based will change over time. At the same time, the plan must withstand change. This means the plan must be adaptable without compromising its integrity. Finally, a plan must not rely on logic alone; it should have an intuitive aspect. In fact, the essence of the plan is its intuitive aspect, the feeling you have about why it will succeed.

◯ Holden Planning Model: The Holden Planning Model is ideal for selling high technology

The Holden Model to Strategic Planning is an ideal tool for selling high technology products.[1] The Holden Model has five components.

The *current status* describes where you are right now. It qualifies the account by describing the customer's organization, the political structure, the sales issues, and other pertinent data.

The *objective* is exactly what you intend to accomplish. This second component should be simple, quantified, tied to time, and logical.

The *strategy* develops the plan to use resources to achieve the objective in terms of the competition. It is not dependent upon a set of assumptions that could easily change.

Resources include the time, money and people needed to execute the strategy and achieve the objective.

Tactics follow the strategy and describe the methods to be used to implement the strategy. Tactics are dynamic actions that will create the effect described in the strategy.

◯ Testing the Plan: Examine the sales plan against all its elements

Once formulated, the plan must be tested. If there is a possibility that the plan or strategy will fail, the time to establish that is early, when you can still make the necessary adjustments.

The first test of the plan is to determine if it makes sense. Your common sense is a valuable evaluation criterion. Next,

[1]Holden, *Vanguard*, (Referenced).

determine if the needed resources are available. If the plan requires a new product, the availability of that resource may be in question. The third test verifies direction. Is the plan a puzzle, or a clear path that can be followed? Will the plan lead to stability? If properly executed, will the plan lead to a continuing relationship with the customer? If it destabilizes the situation, even if it is successful, it may compromise future business.

The fifth check looks for a radical departure from company philosophy. If the strategy requires a significant change, obtaining management support or approval may be difficult.

The final test is to project yourself into your competitor's shoes and surmise what the competitor could do to defeat the plan. This is the acid test. Is the plan's success dependent upon one individual who could be transferred? Is it only aimed at the market leader, or does it also take into account dark-horse second or third competitors who could cut you off at the pass? It sometimes happens that two competitors become so focused on one another that they overlook a third competitor who sneaks in and snatches the prize.

If you find it difficult or time-consuming to test your plan and would rather avoid this exercise, rest assured that if you don't test it your competitors will.[2]

One of the first applications of the plan is in the area of problem finding. What better way to position your product and establish the ground rules for how the competitive battle will be fought than if you find the problem the customer has that must be solved? You will have truly set the pace for the competition. Once you have identified or found a problem, who can better offer a unique solution than you?

○ ## *Problem Finding: The customer should find the problem much the way you did*

You may find the most wonderful problem, but it is useless unless it is accepted by the customer. This implies it must have real meaning for the customer. Sometimes meaning must be managed. To manage the problem-finding process, carefully develop a support system for the identified problem. This can be done by announcing relevant facts in advance of announcing

[2]Ibid.

the problem, or briefing key contacts and explaining to them the problem uncovered. These implentation steps are necessary if the identified problem is real but not obvious to the customer.

Finding real problems requires creativity. To create, you first need facts and information to understand the customer better, then you must act upon that understanding. Therefore, great emphasis is placed on learning all the details about the customer's situation. It is from these details and their context that you will create or find new problems and generate new methods for solving them.[3]

Once you have defined a new problem, develop a plan to obtain the customer's acknowledgment of the problem and the customer's acceptance of the solution.

Problem Solving: There is a process to solving a problem

Problem solving is a four-step process: define the problem, list the alternatives, select one alternative, then implement it. For successful implementation, it is important to establish an early relationship with the customer and get the customer involved in the interpretation.

Through this involvement you can establish goals in solving the problem that are in concert with the goals and objectives of the company. You may also find ways to advance the political position or visibility to management of the involved individuals.

Also review the situational and environmental issues around the selected alternative.

How will it affect those with political power and influence in the account?

How will it affect your political position?

Will it solve the technical issues?

Will your alternative require direct intervention into the account or can you sell it through promotion by an employee of the customer, an in-house salesperson?

---

[3]Leavitt, *Managerial Psychology*, pp. 304-309.

After you have answered these questions, test the water. Tentatively present your alternative to a key decision maker as the solution to the problem. If accepted as is, develop the strategy to implement it. If rejected, you have three choices: abandon it and find a new alternative, define a new problem, or develop a strategy to sell the customer on it anyway.

If the customer accepts your problem but alludes to new issues or other problems your solution surfaces, these must be addressed in your implementation strategy.

○ *Implementation Strategy: Learn how to lead others to see the solution*

In developing the implementation strategy, first answer the following questions:

- How will I achieve internal acceptance among the other decision-makers and influential individuals in the account?

- How will I strategically position my product or service so that it will be perceived as the only or best choice?

- What will the competition most likely do?

- Will the impetus to execute the strategy come from outside or inside the account?

As a salesperson without formal authority over the customer, you cannot implement the solution, you must convince someone in the account with authority or influence to implement it for you.

All things being equal, if you develop a solution only you can implement, it will differentiate you from your competitors.

Gunther Klaus in his "Marketing By Objective" lectures calls this the *Principle of the Fine Edge.* Simply stated, the principle says, "Figure out what makes you different and sell it like hell."[4]

---

[4]Klaus, *Marketing by Objective,* (Referenced).

CHAPTER

Sell strategically

Many salespeople have been successful without systematic attention to strategy and think strategic selling is a lot of nonsense. A salesperson may have a product that sells itself, or the capability and capacity to exploit a growing market. According to the theory of evolution, he or she survives and dominates others of the species.

Unfortunately, when the product no longer has acknowledged superiority, or if the market stagnates, and a competitor makes a creative strategic thrust, the salesperson, unless prepared for the thrust, will react and a new star will be born. If the salesperson had had the insight early in the selling process to adjust to the lack of clear product superiority or the down marketing, a competitive sales strategy would have been developed that could have kept him or her on top.

◯   ## *Developing a Sales Strategy: Sales are won consistently through strategy*

Developing a successful sales strategy requires some vision and a touch of imagination. A sales strategy is aimed at defeating the opponent's strategy. The opponents include customer resistance and the competitor. Both must be considered in developing the strategy.

Although generals and politicians have studied strategy for thousands of years, it is only recently that businesses have embraced strategy. The Japanese, in their usual manner, studied it fervidly, and their phenomenal worldwide economic success speaks well for the strategic approach to business in general and sales in particular.

A company develops a business strategy. Marketing develops a product strategy to address the market in general. Sales develops a sales strategy that is competitive in nature, and modifies marketing's product strategy as required to capture specific accounts in specific sales situations. In essence it marries product strategy with political strategy.

Churchill said, "Only when military and *political* thought are joined could leaders discover easier ways of achieving the main purpose."

As he saw it, the "distinction between politics and the military diminishes as the point of view is raised. At the summit, true politics and military strategy are one."[1] Churchill's product was the military.

The famous desert fox, the World War II German Field Marshall Erwin Rommel was a master technician, but, in the words of another Field Marshall, Gerd Von Rundsteadt, an *unlicked cub* when it came to strategy. As a strategist, Rommel was shortsighted. He saw only the tactical release of his own troops as an issue, while blindly refusing to accept that political considerations might demand a course of action that seemed tactically unacceptable.[2]

Although not directly responsible for the battle, Dwight Eisenhower was in essence defeated by Rommel in Africa at the Kasserine Pass. Ike was to blame because of the lack of a plan

[1]Manchester, *The Last Lion*, p. 569.

[2]David Irving, *The Trail of the Fox*, (New York, NY: Thomas Congdon Books, E.P. Dutton, 1977), p. 453.

with clear direction.[3] Yet Ike was a general with rare and valuable gifts. He united the allied forces through political accumen, did not permit a compromise strategy and later defeated Rommel at Normandy. Ike understood that a successful strategy must combine the product, in this case military capability, with political reality, even if it meant tactical compromise. He was a politically astute salesman.

In terms of a sales strategy, these historical perspectives point out the necessity of adding to the product strategy a political strategy to address the political structure of the account. Therefore, a sales strategy must have two components, a product component and a political component.

If the political component is not considered, the strategy will be doomed to failure. Politics are an integral part of any sales strategy because people and organizations—politics—are involved in the decision process. It is essential to appreciate the importance of the political component of a sales strategy.

By developing a sales strategy with both a product and political component, you create an opportunity to circumvent the competition by keeping them focused on the product component.

○ Product Strategy: Aim to be the sole supplier of your product

The product component exploits the features and benefits of the product. It addresses the specific needs of the targeted account, and provides solutions. The objective of the product strategy is to develop a monopoly within the account. The product strategy is designed to make you the sole supplier to the account for the type of product or service you are offering.

In high technology, a golden opportunity exists to become a sole source to an account, especially in selling capital equipment.

In the case of most materials that are used by the customer in the end product being manufactured, a second source is demanded and actively sought. This is not always true with OEM items such as computers or capital equipment such as computer-aided tools, automatic testers, and other production

---

[3]Bradley and Clay, *A General's Life*, p. 130-131.

equipment used in managing the facility or in designing and manufacturing the product.

By developing a product strategy that is clearly perceived as solving the customers' problem, you can focus on the more qualitative issues that differentiate your product.

◯ *Business Strategy: Focus on cost of ownership*

You allow your competitor to focus on the product features and benefits while you concentrate your efforts on the business issues through qualitative differentiation.

The high technology industry for the most part is overcrowded, and product differentiation is slight. Consequently it is necessary to sell less tangible advantages. It may be necessary to sell your company by stressing brand awareness like IBM, Apple, or Tektronix. Reliability may be sold based upon internal quality programs or a field-proven track record. The latest technology may be the focal point, or business competence, which means you are probably going to be around awhile, unlike many high technology companies that grow at a rapid pace, then disappear or fade away.

Friendliness or ease of use is another high technology sales buzz word which attempts to demystify the use of complex products making them easier to use. Programming menus, touch screens, the *mouse,* function keys, automatic set-up and initialization, robotics and other built-in humanizing features reduce the technical knowledge level required of those who operate, program, and use this equipment. This in turn reduces the cost of ownership.

More mundane yet important issues such as price, location, packaging, and availability can also be used in an attempt to monopolize an account.

A monopoly will enhance your control and lower your cost of sales. This translates into profits for your company. With high technology products, to concede a portion of the account to a competitor, or to assume a second source is necessary, is an error. No matter what the customer tells you, you have an opportunity to become the sole supplier, if you cement the relationship with the customer by serving their needs after the product is delivered.

○ Political Strategy: Tap the customer's power base

The political component of sales strategy utilizes the political structure of a company to your advantage. Companies or organizations are no longer productivity driven. Today, marketing drives organizations. Information has become an asset and socio-political issues are of concern to most corporations.

Organizations are both responding to these charges and acting as the impetus for the changes occurring. High technology is playing an active role in making these changes possible and, for that matter, inevitable. The process is not serial but additive. Automation is creating a new blue collar worker and middle management is participating in decision-making rather than simply implementing decisions.

Staff people, particularly planners, are growing in importance, and focusing on better utilization of human resources, automation, and information processing.

Top managers are more arbitrators and negotiators than commanders or dictators. They must deal with the sophisticated political components inside their organization.

In this changing world, salespeople must learn how to interface with the political structure and use it to their advantage.

A modern organization is a society unto itself, consisting of a complex set of interacting power groups. To sell to these organizations it is necessary to understand their backgrounds, objectives, beliefs, and motives. These power groups form the power base of an organization. Those within this base exert influence on the organization. Power within a company flows out of this base.[4]

Your objective is to tap into this power flow, but without a clear and definitive sales strategy consisting of both a product and a political component you will have little if any chance of channeling powerful organizational influence in your direction.

---

[4]Holden, *Vanguard*, (Referenced).

CHAPTER

(22)

Don't depend on luck

Luck, that mysterious force that brings good fortune or adversity, and controls the events or circumstances that operate for or against you, may not be mysterious at all.

Lyndon Johnson said to look into a situation and you will find it is a lot more than luck.[1] If you depend on luck, chance, fortune, destiny, fate, or Providence, you are bound for disaster. Napoleon said luck is a form of intelligence. If you are diligent, you will be lucky.

A chance happening of events may coalesce and bring you the good fortune of an order. A bluebird may fly in your window or you may benefit from chance by unwittingly introducing the right product at the right time to the right customer.

But if you want to be consistently lucky, you must learn how to do things intelligently, through careful planning. Dilettantes

[1]Caro, *The Path to Power,* p. 225.

may *luck out* but you can be sure they won't be consistent. Consistency in sales depends upon knowledge, decisiveness, and wit. Consistently winning orders is a direct result of skill in planning, managing, and directing the sales strategy.

◯   *Types of Strategy: There is more than one type of sales strategy*

Selling is neither an art nor a science. Success in selling is not due to luck. Success in selling is the consequence of the intelligent execution of a well-thought-out sales strategy.

To win the high technology sales game, you must think strategically. There are two basic strategies: direct and indirect. A variation on the direct strategy is divisional, a variation on the indirect strategy is containment. There are no other strategies.

The USA's grand strategy in World War II was an example of these two strategies and their variations in action. An indirect strategy was used to gain the support of the public for the war. When Japan attacked Pearl Harbor, a strategy of containment was employed by the USA. The objective was to hold or contain Japan in the Pacific, while a divisional strategy of a two-front war in Europe, French Normandy and the invasion of Italy one and the Russian front the other, was used to defeat Germany. Then a direct strategy made possible by $E = mc^2$ was executed to crush Japan.

The Romans normally employed a direct strategy during their conquests. They locked shields and, through discipline and might, put fear into the hearts of those who attempted to stand against them.

Hannibal, using both the Alps and elephants, resorted to an indirect strategy and defeated the Romans in the Po Valley. Napoleon usually executed a divisional strategy in his wars and battles. Meeting his adversary head on, he would divide them in two, then turn all his forces on one half. After defeating that half we would turn around and conquer the others.

Nelson turned the tables on Napoleon in the battle of the Nile. At Abouxier he used Napoleon's divisional strategy and brought his ships up the Nile, positioning them between Napoleon's land forces and the supply war ships. First he disposed of Napoleon's fleet, then he landed marines to dispense with Napoleon's provisionless army.

Containment strategy was executed by the Romans as Masada. In more modern times Americans used a containment strategy in Vietnam and the Russians used it in Afganistan. Neither the Americans nor the Russians exercised their full might with a direct strategy.

Business strategies in general and sales strategies in particular are not much different than military strategies. Successful salespeople are like successful generals, they think and plan strategically. The creative strategist does not sit back and hope that lady luck will bring in an order, but goes out and wins orders. The strategic salesperson qualifies the account so as not to waste time, then, based on this qualification, develops the sales plan, strategy, and tactics.

With regard to the competition, the creative strategist is skilled in the art of maneuver. The strategist focuses on the competitor's mind and strategy to create situations that garner a significant advantage toward securing the order. Strategists know they must find new applications for their products, find new customers, and find new ways to sell. They may appear to act like a foot soldier, but they think like a general. They consider the big picture when they develop sales strategies and tactics.

○ Organization Variables: Be aware of what variables within an organization can affect your sales

An organization is a dynamic network of task, structure, information, and people.[2] When selling to an organization, the task of the organization in terms of what you are selling is to make or not make a buy decision for your product.

Normally you will work with the people-variable to obtain a favorable decision, but in doing so, the structure and information variables should not be overlooked. Structure is the formal organization and authority work-flow system. Information is the informational and control technology of the organization.

The people-variable or system can be controlled by changing the people, their attitudes and behaviors, or their relationships. The structure and information variables can also be

[2]Leavitt, *Managerial Psychology*, p. 282.

controlled. Because they interact, any change to one may affect the others. In addition to these variables, the environment in which the organization functions must also be considered.[3]

Assume you are addressing an information and control application with a computer system for data processing. Further assume that a three-person committee will decide whether or not to purchase such a system. The first person feels that your product may be helpful, but since the division is decentralizing they can function without it.

The second person feels that since they have a very open and communicative organization, such a system may interfere with personal interaction and depersonalize or formalize communications.

The third person is a firm believer in your competitor's product and feels that if they choose to purchase an information and control system, it will only be from your competitor.

Finally, this division belongs to a corporation that has a policy recommending that all divisions, wherever possible, automate their operations. At the same time it has a policy of autonomy for each division, and will not dictate or impose automation.

You are now faced with four interconnecting variables that bear upon whether or not you make the sale. The division's planned decentralization is a structural issue. The communication interface is an information issue. The attitude toward the competitor is a people issue. The environment is conducive to automation.

This chapter is not intended to develop a sales strategy, but to show the various alternatives relative to each issue.

In terms of structure, you can work to change the person's attitude by showing that your product will provide even better benefits with decentralization, or work to convince the division not to decentralize.

In terms of the information variable, you can focus on changing the person's attitude by convincing the individual that your system will not depersonalize the department, or that the current information system needs to be changed even at the risk of depersonalization.

In case of the people issue, you can either deal with the objection directly and sell the individual or your product, or work to have the individual nullified through a promotion, transfer, or some other neutralizing method.

---

[3]Ibid., p. 290.

Changing each individual's attitude and behavior is the classic sales approach. Stopping decentralization, changing the current information system, and eliminating or neutralizing the opposing party provide more sophisticated alternate strategic paths to getting the order.

As for the environment, working at corporate levels to have them influence the division to automate is another alternative. Since all these variables interact, the strategy and tactics employed must be carefully planned.

Unless these organizational variables are known, understood, and dealt with in your sales strategy, you are in danger of failing. Concentrating all your efforts on the people variable and working to change peoples' attitudes and behaviors is one approach, but if this approach is not working or is blocked, and if you have also focused on the other organizational variables of structure and information, as well as the environment, you can still win. By dealing with these factors in your initial strategy, you will enhance your chances of success and when you win others will say you were just lucky.

CHAPTER

23

Never change your sales strategy

True strategy is immutable. When you develop a sales strategy for selling to a particular account, first establish your objective. Then determine how you will accomplish it. The "how" is your strategy. Next decide "what" to do to execute the strategy. The "whats" are your tactics.

○ ### Changing the Ground Rules: Remember that your tactics must anticipate changes in the ground rules

For a given objective, a strategy or direction should remain fixed while the tactics, the implementation, will change over time until you accomplish the objective. By keeping your strategy fixed for a given buying criteria or set of ground rules, you will be able to maintain control, stay on schedule, and not compromise the effectiveness of your plan.

If the ground rules shift and a new criteria for buying is introduced, your strategy will be in disarray unless you planned for such a contingency and have a tactic to deal with the shift. On the other hand, an effective strategy has a tactic that either changes the ground rules for the competition or appears to change them at the eleventh hour. This planned move on your part may force the competitor to react and change his strategy. If the change was not anticipated, the competition is likely to make mistakes and lose.

Assume that your objective is to capture an account where your competitor has been entrenched for years. To develop your strategy, first study the competitor and identify their outstanding characteristics relative to the account. Next determine the competitor's attitude and behavior. Let's further assume that the competitor has put a junior salesperson on the account in a maintenance capacity. The competitor assumes the customer will continue to buy because of the installed base, and their investment in the existing product as well as perceived product superiority.

Once you understand the competitor's attitude and behavior concerning the account, evaluate the environment in which the battle will take place.

Suppose the customer is making a major change in their product line and will be purchasing a large amount of capital equipment. Your competitor is firmly entrenched and has a new enhancement to their product that will meet the customer needs. The environment is conducive to the competitor's success.

Do Not Base Your Strategy on Your Strength

Now analyze your strengths. Why should this customer purchase from you? What benefits do you offer that your competitor does not offer? Assume that the competitor's product is hardware-intensive. They provide a solid reliable product and, although it is difficult to modify since it is hardware-oriented, it does the job well. Your product is newer and software-intensive. Response to change is quick and easy. Your value or strength is flexibility from software-intensiveness.

The first thought that comes to mind is to base your strategy on your strength and sell flexibility. A smart strategist will hold back the strongest point because every strength will eventually become a weakness. Do not base your strategy on your strengths. Instead, develop your initial thrust around software technology. Software is the wave of the future, the thing to do in keeping with the information age; it provides better investment protection. You apparent strategy is to directly promote technological leadership through the product software. Your true intent is to indirectly promote the value flexibility.

To establish credibility, you demonstrate software solutions to the problems that your competitor solves with hardware. Your major advantage in terms of the competitor, flexibility, is held in reserve.

The next step is to determine if your strategy will lead to stability so that your product will be successful in this account. Will securing this order mean you will destabilize the account, jump the decision-maker, get the management to overrule the user, or force you to expend excessive resources trying to make your product successful in a hostile environment?

Account stability is a prerequisite of a successful sales strategy. With high technology products, success depends on the commitment of the customer to the product as much as it does on the inherent quality and functionality of the product. Let's assume it soon becomes clear that with proper management support your product will lead to stability.

Let's further assume the new, young software-oriented department manager with the new management direction he is advancing could perceive your product, if properly positioned, as valuable in helping him promote his ideas. You now have a political focus to your strategy.

The last prerequisite to developing a successful sales strategy is to ensure it is explicit. It must be clearly and simply stated, and definitive. In this case the product component is flexibility, i.e., response to their product changes. The political component is gain, i.e., a change from old hardware to new software will enhance the manager's ability to achieve his personal objectives.

Since the competitor is aligned with the majority of the customer's power base, the competitor is in a strong political position. If not so aligned, the competitor's position would be weak. Since your competitor is firmly in position from both a product and political perspective, you do not want to launch a direct attack.

You could use a divisional strategy but your technical and political superiority is not yet obvious. Additionally, the competitor is doing the job and everybody is happy. The best solution is a containment strategy, designed to upset the competitor's equilibrium.

Before you launch the real attack, you appear to be attacking the firmly entrenched competitor directly. Your true intent is to indirectly change the ground rules, but first you execute a diversionary tactic and attack the competitor's position head-on, by directly offering a software-intensive product to replace their existing hardware-intensive systems.

The competitor's strategy has been repeat business through product superiority with hardware enhancements, to keep abreast of the customer's needs. When you directly attack this strategy by showing the benefits of the software approach, the competitor responds by countering with the benefits of the hardware-oriented system which works just as well. The customer sees some benefit in your offer but not enough to justify changing vendors.

The competitor successfully beats back your attack, falling into your trap, just like Jacques Jaffre, French commander-in-chief in World War I, who entered Lorraine not suspecting the retreating Germans were luring him into a trap.

It is now time to change the ground rules. Just like the German commander, Alexander von Kluck flanked the French, you flank your competition by surfacing your major product benefit, flexibility, the ease of making changes, and aligning it with the customer's new product line, which is in a state of flux. You also use the influence of the new department manager to promote your solution within the company's political structure.

The competitor will keep the old product line application and its repeat business for now, while you partition the business with a divisional strategy and focus on the new product line business. Your software can quickly and easily be changed to meet their changing product needs, whereas the competitor would have to modify or design new hardware, which takes significantly more time, effort, and money. You convince the customer that the competitor's solution for the new product line is time-consuming and expensive. The hardware changes would have to be duplicated on every system, whereas software is easily transportable. Since you have already proven your product will do the job, it is difficult for the competitor to counter your argument.

Your containment, or surround-and-disturb strategy, keeps the customer's environment stable, but it surrounds the competitor with confusion, containing the competitor to the old product line, while disturbing their future position, since you will take the new product line business.

○ ## *Attack the Competitor's Strategy: To beat a direct strategy, give the customer something new to consider*

You have successfully attacked the competitor's strategy and changed the ground rules. The new buying criteria is "flexibility" for new products whose design is not stable.

The environment is now emotionally charged. The competition reacts and changes their strategy offering a software enhancement they are designing. Although this enhancement will make their product more flexible, it is too little, too late. The competitor has played right into your hands. By offering a software solution, the competitor has substantiated your position. This will confirm in the customer's mind the value of your solution.

If the competitor had not taken the account for granted and had kept a top salesperson on it, chances are they would have maintained control and effectively countered your strategy by introducing their new software enhancement early, selling futures to the customer.

In fact, this was not the case and your containment strategy worked because you hid your true intent from your competitor and established credibility with the customer, proving you could do the job. You then executed an indirect strategy and changed the ground rules by offering a unique benefit, flexibility, which solved the problem associated with the unstable new product line. Although you appeared to the competitor to be executing a direct attack in the customer's eyes, you did not try to unseat them where they were strong, but attacked their product-superiority strategy relative to the new product line and changed the buying criteria from rigid hardware enhancements to flexible software enhancements. Thus, you won the new business and successfully contained the competitor to the old product line.

Later you will disturb the competitor's old product line business position and eventually capture that business as well. The competitor's volte-face caused their downfall. They lost because they were unprepared and reacted by changing their strategy from hardware to software at the eleventh hour.

CHAPTER

24

Keep others ignorant of your strategy

If the account was properly qualified as having sales potential and if you decided to actively pursue the sale, and lost, then 99 out of a 100 times, you were outsold. This is the *only* reason you lost.

○ ***Control Through Strategy: The timing and the competition are important factors***

Sales situations, conditions, circumstances, and competitors are continually in a state of flux. If you are not in control you will react to these changes and chances are you will lose the sale. If you put yourself at the mercy of chance, the wheel of fortune may roll over you.

A strategic approach to selling will put you in control of the time frame during which the order will be placed. With many salespeople, their strategy tends to be based on what worked before. In the high technology environment, strategy based solely on experience is rarely adequate. Different sales situations require different strategies. If you develop a sound strategy and execute it tactically and win, the competition will probably understand your tactics but it is unlikely that they will comprehend your strategy. Fortunately you never have to repeat the same tactics, since there is an infinite variety of ways to execute a strategy. Tactics are unlimitable.[1]

Strategy formulation does not come easily even for the seasoned salesperson. Developing a successful strategic sales plan requires systematic analysis of your product, the customer, and the competition. Your objective is to upset the competitor's equilibrium so they will never know what happened even if they think they do.

For a given objective or a given set of ground rules, a strategy does not change. It is an irretrievable commitment to a course of action that, if properly formulated, cannot be beaten. It is immune to the state of flux that surrounds you. It is not visible to your competitors, hence it will force them to act in a manner advantageous to you. They may react, they may restrain themselves, or they may cooperate. Reaction will throw them into confusion or disorder. Osborne's reaction to lack of IBM compatibility in their computer threw them into bankruptcy. Restraint will allow you to pick and choose the accounts you want. When it comes to oscilloscopes, Tektronix can have any account it wishes. Cooperation will result in stability. The major semiconductor manufacturers cooperate through second source agreements which leads to stability.

Remember that your objective is to meet your sales forecast and achieve the objectives of your company. It is not your objective to annihilate the competition. One hundred percent

---

[1]This and subsequent chapters on strategy are a summary of the thoughts of many people. The major sources are listed below.
*B.H. Liddell Hart, *Strategy*, (London, England: Faber and Faber Ltd., 1954).
*Samuel B. Griffith, *Sun Tzu, The Art of War*, (New York, NY: Oxford University Press, 1963).
*Bruce D. Henderson, *Henderson on Corporate Strategy*, (Cambridge, MA: ABT Books, 1979).
*Boris Yavitz and William H. Newman, *Strategy in Action*, (New York, NY: The Free Press, A division of MacMillan Publishing Co., Inc., 1982).
*Holden, *Vanguard*, Training Course.

market share is not the objective of a well-advised management.

If the competition knows they can also win, their positions will remain in check.

Abdul Aziz conquered many enemies as he united modern Saudi Arabia but he, contrary to Bedouin custom, forbade all looting or killing. When talking about his enemies he said, "When they punished us, it stirred us to revenge. So let us not punish them."[2] If the competitor has an alternative, they will not fight as hard. If the competitors act rationally you will always know where they are coming from and you can control where they are going.

If you appear irrational and unpredictable to them you have a significant advantage. The ultimate strategy not only puts you incontrol of the timing of sales motion, it puts you in control of the competitor as well. Maneuver and surprise will give you a significant advantage. The successful salesperson wins strategically.

○ *How To Use Strategies*

If you are three times stronger than your competitors, you may wish to meet them head on and overcome them with your superiority. But beware! They may change the criteria for buying. If they successfully change the ground rules, you lose.

They may partition the business. Again you lose because you have given up part of the business. They now have a foothold. If, in the euphoria of your direct attack, you failed to cover all the technical bases or failed to penetrate top managment, they may contain you by labeling you with a classification that relegates you to addressing only a portion of the business, while they take the rest.

The **direct strategy** is always vulnerable to a wily competitor who is skilled in using indirect strategies. The direct strategy is most effective when you are very visible, have adequate resources, and your sales strategy is based on selling company or product superiority. It only works if you are perceived superior in terms of the value you offer from a product, business, and political point of view.

[2]Lacey, *The Kingdom*, p. 163.

An **indirect strategy** works best when the objective is to change the criteria for buying. It also works well when executing a power stratagem focused on the people and politics of the account. The most likely competitive counter-strategy is a direct or divisional attack intent on collapsing the time-frame and forcing a buy decision before you have had an opportunity to complete the execution of your indirect strategy.

An indirect strategy takes time to implement unless your product or political position is strong and you offer the best business solution. You cannot convince the customer to change the buying criteria overnight, nor are you able to develop the contacts and influence the management to execute your power stratagem quickly. Hence it is essential to lull the competitor into a false sense of security. Your objective is to catch them unawares. As Kubilai Khan once advised, "Never ride on the skyline of the hills, but always a little way below the crest." When you appear, they will not have time to act, and can only react to the situation you have created.

To generate a reaction, conceal your true intent. Appear to give up, or outwardly appear to be employing a direct strategy. If the competitors become complacent, by the time they realize your true intent, their strategy will be in disarray. It will be too late, because their strategy was direct and you attacked that strategy indirectly, changed the ground rules, and got the order.

If you are politically or product-wise superior but your competitor is strong in the account with an installed base of equipment, has a good rapport with the customer, or is in business control with the product use a **divisional strategy.** Complement by second sourcing the competitor or by partitioning the business.

As you execute the divisional strategy, your competitor may respond with a direct attack to force the customer to order before your strategy takes effect, but is more likely to respond indirectly to delay the decision to buy time if you appear successful. The delay will give them time to counteract your proposal.

If the competitor is entrenched in the account, and is strong technically, financially, and politically, with a large base of installed equipment, execute a **containment strategy.** Look for a soft spot. If the competitor becomes careless and assigns an inexperienced salesperson to the account, makes it a house account by managing it from the factory, or becomes lax about support, attack!

If the competitor is vigilant, attempt to gain a foothold in a possibly insignificant department or for a minor or specialized application, then try to unbalance them. Seize every opportunity to take or challenge something the competitor values.

Change your actions and alter your plans so the competitors do not know what you are doing. If the competitors do not know how or where you intend to penetrate the account, they must prepare to counter you in many ways and places.

If you can keep them off guard, if you can disturb them, they will have to maintain a defensive position and will have little time to prepare a plan to counter you. Surround them with hyperbole. Disturb their equilibrium, and eventually they will make a mistake. Then you strike and create a sale.

Five Strategic Rules

In a sales situation there are five rules a good strategist should follow. They are based on the writings of Sun Tzu, *The Art Of War*, China, 500 B.C.

1. Approach your objective indirectly.

2. Attack the competitor's strategy.

3. Develop your strategy based on the following rules:

   — If you are three times as strong as the competitor in all respects, execute a direct strategy.

   — If you are not three times stronger than your competitor use an indirect strategy.

   — If your competitor has an installed base but you are potentially stronger, employ a divisional strategy.

   — If your competitor has an installed base and you are weaker, execute a containment strategy and wait for an opportunity.

4. Engage an in-house salesperson. Use this person to:

   — Address the political component of the sale.

   — Promote your product internally.

   — Obtain for you competitive information.

   — Find out who has the real power and influence.

   — Advise you on what others think of you, and your product, company, and proposal.

5. Keep others ignorant of your strategy. The less people know about what you are doing the better chance you have of winning. If they have no need to know, even if they work for you or your company, you have no need to tell them.

Figure 4 illustrates the best strategies and counter-strategies to employ depending on the customer's perception of the value you or your competitor offer. The goal of the true sale strategist is success through a controlled plan. The strategist wins the battle before it is fought.

STRATEGIC PLANNING MATRIX

CUSTOMER PERCEIVED VALUE			OFFENSIVE		DEFENSIVE	
PRODUCT	POLITICAL	BUSINESS	STRATEGY	TIME-FRAME	COUNTER-STRATEGY	TIME FRAME
STRONG	STRONG	STRONG	DIRECT	COLLAPSE	CONTAIN	EXTEND
WEAK	STRONG	STRONG	INDIRECT	COLLAPSE	INDIRECT	EXTEND
STRONG	WEAK	STRONG	INDIRECT	COLLAPSE	INDIRECT	EXTEND
WEAK	WEAK	STRONG	INDIRECT	EXTEND	DIVISIONAL	COLLAPSE
STRONG	STRONG	WEAK	DIVISIONAL	COLLAPSE	INDIRECT	EXTEND
WEAK	STRONG	WEAK	INDIRECT	EXTEND	INDIRECT	COLLAPSE
STRONG	WEAK	WEAK	INDIRECT	EXTEND	INDIRECT	COLLAPSE
WEAK	WEAK	WEAK	CONTAIN	EXTEND	DIRECT	COLLAPSE

THIS CHART LISTS "MOST-LIKELY" STRATEGIES AND COUNTER-STRATEGIES

Figure 4: Strategic Planning Matrix

CHAPTER

(25)

Execute your strategy tactically

Tactics allow you to adapt to the customer and the environment as well as to the competitive thrust or counter thrust. Tactics flex your strategy. They are the dynamic component of your strategic sales plan.

○ *Executing Tactics: Tactics are dynamic*

Strategists executing tactics act quickly and decisively. The strategist knows what is at stake for both them and their competitors, but make sure their competitors do not know what they have at stake. They know when to yield or withdraw and when to attack or advance.

Developing successful tactics requires an understanding of the customer's and competitor's attitudes and motives. Once the tactics are developed they are executed to effect the strategy in a sequential fashion where each tactic begets another tactic until the close.

When the attitude or motives of the customer or competitor shift, or a shift is predictable, the tactics should immediately be reassessed and modified as required. The sequence previously set in place may be upset. You may be forced by competitive tactics to compress or expand the purchasing time frame. If the ground rules change, and if in your strategy you anticipated such a change, you can draw on an alternate tactical sequence. If unanticipated, you can develop entirely new alternatives. The important point to remember is not to react, just appear in the competitor's eyes to react.

The more unreasonable, capricious, or arbitrary you appear, the greater your tactical advantage. Attract the competitor's attention, but appear confused or weak; play down the significance of your actions, and simulate emotion. To the customer, project poise and emphasize your product's value and solution.

Tactics must be managed in real time as various situations arise and circumstances dictate. Tactics can be planned, but the ones you will actually execute cannot always be predetermined.

○ Competitive Tricks: Keep your competitors off balance

The competitors, especially if unsure of their positions, will tend to react. Your objective is to bring about a reaction so that they will lose control. If out of control, they may try dirty tricks such as negative selling by focusing on your company's or product's vulnerabilities rather then their strengths as the basis for the customer to decide in their favor.

Arranging for clandestinely obtained internal, possibly compromising, literature or memos from your company to find its way into your customer's hands can also be extremely damaging. Some customers have a policy against accepting such data, but often the damage is done in the offering or illegal receipt. It is like the judge telling the jury to disregard what they just heard.

Sometimes the competitor will set up distractions during your presentation by arranging for key individuals attending the meeting to be called away. The competitor may arrange a meeting with an individual not attending your presentation, so that he or she is in the building during your presentation. This can have a distracting psychological impact on you (Who is he visiting? Is the person important?). Just by being there the competitor may quickly obtain information about your presentation. The competitor's presence alone will be disquieting for both you and the customer.

There are many other dirty tricks which, if you are not careful, can eat you alive. But if you have generally accounted for them in your strategy, the competitor will lose credibiity when they try them.

○ *Execute Tactics Early: Use your tactics before your competitor forces you to*

As opposed to attracting the competitor's attention, avoid the competitor's attention by concealing your intent and being obscure until it is too late for them to respond effectively. Redirect their attention to another competitor by seeming to be unresponsive and not a contender for the business.

Another tactic is to appear unworthy of serious attention, by pursuing a minor, possibly unprofitable application, or by the pretense of focusing on the wrong application or personnel in the account.

To be successful with these tactics, you must execute them early in the sales process, and gain the advantage before the competitor knows what you are doing. Of course, if you have a superior product, political or business position, and are executing a direct strategy, your tactic is to appear unbeatable. You want the competition to believe the effort is not worth their time so that they will pursue other, more likely opportunities.

Suppose a sales situation exists where a major division of a corporation has a large installed base of your competitor's product. A new division is formed by this corporation in an out-of-the-way place. This division has little growth potential in the short term, but is influential with the corporation.

Your strategy is to capture the small division and use it to eventually break your competitor's hold on the larger division. To do this you employ an indirect strategy.

Your objective is to get an order from the new division, and use it as an indirect route to penetrate the larger division.

○   ***Appear Irrational: Appearing irrational can delude your competitor into false security***

One set of tactics is to attract the competitor's attention by making an all-out direct attack for the large division's business. By attacking the competitor's strengths you appear confused because the competitor knows that tactic won't win. You make certain credible concessions, knowing the large division may not accept them because they are not significant enough to cause a change in suppliers. Yet they are significant enough to appear irrational or emotional on your part to the competitor.

In the meantime you work with the new division, but play down the significance of this activity. The competitor, by virtue of their position in the large division, assumes they will also get the business of the new division by exerting influence through the large division, and by virtue of their large installed bases.

During this tactical execution you at all times maintain credibility with the large division. They appreciate your efforts. They even get to like you, and understand the worth of your product over the competitor's, but they just can't justify a change; the risk in their minds is too high. You appreciate their feelings but you keep pursuing the business.

The competitor views your position as weak, which it is in terms of this division. Thus the competitor relegates you to the nuisance category. The large division benefits to a certain extent because, provoked by your proposals, the competitor steps up its support and makes a few concessions for which you get the credit because it was your activity which motivated the competitor to improve their support.

In working with the new division you carefully promote the concept of them standing apart, of not being a me-too division, of corporate visibility, and you show how you can provide this value to them through your product. You also focus on the similarity in your positions. They are a small division with potential. You are a potential supplier to the corporation.

They see the value of being able, through your product, to make their mark in their corporate world. They see the benefit in not blindly allowing the large division to dictate their decision. You provide a balanced and stable solution. You are sensitive to their position and they have confidence in you.

Before the competitor knows what happened, you have the order. They react. They attempt to solicit corporate help but by virtue of the new division's influence with corporate, the competitor finds you have already covered that base.

The competition tries to use the large division as a hammer, but because of your rapport with them even though you haven't sold to them, the larger division's attempt to turn the order around is half-hearted.

You can now execute the tactic of discrediting the significance of your win by stopping your direct attack on the large division as you develop strength in the new division. The new division is used to "sell" for you at the large division.

Slowly you break down the obstacles to the penetration of the larger division. The competitor becomes confused. They start to react again. They start losing control. You wear the competitor down. You keep them constantly occupied. They rush around, offering concessions. You maintain a low profile but encourage arrogance in the competitor. Eventually, the large division asks to buy your product.

Although you appeared to the competitor both irrational and unpredictable, the sale was inevitable because you were always in control. You decided where the battle would be fought and you understood the competitor's strengths and weaknesses. You agitated them while you concealed your true intent. You tactically executed an indirect strategy that by a circuitous route confused the competitor and accomplished your objective.

You got the sale and the customer benefited in several ways. The new division had a good product, established their independence, and made their mark in the corporate world. The large division, through the interface with the new division and the performance of your product, saw the value you offered which in turn diminished their risk. Consequently, they eventually purchased your product. Finally, through your efforts and due to your tactics, they received better support from your competitor for the existing equipment. What's more, you got credit for it![1]

[1]The following books and articles were referenced:
*Henderson, *Corporate Strategy.*
*Holden, *Vanguard.*
*Jim Holden, *Winning Control Over The Buyer and Competition,* (Industrial Marketing, December, 1982).
*Hart, *Strategy.*

CHAPTER

26

Prepare for unsavory competitive tactics

Never compare your product to the competitive product. Never slight the competitor's product or the competitor. There are various reasons for this.

First of all, the buyer may not even be aware of the competitor you mention and by mentioning them you may motivate the buyer to investigate. Belittling the competition whom the buyer has bought from or plans to buy from is tantamount to calling the buyer an idiot.

If you knock the competitors too hard, you may cause the buyer to defend them. This is especially true if the buyer likes the competitor, or the competitor's salesperson.

The customer may start talking about the competitor's product. In this case it is permissible to carry on a short dialogue about the competitor, but do not fall into the comparison trap. The minute you allow yourself to start comparing, you are abandoning your strategy. Your new strategy will become yours versus mine. This strategy always puts you on the defensive even if you have a superior product.

Moreover, it is below your dignity as a high technology salesperson to grovel in polemics or cast aspersions at the competitor.

If, on the other hand, the customer asks you to help them make a good, logical evaluation of the relative merits and values of your product versus the competitive offerings, this request for help can be effectively and tactfully used to your advantage through the Holden technique called *Trapping*.[1]

◯ *Trapping: It is wise to lay defensive traps*

The only reason to make a product comparison is to establish the fact that the buyer will lose something if he or she buys from the competitor. This only works if the buyer is able to visualize the gain through your product's value and aligns it with her or his buying criteria.

For example, a salesperson may be talking to an engineer.

"Our product computes a measurement and analyzes the results while the next measurement is being made. Essentially you realize twice the throughput compared to conventional systems, which first make all the measurements and then analyze the results."

The salesperson selling the conventional system now has a problem because the engineer will visualize the gain *twice the throughput* with your system.

If the salesperson tries to promote the throughput of a conventional system, the competitive tactic is contained or trapped.

It is wise to lay defensive traps, but for these traps to be effective, they must be planned well in advance and used from the start of the selling situation. The trap predisposes the customer against the aggressive or negative tactics the competition may use. Traps also facilitate comparisons that increase the effect of your benefits without directly attacking or naming

[1]Holden, *Vanguard*, (Trapping is a Holden Tactic)

a specific competitor. The competitor, on the other hand, finds you where he or she least expects you.

TRY IT, YOU'LL LIKE IT:

In any sales situation, the competitor will try to make you alter your strategy. A knowledgeable competitor knows it is more effective to attack your strategy than attack you, your company, or your product.

A competitor may plan to install a piece of capital equipment free for a trial period, knowing full well that the customer will use it and become familiar with it. After that, the customer is unlikely to exercise the return-with-no-obligation option.

This sales tactic, called the "warm puppy close," can freeze your product out of the picture quite effectively. Before the competitor attempts the "try-it-you'll-like it" trick, subtly plant in the buyer's mind the idea that vendors with high inventory and poor selling records often procure sales by manipulating buyers with free installation offers. Would the buyer give his or her child a puppy to evaluate for a few days and expect them to return it? The competitor knows that once installed the chances the of the customer removing the equipment are slight. Due to the customer's commitment of resources to the "free" trial offer, the customer will try to make the installation successful.

This will alert the buyer to this manipulative tactic, and if the competitor tries it, it is likely to fail.

PRICE CUTTING

A similar approach will protect you against price cutting. Mention to the buyer during lunch, a plant tour, or some other informal meeting your company's philosophy of a one-price-to-all-policy, that every customer gets the best price and that quantity discounts are available to all.

Talk about price cutting as a method of moving obsolete products, and refer to last-minute price cutting as a lack of integrity.

"Why were you not offered the best price initially?"

Then when the competitor realizes they are losing the sale, if they cut the price at the eleventh hour, they trap themselves and lose their credibility. You may have to make some other concessions to keep the sale, but it will probably be more token than substantial.

NEGATIVE SELLING

If the competitor attempts negative selling, you can facilitate self trapping by mentioning to the customer during a casual conversation that your company never slights the competition, that your company's professional standards do not allow this, and that negative selling is an insult to the intelligence and ability of buyers to see pros and cons for themselves. With this trap set, the unwary competitors who try negative pitches will immediately label themselves unprofessional in the buyer's mind.

Traps may be set for competitors who know your product's weaknesses and intend to exploit them. By admitting to them up front and explaining how you have compensated for them, the competitors who bring them up will, to their chagrin, find the buyer defending your product.

On the other hand, by carefully explaining specifically what to "look for" in a product such as yours and carefully mentioning items that are your strengths but your competitor's weaknesses, you will force the competitor into a position they may not be prepared to defend. When the customer brings these points up, the competitor will have to address them honestly.

Another form of trapping is by association. If your competitor is known to use dirty tactics, subtly associate negative selling with a prejudice or bad experience the customer has had. Work on the buyer's insecurities about buying wisely. Plant the idea that anyone who sells negatively, cuts the price, or the like may be hiding something. If reinforced properly through casual repetition, the buyer will be wary of these unsavory tactics if the competitor tries them.

The wise tactician lays traps for the potentially deceitful adversary. These adversaries will only fall into the traps if they use these tactics and trap themselves.

◯ *Blocking: Use blocking to control the closing*

If the competitor is closing, you have two choices: shake hands with the winner of a well-fought battle, or block. With the technique of *blocking*, you turn time to your advantage.[2] As long

[2]Ibid., (Blocking is a Holden Tactic)

as you are winning, close as quickly as possible. When losing, the longer the close is delayed, the better opportunity you have to win. In this case, time works to your advantage.

A customer will close after reviewing the vendor's proposals, receiving all the information needed from all potential suppliers and from his or her own company, and when they can commit funding. Once this situation exists, the customer is ready, willing, and able to make a decision and select a supplier. They are ready to close. You can delay the timing of the close through blocking.

HOW TO BLOCK

To block and delay the close effectively you must challenge the customer's willingness to close by providing new information that will be available after the anticipated decision date. This will delay the decision, effectively blocking the competitor.

You now have more time to respond. Of course you must convince the customer it is in their best interest to wait. Typical blocking tactics include a new product enhancement, a change in delivery if delivery is a sensitive issue, a management meeting, a new support commitment, or a revised financial proposal. A revised financial proposal does not necessarily cut the price but changes the overall value of the financial package in some other way. In any event the block should not be perceived as a price cut. A price cut at the last minute is dangerous if your competitor has trapped for it.

It is important to remember that although a number of such blocking approaches can be successful, you must start laying ground work to implement a block early in the selling process.

Allude early to any issues you intend using, in case a block becomes necessary. If you try initiating a surprise block when the sale is about to close, it may be ineffective. In fact, it may be perceived by the buyer for exactly what it is, a blocking tactic.

New data can delay a decision from a day to a week, but by introducing a new idea or a new technology you can delay a decision by months.

BLOCKING TACTICS

If the technology is changing, convince the buyer to wait, making do with the existing technology until the new generation equipment is available. This is effective if you have new technology in the making, and your competitor is selling current or older technology.

Often in high technology, especially with capital equipment, a customer will find other ways to accomplish a task while waiting for the *right* product. This *waiting* is reinforced if the new technology brings with it a long-term cost savings. New technology alone might not be enough to block, but by showing corresponding and significant cost savings, you will get management's attention.

An example of the most common blocking technique used in high technology selling is the delay block, or the *"information-you-got-to-see-but-won't-be-available-to-see-until-after-you-visit-my-competitor"* technique.

Assume the customer has two days available, Wednesday and Thursday, to visit you and your competitor for demonstrations, after which they will decide which product to purchase. You have first choice and naturally pick Thursday because of the "last in" rule. The "last in" rule says the last supplier to talk to a customer before a buy decision has an advantage, everything else being equal.

After all arrangements have been made, your competitor executes an effective block by rearranging the schedule so that the customer now visits them on Friday. They are now first in. You must now convince the customer to delay the final decision until after Monday morning. You tell them you have some new important information but you cannot supply it until Monday.

When the competition tries to close on Friday, the customer will say they cannot make a decision until they get this one last piece of information from you. The decision will be delayed until late Monday or early Tuesday. You have effectively counterblocked.

The information you provide Monday had better be credible. If you planned in advance for this eventuality, you will have some key information that you can now use.

A second possibility in this situation is to choose Wednesday. The competition may then develop a false sense of security of being "last in." When they try to close Thursday they will find that the customer is waiting for that *"last-bit-of-information"* that you will provide Friday.

In this case, you effectively block Wednesday and close Friday. It will be difficult for the competition to block Friday since they are secure in believing they will close Thursday, a last minute block attempt after they try to close and find out what you have done will probably not work.

Of course you can close Wednesday if you are in control, the demonstration being a mere formality. No amount of blocking will help your competitor in this case.

○ Linking: Link each step in the sales process to the next

Linking is a process of ensuring that as you execute each tactic in your sales strategy, you also set the stage for executing the next tactic.[3] It is an organized method of using conditional closes to maintain control over the selling process.

Salespeople will typically attempt to close five or six times before they are successful. There may be customers out there who will buy your product the first time you try to close, because your company was clever enough to design the product to meet their needs exactly. In this case you're not selling, you're taking orders.

It is the neutral customers, the pro-competitor customers, or the customers *who never heard of you or your company or your product and who for the life of them can't think of any reason in the world to buy your product even if they had heard of you*, that must be sold. The more times the customers say "yes," the more times they commit to something, even a minor point, the better your chances of obtaining the ultimate commitment: the purchase order.

FOCUS ON "YES"

Your objective is to close. But failing this, your objective is to motivate the customers to say "yes" as often as possible, to obtain small commitments as often as possible, to ensure the customers are so used to responding to you in the affirmative that as you pop the question each visit, the "yes" response will become easier to make.

Random "yeses" are better than "nos" but are not as effective as a tactically directed series of "yeses" linked together through the selling cycle to the final "yes." Care must be taken not to mar a sound and farsighted strategy through a chain of errors in execution.

The complexity and duration of the sales cycle will vary, but in general for high technology products, it takes a series of steps. Each step embodies a tactic that must link to the next tactic. Your current tactic may be to present your product and try to close.

If you cannot close, then your next tactic might be to invite the customer to the factory for a demonstration of your product.

---

[3]Ibid., (Linking is a Holden Tactic)

The time to get the customer to commit to the demonstration is after you've made the presentation and failed to close, but before you leave the customer's presence.

This linking provides continuity from tactic to tactic and assists you in building positive momentum. The conditional closes are not random but a planned part of your sales strategy.

If your sales strategy was not properly tested or if it starts to fail, one of the first indications will be the failure to link from one tactic to the next. If you fail to close and the customer doesn't wish to see your demonstration because the competitor's demonstration has convinced them the other product will do their job well enough, you have also failed to link.

You are now in trouble. A random "yes" or interim close not in line with your strategy will be ineffective. At this point you have lost control, and must either try to link to an alternate tactic (which can put you back in control), or transition into a loss-recovery mode.

By being prepared with traps and blocks to counter the competitor and by linking your tactics within the overall sales strategy, you will build continuity and win.[4]

---

[4]Ibid. This chapter summarizes Jim Holden's streetwise tactics which focus on the competitor and deal with developing a competitive advantage.

CHAPTER

(27)

Salespeople influence without authority

A person who exercises power has authority or influence over another. Authority is a delegated power. Authority is formal and bestowed through an organization. The person with authority has the legitimate right to lead, take action, and make decisions within his or her sphere of responsibility. The buyer uses authority to make a buy decision.

Conversely, influence is a derived power. It is derived from skills, personality, possessions, or association with authority. A person with influence can exercise it anywhere at any time. A salesperson has no authority but uses influence to ensure the buy decision is favorable.

◯ Coercive Influence: Education is a coercive influence

Influence can be coercive, manipulative, or collaborative.[1] A salesperson applies coercive influence through the process of education. A new employee may join a company in a key decision-making position and have a preference for the competitor's product. In a new company, the employee will be isolated from his or her previous group and environment. The salesperson *educates* the new employee by providing portentous reasons to buy from the company's perspective. In this new environment, the employee will be more vulnerable to influence than in the old company since he or she may feel alone.

The new employee may not have the peer credibility enjoyed at the old company. If the salesperson moves swiftly and if there is local support for the product, the process of education is used to influence the new employee and show how others support the product, implying that if the new employee also supports it, group acceptance will result. The salesperson can enlist members sympathetic to the cause to help persuade the new employee not to buck the system.

Fear is a strong motivating factor. If a customer needs the salesperson's product and the salesperson is the only supplier in the required time frame, the buyer can be coerced into meeting certain demands. This is obviusly short-term thinking. If everybody is buying the product, the power of numbers may be used to play on the customer's fear of being wrong, thereby influencing a buy decision.

Another coercive tactic is for the salesperson to leak unflattering information anonymously about an adversary in the account to key individuals who have influence. This can result in pressure on the holdout to purchase the product. This tactic is more commonly used secretly by one competitor against another to influence the sale and often involves the press. Coercive influence, although rarely sanctioned officially, is nevertheless widely used.

A more ethical derivative of coercive influence is influence based on the salesperson's prediction of how the customer is likely to respond. With the predictive approach to influencing, the salesperson says in effect, "I am going to convince you my product is best for you." And the customer says, "OK, try."

---

[1]Leavitt, *Managerial Psychology,* (Referenced pp. 148-172).

In using this approach, the salesperson has already pre-dicted the expected results of a particular approach and is directly and overtly going about attempting to change the customer's behavior in a direct manner.

○ Manipulative Influence: Think of manipulative influence as unconscious change

Manipulation conjures thoughts of Machiavellian methods and other disreputable conduct. Manipulation relies upon rela-tionships to effect the sale. The salesperson forms a close relationship with the customer, then uses this relationship to influence the customer to buy the product. This does not mean that the salesperson is insensitive to the needs and feelings of the customer. On the contrary, by virtue of the close association, the salesperson understands the customer and takes joint responsibility for the decision. This is important because the objective is to develop a long-term relationship.

Influence through manipulation implies the customer does not consciously know exactly what the salesperson is doing. In fact, it is difficult for a salesperson to keep his or her motives secret. The customer knows the salesperson is not there on a social call but to sell the product. As a customer begins to value the relationship with the salesperson, the salesperson can create dissidence between the customer's belief system and the relationship. If the relationship is one where the customer is dependent, the dependency can be exploited. Otherwise, the relationship is exploited in terms of recognition, need for approval, need to be first, or some other such emotion.

Execution is not precipitous, but slow and indirect. Change is produced incrementally. The customer will be cognizant of the change taking place within, but may not be aware of how it is being done.

Change is more powerful and more difficult to reverse if it is kept at the unconscious rather than the conscious level. People do not like to think they were unconsciously managed even if it were for their own good. If customers realize they were manipulated, reactions will be negative. Manipulation has deplorable connotations and raises ethical questions. Yet, manipulation often forces the customer to look at things dif-ferently. It gives the customer the opportunity to explore new methods and processes and to test their applicability and workability.

If the salesperson cannot achieve the expected results or does not wish to be manipulative and does not wish to risk the possibility the prediction may be in error, the customer can be approached using various stimuli. The customer's response is then compared to a set of norms. The salesperson divides the responses into categories looking for similarities and differences, such as personality characteristics and leadership styles. Based on this data, attempts are made to influence the customer to purchase the product. If the customer is not aware of what the salesperson is doing, one might deduce the customer is being manipulated. In effect, the salesperson is trying to direct the customer's response based on the customer's personality. The salesperson's influence is comparative since he or she has classified the customer into a personality category and is attempting to influence based on a set of influencing norms for people who fall in that particular category. This comparative approach is a more palatable derivative of the manipulative influencing method.

Collaborative Influence: If a customer has decided on change, salespeople can collaboratively assist in making the changes

Influencing through collaboration places the responsibility for change on the shoulders of the customer. The salesperson acts as a facilitator of change and assists in the process. The dynamic is sharing rather than controlling. There is a certain uncertainty about collaborative selling. In essence, a partnership is formed between the salesperson and the customer. The salesperson acts as a consultant or counsellor to advise the customer. His or her role is to develop a helping relationship to facilitate the customer's understanding of how to solve problems.

Collaborative selling involves interviewing in which the salesperson listens and tries to understand the customer and the problem. The customer is expected to purchase the product but the process is interactive and the decisions are mutual.

The salesperson's objective is to use interpersonal communication skills and provide information that will show the way to the salesperson's solution; but the customer makes the choice. Coercive or manipulative pressures are not brought to bear. The influencing behavior is not exerted by the salesperson but is a function of the relationship. The difficulty and uncertainty of selling collaboratively should be obvious. On the other hand, if the relationship and the collaboration are successful, the customer will develop confidence in the salesperson, and a mutually beneficial relationship will result. The customer will appreciate the value the salesperson represents, and the competition will have difficulty breaking the bond between them.

In the case of collaboration, rather than risk an erroneous prediction or an incorrect comparison, the salesperson chooses to interact with the customer. Through interaction, risk or chances of failure will be reduced because of the joint working relationship. The customer will also help lead the salesperson in a direction where the salesperson can be of value to the customer and help them achieve their objective through the product the salesperson is actively selling.

The interactive approach advances the customers toward achieving their personal agenda. Through interaction, both win. In this case, the salesperson is influencing indirectly.

◯ *Unknown Problem: Deduce the customer's need*

In these three cases the underlying supposition is that the salesperson has identified a need and that the need, product, business, or political, can be fulfilled with the product being sold. In the situation where the need or problem is unknown, the salesperson is faced with finding a problem to solve with the product. A need or problem with which the customer can identify must be deduced. In effect, since the salesperson is not part of the customer's world or more specifically, company, the deduced need must have universal validity. In problem finding, influence is deductive until a unitary need is found. Once found, a predictive, comparative, or interactive mode of influencing will be employed to approach the customer. Until then, the salesperson is in a missionary mode thinking deductively while searching for a need to fulfill or a problem to solve.

The four influencing strategies or modes; predictive, comparative, interactive, and deductive,[2] are based on Steven Peppers *World Hypothesis*[3] and developed by the Seon Consulting Group of California as a sales training course on influencing. These influencing models offer the salesperson an alternative to the hard-core coercive and manipulative styles and the classical collaborative method. They also add a fourth method useful for problem finding. These influencing models are a means of making proofs and of refining arguments for a decision.

○ Sales Influencing Strategies: You can influence sales strategically

The sales influencing strategies illustrated in Figure 5 parallel the sales product strategies and are executed in a similar manner.

In summary, when the salesperson is in the *predictive* influencing mode, in effect, he or she is saying, "If I can predict the results of my actions, then I can authoritatively act to change the behavior of the customer." The influencing strategy is direct, authoritative, or predictive. This is similar to a direct sales strategy.

In the *comparative* influencing mode, the salesperson says, "If I can compare my customer's personality to a set of norms, then I can act to change my customer's behavior based on these generalizations." The salesperson then works to direct the customer's response by partitioning the customer's reaction to various personality-directed stimuli, focusing on those that will complement the objective. This is similar to divisional strategy.

The *interactive* influencer says, "If I can work jointly with my customer, we can together satisfy our mutual goals." The influencing strategy is indirect but executed in a cooperative fashion. This is similar to an indirect sales strategy and is aimed at goal satisfaction.

[2]Seon Consulting, 850 Kenyon Avenue, San Leandro, CA 94577. (For additional information on influencing strategies write to Dr. David Fry at Seon).

[3]S.C. Pepper, *World Hypothesis*, (Berkeley, California: University of California, 1942.)

INFLUENCING STRATEGIES

STRATEGY	PROCESS	RESULT	SIMILAR SALES STRATEGY
PREDICTIVE	AUTHORATATIVE	BEHAVIOR MODIFICATION	DIRECT
COMPARATIVE	MANEUVER	PERSONALITY DIRECTION	DIVISIONAL
INTERACTIVE	COLLABORATIVE	GOAL SATIFACTION	INDIRECT
DEDUCTIVE	MISSIONARY	NEW VALUE	CONTAINMENT

Figure 5: Influencing Strategies

In a *deductive* influencing mode, the salesperson says, "If I do not know how to sell my product to this customer, I must deduce a need or problem and then act as a missionary to convince the customer of the value of the solution I offer." In this case, the salesperson is in a deductive mode of influence until he or she can deduce or discover a new value to offer the customer. This is similar to a containment sales strategy.

The influencing models shown in Figure 5 and employed by the salesperson will differ among individuals and circumstances. Most salespeople at one time or another have used all four influencing methods. Sometimes, a salesperson will use them all at the same account during a single sales situation.

CHAPTER

(28)

Develop an in-house salesperson

An excellent way to extend your time in an account and quickly develop credibility is to establish an inside salesperson. This person will promote your product behind the scenes. There are many ways to find and develop an in-house salesperson, but the most effective method is by developing a professional relationship. People like to be liked, professionally as well as personally. Your objective is to initiate and cultivate these relationships. There is nothing dishonest or insincere about developing friendly relationships in your business life. If the customers like and respect you, they will welcome being with you, for they will expect to benefit from the relationship.

○ *Common Interest: Find a common interest with your customer*

Developing a personal but professional relationship requires sincerity. If you are dishonest, insincere, a glad hander, or otherwise not in tune with the customer, you will be perceived as a "phony." The customers will be very sensitive to any attempt on your part to manipulate them. A genuine and sincere relationship with the customer is dependent upon two factors. The first is a common interest. The business, an organization, a hobby, an entertainment such as wine-tasting, gourmet food, the theater, or sports can provide the basis of a friendly relationship. The second factor is how you go about expressing yourself relative to the first.

It is important to understand the personal side of a professional relationship. Form a personal impression of the customer, and allow the customer to form a personal impression of you. This is accomplished by sharing yourself genuinely during the sales encounter. Your courage to be known, to say it like it is, is critical in developing an in-house salesperson.

To achieve authenticity and genuineness as a person, you must be willing to look inside to see yourself and to self-disclose. Through introspection you will be more objective and discuss more openly the pros and cons of a given situation.

It is essential to understand yourself so you can select the most compatible means of relating to the customer, your most compatible qualities in terms of the customer's personality. Then you can better express yourself honestly. Where there are incompatibilities or incongruencies you will be better able to avoid them or to deal with them up front.

When you and your customer honestly discuss a difficult point or share an experience, you are in effect self-disclosing. This sharing can be close and warm or more distant, as long as it is an honest sharing between people of their experience. This assumes you have determined how to relate to the particular person you are trying to develop as your inside salesperson. It assumes you have developed people skills in evaluating and understanding others. You must take the initiative and accept responsibility for the relationship. It is your responsibility to know your customer, not your customer's responsibility to know you.

◯ Tactical Advisor: Ask your business friend for advice on tactics

Once you have cultivated your inside person, and sometimes even during the cultivation process, you will have a primary supporter within the group or on the committee. This person can monitor the group, observe individual committee members, and keep you informed on the competitor's position and tactics. The person is not your agent provocateur to your competitor or internal unbelievers. Your inside salesperson must be convinced of the merits of your product or service, so he or she can subtly sell for you to other group or committee members, and to management.

The inside salesperson is your tactical advisor, telling you how you are progressing, and suggesting your next move. Sometimes it is not necessary for you to cultivate an inside salesperson. Your product does it automatically. At other times, someone in your company may have a close relationship with your customer. In this case you can piggy-back off this relationship and accomplish the objective.

The advantage of having an inside salesperson should not be underestimated. It is rare that a sale is made to a committee without the help, direct or indirect of such a person. Consequently, your sales tactics should specifically include the cultivation of an inside salesperson from the beginning.[1]

○ *Corporate Planners: Corporate planners make good allies*

The corporate planner is a person near the top and makes an excellent inside salesperson. He or she performs a significant and necessary function at the highest levels of management. Often the corporate planner is an officer with direct access to top management. For this reason, he or she can be effective in influencing the thinking of top management.

Corporate planners are salespeople and educators. They teach and sell to management new ideas, and the best techniques for an efficient planning process. They stimulate the use of new tools, methods, and concepts. They clarify corporate ground rules, consult, and integrate. They evaluate divisional plans. Corporate planners are also involved in high-level decision making and in initiating new development activities and nurturing them.

The corporate planner has been called a *chief of staff* and a *technologist of change* who not only sees that objectives are established, but also helps management shape them and devise the strategies to achieve them.

[1]Kaplan, *Selling Effectively to Committees.*

In some corporations, the planner may be called a strategic planner, planning coordinator, vice president for corporate development, director of development planning, or special assistant to the president for planning. The title is not important. What is important is that this person is concerned with the formal corporate planning process, has influence at the top, and is usually accessible.

Accessible people in similar positions include corporate directors of quality, financial planners, and organizational development managers. These people may not be directly involved with the departments or subsidiaries you have targeted to penetrate, but, if properly cultivated, they can certainly wield influence on your behalf. Since they, especially the corporate planner, spur new ideas, methods, tools, and systems, they are the ideal target for promoting new high technology products throughout the corporation.[2]

○ ## Technology Interface: Incorporate the financial benefits

Since the corporate planners understand both the short and long term objectives of the company, they are ideal interfaces for your technology. Since they are close to the top, they will also be concerned with the financial aspects of your proposal. Through these planners you can influence people across the organization if the planners buy into your solution.

Assume you have a product that will solve a problem in the corporation and result in a cost savings as well. One facet of your strategy should include selling the corporate planner. The planner's interests include increasing the corporate profits, long-term stability involvement in new developments, and a relationship with a qualified vendor who will continuously provide viable solutions and standardization of company operations where feasible and beneficial.

Your objectives in dealing with the planner are to obtain the latest data on budgets and implementation plans, to convince him or her to help you sell your concepts, to better

[2]George A. Steiner, *"Rise of the Corporate Planner"*, (Harvard Business Review), September-October 1970.
Portions of this chapter are based on G. Steiner's excellent article. The strategic planner as G. Steiner predicted has become a valuable resource in the 1980s in most corporations.

understand the political structure and power base, to create support from the top, and, if necessary, to ensure resource commitment to your product's success.

By presenting the planner with your proposal, together you can develop an action plan that will help you win with line management and the key decision makers. The proposal to the planner may either be a subset of your overall account proposal or the complete proposal.

○ *Use the Proposal: Tailor your proposal to the corporate planner's needs*

The proposal concentrates on your technology, product, or method, its advantages, and the financial implications. The advantages are tailored to the planner's specific interests and needs. One impressive sales technique is to provide each recipient of your proposal with an advantage section tailored to the specific executive and their particular interests, rather than to the company as a whole.

Recommend your product be appropriately configured to support the application requirement. Arrange benchmarks if necessary to prove performance advantages. Often specific points can be made by the use of previous benchmarks conducted at other sites for other customers. Present the conclusion of the benchmarks in terms of benefits and dollar savings. Next provide a procedure that points out areas of present customer operations or methodology that your recommendation will improve. State the support and commitment from your company to help them with a partnership arrangement to achieve the results desired. Finally, present your cost savings in terms of payout, cost of ownership, or investment return.

If successful in selling the planner, concentrate on developing a plan of action with the planner's support. He or she must be in agreement with the division of responsibilities and dedicated to the success of your joint plan. Your support must also be committed positively and permanently.

Armed with the plan, you both work on convincing key decision makers of its virtue.

(29)

Penetrate upper management

It is essential to penetrate upper management early in the sales process. In fact, exploit every possible credible reason to contact higher levels of authority and influence. Through this penetration, identification of the influential individuals and alignment with them can begin. If you start too low in the organization, you will have difficulty moving up. It is best to start as high as appropriate and move down. You cannot establish and maintain account control without upper management penetration.

○ *Penetrate Early: Talk to people at all levels of the customer's company*

If you have contacted or must contact lower echelons before you contact upper management, you may either have to go through your lower level internal contacts or orchestrate direct contact from your management to interface with the customer's top management. In this latter case, keep your inside person informed concerning the upcoming contact.

Starting too low opens you to being blocked by the buyer or key decision-maker. These people may advise you that they alone will make the decision and you should not interface with anyone above them. What they say may be true, but it is also true they will at least discuss and get tacit approval from their management before buying.[1]

Management may introduce a new criterion to the decision-making process. If the competitors have penetrated upper management, they will have this information and you will not. By the time you get the word it may be too late, or the information may be distorted causing you to react. You will then be out of control.

Early penetration allows you to talk to upper management without permission of the decision-makers since you have already established a relationship. If things start to go against you and you must use these contacts to influence the decision through your relationship with upper management, you will not be perceived as going around the decision-makers. This will lower your risks of angering them.

Early penetration also builds your influence with non-influentials and lower echelon individuals. You may even be in a position to use your upper management relationship to do them a favor. It is not unusual for the key decision-maker to solicit your help in selling management. This upper management contact gives you legitimacy and helps you control the selling situation. Finally, it gives you visibility with upper management, which can be helpful as you build a long-term relationship for yourself and your product.

○   ## Who to Contact: Be sure to contact the decision-makers and those who influence them

The specific individuals you should target for penetration are those who are making or influencing the decision, and

---

[1]The following Holden sources were referenced in developing this and subsequent chapters on the political component of sales.
*Jim Holden, *Power Base Selling*, Training Course, (Schaumberg, IL: Holden Corporation, 1982.)

those responsible for approving the purchase. Your objective is to be perceived as a resource to management but, more important, to the key decision-maker. You are not there to interfere but to help. Always start at the top, that is, the highest appropriate level in terms of the product being sold. To win attention at the top requires a proposal that promises incremental profits for the customer as a result of economic savings, increased productivity, better marketing methods, or improved conditions for the employees.

Top management should be approached if the value is real and significant; otherwise, do not waste their time. You are better off not meeting top management, except socially, unless you have something substantial to impart.

Since management penetration strategy dictates you start at the top, search for the highest individual in the account who is involved in the decision or has a rapport with your competitor. Be open and flexible in making the appointment. If the response is positive, the individual is likely to send you to one of his or her lieutenants. In this case, make sure you arrange an open door for you to return and close the loop in the future. If you can convince your own management of the importance of this contact, use them to get an audience with the individual by arranging a visit.

Other methods of meeting these high-level people include having someone on their staff or someone outside the company who has a social or business relationship with them arrange a meeting. You can arrange to meet them *accidentally* at some social event or high-level seminar. If they belong to a business organization such as the American Electronics Association, arrange to join and meet them there. In spite of all these ploys, the easiest method of meeting management is a direct telephone call by you or your management.

◯   *When Else to Penetrate: Do not approach top management when you are losing the sale*

If you do not have a rapport with upper management and your competitor does, you have an odds on chance of losing the

---

*Jim Holden, *"Fox Hunting, Tracking the Buyer With Clout,"* (Industrial Marketing, June 1982.)

Chapters 29 through 31 summarize the Holden one-day seminar on understanding and using the politics of a company to the salesperson's advantage.

sale. If you have failed to penetrate management early, the next best time is after a successful installation. At this time, give credit for the success to the manager's staff.

The worst time to contact top management is when you are losing the sale. Top management should not be approached to overrule a decision-maker who has decided against you unless you can show just and significant cause from their viewpoint and have the support of key individuals in the account.

Even so, if your management contact takes place at the eleventh hour, you have little chance of success.

If you have not properly cultivated upper management, jumping over key decision-maker's heads in an attempt to secure the order after you have failed to sell them on your product is a dangerous last resort. You may succeed with this tactic, but you will have alienated the people you bypassed. It is unlikely you will ever sell to them in the future. What is more, if upper management overrules them, it is tantamount to saying they made a bad decision in rejecting your product, and management made a bad decision in assigning them the responsibility to make the selection.

The other less-than-desirable time to meet with upper management is when a previous installation has problems. It is better to wait until all problems have been solved.

What to Do: Here are guidelines for dealing with top management

Sometimes top management people will attend your presentation or drop in during it. If they attend, they will probably leave early and rely on their middle managers or the committee members for their information and to sort out the technical and competitive details. If they drop in, it may be your only exposure to them, so be prepared to deliver your value message at a moment's notice.

One way to attract top management to your presentation is to bring your management along. Often they will go off together and strike up a relationship while you are making your presentation.

When you finally meet with top management, make a short presentation to introduce yourself, your management, if present, your company, and your product as a solution with value to them. It should be brief and general. Even if your management is present, make sure you stay in control of the meeting. No matter how knowledgeable or well-intentioned, they probably have not lived and bled with the account and are more likely to make a mistake.

If this is the first time the account has been called upon, you still want to maintain control, because you are the one that will have to live and bleed with it after your manager goes on to other pressing issues.

It is best if the meeting takes place in a relaxed and informal manner. It is important to listen to what the manager is saying. Be overly eager to understand their objectives; do not be too eager to present your product.

◯ First Encounter: Use care in setting up the first encounter

When you make a direct contact, always make an appointment for a specific time, but never on the hour. Make an appointment for 2:15 P.M. instead of 2:00 P.M. It is easier for the executive or the secretary to remember. It also allows a little overtime for an earlier meeting or for a break between interviews.

If the appointment was made several weeks in advance, call to confirm the time of the meeting. They may have forgotten and your time is too valuable to waste.

Don't grow pale or get nervous at the thought of a belly to belly encounter with the president or general manager. One technique to get you started, reduce the butterflies, and, more important, get you the information you want, is to draw on the white board, flip chart, or a tablet the organization chart of your company. Never use a predrawn organization chart. Always start from scratch and draw it yourself.

Draw the blocks, add names, make comments about each key person's success story, touch on human interest and relate your management to his in terms he can appreciate. This assumes you have done a profile on the executive and know his or her likes, dislikes, hobbies and hot buttons. After you finish, no longer than five minutes, offer the felt tip pen or chalk and say, "Incidentally, would you please take a minute to explain your organization."

Most general managers are hams at heart. They will grab the chalk and start at the top. Now you know who they work for. You can interact with them. They add a name, you ask questions. Find out who is responsible for what. The longer you keep them talking, the more valuable information you will obtain.

When they're done, if you used your listening skills and probed deftly, you will know the total organization, who is responsible, who the decision-makers are, who has influence, and possibly something about the personalities involved. Keep in mind this information is only one person's opinion, even if a rather important person. They may not know how their organization really works. Their perceptions may not match reality. So file it away, then continue probing the organization to verify what you were told.[2]

Incidentally, had you used a pre-drawn organization chart, the executives might have thought you expected a copy of theirs and usually these charts are company confidential.

It would also give them an easy out by saying they don't have one to give you. You want them to follow your lead. By drawing your chart, they are more likely to draw theirs. They can always leave sensitive items off the chart, or be ambiguous.

After the organization chart, start communicating your sales value. You should prepare it in advance, limit it to five or ten minutes at most, and word it to both deliver your message and find out how they feel about your product or service. Try to determine their plans and budget constraints if any. Also do something positive that will ensure they remember you. These executives see numerous people daily and will not remember many of the people, let alone what they say. To use their influence effectively, you must get their attention and they must see value in what you propose.[3]

⭕ *Rejection: If an executive refers you to someone else, use the executive's name to request a meeting*

If the executives or general managers decline a meeting, they will probably refer you to someone else. In that case, use

---

[2]Frank J. Burge, *Sales Training News Letters,* (Fairchild Camera and Instrument Corp., 1968) various.
Frank Burge, while Marketing Manager of Fairchild Instrumentation, published various Sales News Letters based on material from the masters of sales training Zenn Kaufman, Morris Pickens, Red Motley and J. Douglas Edwards.
[3]Ibid.

their names to your advantage. The people you are sent to know you were sent by the executive or general manager, and you will have their attention immediately. Additionally, by virtue of your first contact, you have an excuse to follow up with the executives should you need them later. Finally, they know why you are there and your presence is bound to surface at high-level meetings.

If you are persistent and actually create the opportunity for a short meeting with the executives, when they refer you to someone else, make sure they either introduce you personally or make the appointment for you. It is best if the appointment is made while you are present. Top executives have short memories when it comes to salespeople. Failing this, arrange for their secretary to make the appointment in your presence.

Once you meet the person you were referred to, say, "We have discussed our solutions with the general manager who suggested I contact you. Did he (she) tell you?" By saying "we," you do not appear high and mighty or threatening in this person's eyes. "We" is softer and implies you were part of a group or even acting under your manager's direction.

"Discussed ... solutions," implies the general manager knows what you are proposing, the referee probably does not. "Who suggested" is perceived as a strong request, if not a direct order, by the referer. Switching back to "I" puts you in control. Any implication that someone else in your account is the focal point will be dispelled. After saying, "Did he (she) tell you?" Be quiet and watch the person's body language and eyes. These rather than words will tell you if the general manager has made contact. You will now either be in control or be dismissed.

If the dialogue continues, review with this person your discussion with the general manager. You are now in a position to develop a relationship with this person. If not the decision-maker, he or she is probably influential, otherwise the general manager would not have referred you to the person.

Remember that typical top executives think in terms of profits, productivity, and humanity. If you can communicate with them on that plane and provide value to them in one, two, or all three of these categories, you will have established an excellent atmosphere for your sales campaign.

CHAPTER

(30)

Align with the power

Formal authority is the power that has been delegated to individuals in an organization. Although certain individuals may have formal authority, it does not necessarily follow that they will have influence. The power to influence may stem from formal authority, but it may also derive from other sources based on the associations of the influencers. Those who have influence in an organization constitute the power base.

○ ***The Power Base: The power base of a company may not be entirely expressed in the formal hierarchy***

Every company has a power base. The people in the power base have the real influence and political power in the company independent of their position or title in the organization. A technologist who plays golf with the president, a strategic planner who lives next door to the chief financial officer, a

197

middle manager who is respected by a vice president, or the secretary of the president might be a part of the power base. Each of these individuals may have influence that exceeds their authority. This influence is gained through indirect association with real authority.

Therefore, power base individuals fall into one of two groups. They either have influence and authority, or influence without formal authority. High level individuals who have formal authority and are able to command influence make up the former group. Those that hold more real power than their position suggests form the latter group.

The power base is not obvious from looking at the organization chart. The organization chart distributes delegated authority. It does not identify the political structure or the power base.

Embedded Power Base: The power base is frequently driven by one person

Every account has at least one individual with the influence, if not the authority, to help you get the sale. It is essential you identify the influencer, the *fox*.[1]

Within the power base is a power base. The individuals in the embedded power base are the driving forces within the organization. These individuals are often cunning and skillful gamesmen. They are the *"foxes."* You want them on your side. Jim Holden, in his sales training course, "Power Base Selling," says, "The fox is clever, knowledgeable of major events throughout the company, and above all, knows how to get things done. He may not appear to be involved in areas outside his immediate responsibility, but he indirectly influences the outcomes nonetheless. He is influential in shaping the organization's management philosophy and has the power to act in exception to company policy if necessary."

Risk Takers: One characteristic of power is the willingness to take a risk

The fox assumes risk; risk exists when one's responsibility to complete a task outstrips one's authority to order it.

[1]Holden, *Power Base*, (Referenced).
The fox is a Holden term for the person or persons in an account with the power to influence the sale.

Responsibility is the performance of an obligation that an individual assumes. Responsibility is an individual rather than a group phenomenon. Authority is a derivative of responsibility. Authority consists principally of the right to command. If a person has the responsibility to accomplish an objective, it is only natural that he or she should also have the authority to command the necessary resources to satisfactorily accomplish it.

The individual with the responsibility and authority to accomplish an objective is accountable for how well he or she performs. A person can delegate authority and responsibility but cannot delegate accountability.

On the other hand, if a person assumes responsibility without authority, the person is both accountable and taking a risk. Risk then is equivalent to responsibility without authority.

People outside the power base will avoid risk. Power base individuals will take risk if they can share it. The foxes in the power base often appear conservative but actually alone assume high degrees of risk for short periods of time. A salesperson is compatible with a fox because, like the fox, the salesperson will also assume risk.

A salesperson has account responsibility but no authority over the customer. A fox will assume responsibility to accomplish an objective without the authority to command the resources to make it happen, yet becomes accountable for the result. If something goes wrong, the blame will be laid at the risk taker's feet even though he or she did not have the authority to correct the wrong. If the fox controls the situation so that the high risk period is short, a few months, and if success means a high reward, then the chances of being hurt politically in the case of failure is reduced.

If the risk was taken in the best interests of the company, the individual will enhance his or her position regardless of the outcome. If the risk was taken to advance the individual's position at the expense of the company's objectives, it may be viewed by the company as a power play.

⃝ *Alignment: Align yourself with someone in the power base*

Your objective is to align yourself with one of these power base individuals. This will help you out-maneuver the competition.

To align yourself with a power base individual, a fox, you must be perceived as adding value to the individual and the individual's company. Value is achieved if you can help directly or indirectly in advancing the company to its business objectives.

Therefore, to provide value, you must know their business objectives and understand their philosophy. This information can be obtained during the data-gathering phase of the sales process, and while cultivating a fox.

Aligning with a fox is not necessarily the same as developing an in-house salesperson. When you develop an in-house salesperson, you are developing a relationship to help you better understand and work the account. The in-house salesperson need not be in the power base.

During alignment with a fox, you must determine how to also make a political contribution to this individual. The fox doesn't need to like you—she or he only need to perceive you as a political resource. Your value to the fox may be the enhancement of the individual's position or visibility through your product. The fox will use this relationship with you to show management he or she has control of the vendor, can obtain better service and support, or ensure a lower overall risk to the company. This occurs because you have shown how you and your product are compatible with his or her company's objectives. In this case, both your risk and the fox's risk will decrease. By aligning with you and obtaining your good service and support, the fox will look good, especially if your product has management visibility and is successful.

Your risks are lower because the fox will ensure to the best of his or her ability that your product will be successful. Through this alignment, as the fox's political strength increases, your competitive strength increases and you will be less likely to lose future orders. Your position in the account will be strengthened.

Healthy competition among individuals in the power base should not be confused with power plays. The difference is whether the personal agenda of the competitors provide value to the company or interfere with achieving company objectives. Avoid power plays when aligning yourself with the power base.

Alignment with a fox will significantly enhance your position. Alignment with a fox involved in a power struggle could spell disaster, unless your fox wins.

If you must align yourself with a power play individual or even an individual involved in a healthy internal competitive situation, be cautious; you could end up the scapegoat.

To avoid this risk, maintain an arms length relationship with the power base as a *contact*. A contact does not get directly involved in power plays or in the customer's internal affairs. Such involvement only complicates the sales situation and jeopardizes credibility. Attempting to manipulate a person in the power base, especially another fox, is dangerous. It is like an outsider taking sides in a family squabble—a no-win situation.

Continue to use your inside salesperson to keep you informed as to what is occurring within the account. As for the fox with whom you have aligned yourself, have the fox exert influence with the decision-makers on your behalf. With both individuals, you are relying upon your interpersonal relationships and the value you represent to them to motivate them to support you. In the case of the inside salesperson, the emphasis will usually be on the interpersonal relationship; with the fox, the emphasis will be on the political value you represent.

Once you have penetrated the power base you will represent value to people outside the base since you can now help them penetrate it. It is even possible that through this relationship, you may become part of the customer's power base.

CHAPTER

(31)

Provide value to the power

Fox hunting is the process of defining the political structure within an organization and mapping out the distribution of political strength.

Learning how to properly define the political structure of a company and finding the people capable of influencing the organization on your behalf requires training that addresses the political component of high technology sales. Some organizational development firms provide training in understanding the political structure of an organization. The Holden Corporation trains salespeople in how to interface with the political structure.

○ *Fox Hunting: Here's how you can find the useful individuals in the power base*

The Holden "Power Base Selling" seminar presents an organized approach to spotlighting the customer's political structure, thus identifying the power base for the purpose of increasing sales. During the seminar you will learn how to go about identifying the political structure through an illumination process: what to look for in the political structure, where to align yourself, the basis for achieving sales leverage once aligned properly, and the traps to avoid, including power play activities.

Sometimes, in a given sales situation, the fox or key decision-maker is obvious. In other cases, your inside contacts will tell you who the fox is. But just as often, the apparent fox or person you would logically suspect does not wield the real power. He or she is not influential, is not the fox. In this case you have two choices; to try to sell without the fox's help, or to go fox hunting.

When fox hunting use your data base concerning the company's goals, business objectives, and the management's philosophy. Knowing who historically exerted influence within the organization will help you locate the fox. Since the fox is an influencer, he or she can be identified when exerting influence.

Change in an organization is usually the result of influence being exerted. Promotions, demotions, or resignations, budget and funding allocations, the assigning of key responsibilities, or the making of key decisions are all visible manifestations of influence being exerted.

If you monitor change within the organization, you will learn the political structure and identify the foxes. During a stable period, watch for a situation that destabilizes the political environment and results in change which then illuminates the political structure. In fact, you may have to work to create change.

Securing a buy decision may well depend on a change in the company's policy or procedures. If your competitor is entrenched, it will mean a change in vendors. A change initiated by a fox has a much better chance of being successful than one promoted by an individual outside the power base. Therefore, the fox is critically important to you if you are trying to influence the company to make a major change.

PROFILE OF A FOX

The profile of a typical fox is a person who has been promoted recently and knows why. Foxes use the value they represent to management to their advantage, and can act in exception to policy. They know that past performance or how well they perform in their new job is not as important to getting ahead as being useful and visible to management. They are results oriented.[1]

They are usually involved in working to accomplish the organization's more important objectives, and are rarely surprised by events. They often influence decisions covertly by biasing key individuals in favor of their direction. When involved in a successful project or endeavor, they advertise. This ensures upper management knows what they did to advance the company toward its objectives.

A typical fox is well connected with upper management, key rank and file employees, his or her peers, and major vendors. The fox, although connected with major vendors, will not wear the vendor's label, at least not visibly. Finally, the fox knows that information is power.

Since the fox takes risks, identify the risk takers to find the fox. Find out who takes on added responsibility without commensurate authority, find out how decisions are really made, and who has the ear of corporate management. Ask the little people, the clerks and secretaries. They often know who wields the real influence and gets things done in a company.

Next, look for anomalies between this information and the formal organization. Seek high-level input about who actually influences company policy and procedures, as well as ideas, direction, and concepts.

Since the fox influences others and gets his or her influence by association with authority, to help identify potential foxes other than those with obvious line authority and influence, look for those who spend a lot of time with people in authority. See who comes to meetings, who is ignored at meetings, who does not formally fit into the meeting (why is he there?) and who is listened to at meetings. In meetings, the foxes may reveal themselves.

In general, watch for those who are good at articulating the company goals and ideas, who are noticed by others in the company, who seem to have all the inside information, who seem to influence others independent of their business relationship. Also look for the upwardly mobile individuals who are on the fast track.

Once you have identified the potential foxes, profile them in terms of their major and predominant personality and management style characteristics. Your objective is to develop insight into their interpersonal relationships. The key in profil-

---

[1]Holden, *Power Base*, (Referenced).

ing is not finding similarities but compatibilities in relationships. This is reflected in the amount of time they spend together on both business and pleasure. The level of confidence a manager has in a subordinate or colleague is also an important clue. Profiles may be different yet compatible.

From this analysis, you should be able to select one or two individuals as your target foxes. To qualify them further, feed your data back to your inside contacts and see if they support your assumptions.

INFLUENCING A FOX

Once identified, you must start immediately to build close ties with your fox. Look for ways to help and support him or her. Find areas where you can be of value to your fox providing some added benefits. Next select the influencing mode you wish to employ and develop your influencing strategy. Show the fox how an investment in your product will enhance his or her ability to achieve his or her personal agenda. Obviously, this must be done subtly, with finesse. Deft and indirect references to advancement of the personal agenda of the individual, in an informal atmosphere, will have a profound effect. Sometimes the personal value you offer the fox is obvious, but at other times influencing strategy, which must be executed with adroit maneuver, is necessary. This is not a game for the novice. Sometimes the fox can be influenced through a third party—a person who has influence with the fox that you can influence.

If the fox accepts your value or uses what you offer you will have succeeded in aligning yourself with influence and have penetrated the power base.

CHAPTER

(32)

Welcome objections

An objection is based on a customer's misunderstanding and is given as a reason for not buying.

Customer objections are normal. They represent problems to overcome. They may be a result of information about or clarification of the customer's needs or just a manifestation of the humanity of the customer. They may be real or imagined. Whatever the cause, they are also an indication of interest in your product or system.

If the customer does not buy because of an objection, as a salesperson it is your problem. You have not done a good job of finding and overcoming the objections.

Do not try to stop or delay a customer from giving reasons not to buy. If you avoid objections or stop the customer from voicing them, they will fester and you will significantly delay or lose the sale.

An objection does not result in a lost sale if professionally handled. A clear, direct answer often results in the order.

Welcome objections, for without them you would not know what your customer is thinking. Even more important, use them to your advantage. Objections are your leverage to close the sale.

To overcome objections requires confidence in dealing with them.

○ *Overcoming Objections: Find them, answer them, and make sure your answer is accepted*

Four steps in overcoming objections are: listen to understand, question to clarify, answer completely and succinctly, and confirm that your answer was accepted.

First, *listen* to what the customers are saying. Show sincere interest in the customers' points of view. Observe the customers' behavior. In your mind separate words from feelings. Recognize the customers' rights to their opinions and emotions. Draw out as many of their opinions as possible and make sure you understand the objections.

Your objective is to discover the real objection or confirm the apparent one as real. Use your listening skills and probe empathetically until you are satisfied you have discovered the real objection.

To remove potential defensive barriers, before you proceed allow the customer to vent his or her feeling without interruption. Do not judge or editorialize.

The message you want to communicate at this stage is, "I understand how you feel and it is o.k."

Question the customer rather than trying to immediately answer the objection. By asking a question created from the objection you can verify and clarify that you are addressing the real objection, the issue that is causing the feeling or belief. If the question you ask does not encompass the true objection, the customer will let you know.

Next, *answer* the objection, but do not use the word objection in your answer or in your question and do not respond directly to the objection. Give information that will automatically answer the objection. Be concise and brief. The less time spent answering the question you created from the objection, the better. Use your influencing skills and present only as much data as required to change the belief. Be honest and factual, and do not overstate your position. Above all, protect your customers' egos and show the customers a way out. Finally, *confirm* that you have satisfactorily answered the objection by asking for the order.

C: *"Your price is too high!"*

S: *"In what way?"*

C: *"You charge 10% for the service contract but your competitor only charges 5%."*

S: *"The issue then is the service contract price, is that right?"*

C: *"Yes, that is it in a nutshell."*

S: *"If we can resolve the service contract pricing issue, will you buy the system?"*

C: *"Yes!"*

S: *"We have a full-support monthly maintenance contract and an industry standard on-call contract. We quoted you our full-support contract. Even though the full support is better over the long run we can quote you an industry standard contract at 5%."*

C: *"No ... maybe I should go with the original proposal, it is better for us."*

S: *"Good, why don't we go over to Purchasing and get the paperwork started. I can explain to them our terms and conditions of sale.*

If you can't close on the objection, at least get the customers' agreement that you answered the objections satisfactorily, then get a commitment that will link to the next step in the sales process.

◯ Use Silence: First listen for the real objection

When you deal with objections, it is imperative to remember to be quiet and listen when an objection appears. You will never understand the objection if you do not listen. Even experienced salespeople sometimes forget to listen. Do not start talking before the customer stops talking.

A common mistake is to assume you know what the customer is going to say and blurt out a response before the customer finishes talking, only to find out that the customer was really going to say something else. What is more, now the customer wants to know about the objection he had not thought of, which you have just raised.

Talking before the customer finishes talking will also frustrate the customer and you may never get to hear the real objection and never know why you lost the sale.

Do not even formulate your response while the customer is talking, just listen. Use the silence between the time the customer stops talking and the time you respond to your advantage. Wait three to five seconds before responding. These lulls are difficult for customers to handle. Often the customer starts talking again. This may result in more data about the objection. Sometimes the customer will answer the objection for you, or during this lull period dismiss it. Without any response from you, the objection is overcome. Therefore, make silence your ally.

There are other ways to help customers answer their own objections.

C: *"Your service is lousy; I can't get a service person in here."*

S: *"I can understand why you feel that way. Tell me, have you ever had service problems in your business? What did you do about it?"*

S: *"Well we ..."*

S: *"That's exactly what we are doing. Do we both agree that will correct the problem?"*

The objection has been answered by the customer.
If the customer tries to avoid or delay a decision:

C: *"My boss has to approve this."*

S: *"What is his telephone number? Why don't you call him and tell him I am coming? Am I correct in assuming that I am going to him only to get formal approval? I have satisfied you, haven't I?"*

If your customer says "no," you have an objection. If he says "yes," you win.[1]

---

[1]Burge, *Sales Training News Letters*, (Referenced).

In responding to your questions the customer may answer the objection, realize the objection is absurd, or another underlying emotional objection may surface.

Your time with the customer is both valuable and limited. Therefore you must operate in the here and now.

At each sales interview look for objections. Search for patterns of thinking that are objectionable or irrationally related to your product. Your concern is with what your customer is thinking now, and you must change that thinking if it is not conducive to the purchase of your product.

A customer without questions or objections is unlikely to buy. Remember objections mean opportunity.

CHAPTER

33

Uncover underlying objections

Finding and overcoming objections, changing the customer's belief system, and closing are the real challenges in selling.

Unfortunately, the objection the customer may verbalize is often not the real objection. You must keep searching for the underlying objection. If you jump too quickly and answer the surface objection, you will be forced to answer other objections. Under these circumstances, you will keep answering objections and never be sure if you have discovered the true objection. The customer, not you, will be in control.

This is especially true in high technology sales. The way you manage the customer's emotions in terms of the underlying objection will, when it is all said and done, determine whether you win or lose the sale.

Characterization of an Objection: Objections consist of facts, beliefs, and feeling

There are three parameters to an objection: fact, belief, and consequence. The objective facts, events or behaviors which the customer exhibits, what the customer believes about them, and the emotional consequences of these beliefs make up an objection.

An objection is different from a condition. If the funding is not available to purchase your product, that is a condition. If the customer does not wish to use available funding to purchase your product, that is an objection.

Your objective is to motivate the customer to want to use the available funding to purchase from you. To accomplish this objective, you must focus on the customer's belief system. Dealing with the fact alone will not result in a buy decision.

A fact might be, "Your price is too high!" The customer's belief might be, "You are trying to take advantage of me." The emotional consequences of that belief is to buy from your competitor even if you have a better product. Addressing the fact, the price, will not necessarily win the sale. You must address the belief that you are trying to take advantage of the customer.

If you focus on the fact or the consequence, you can offer a lower price, offer a lower cost product, knock the competitor, or get into a comparison contest of yours versus mine. All of these are loser responses because they fail to deal with the customer's illogical belief that you are trying to take advantage of the situation.

To win, you must address the irrationality of the belief. In dealing with the customer's belief system, concentrate on what the customer thinks about your price, not the price. Find the underlying or veiled objection.

Veiled Objections: Customers may not voice their objections directly

The competitor ostensibly offers the same value you offer, but at a lower price. The customer, exercising sound logic, intends to buy from the competitor, i.e.:

C: *"Your price is too high!"*

S: *"Too high?"*

C: *"Right, you are 15% above the competitor."*

S: *"In other words, you would like me to justify the difference?"*

C: *"Exactly. We do not think your product is that much better."*
("We think you are trying to take advantage of us" is the underlying objection.)

S: *"I can understand why you might feel that way. Unfortunately, you do not have all the facts concerning the investment return you will realize, and I have to take blame for that oversight. Have you and your management reviewed the financial section of the proposal?"*

C: *"We did, but my boss says it does not justify a 15% difference. He thinks you are trying to take advantage of us."*

Up to this point, the salesperson neither agrees nor disagrees with the customer's statement about the price. The salesperson kept questioning the customer to get at the underlying objection. The salesperson respected the customer's viewpoint, encouraged dialogue, did not jump on the first objection, and did not deal with the price issue directly. The salesperson didn't start justifying after the response to his second question, but used the listening skills of aligning, "I understand your feeling", paraphrasing, "We do not think your product is that much better," with the essence of that statement, "If you had the facts, you would not feel that way." Alerted by the phrase following the word "exactly" and by the pronoun "we" to the possibility that this still may not be the real objection and others may be involved, another probing question was asked, and the customer's response "... but my boss says ..." is revealing.

The salesperson now knows the underlying objection and to deal directly with the boss to overcome it. If the salesperson penetrated management earlier, it should not be difficult to get an audience. If not, and if the buyer is unwilling to set up a meeting, preferring to be the interface between the salesperson and the boss, the salesperson is out of control and highly vulnerable to the competition.

In this situation, the salesperson must convince the contact and, more important, the contact's boss, that no one is trying to take advantage of them by charging more than the competitor. They must be convinced their conclusion is unfounded and has no basis in fact.

But before doing this (that is, once the salesperson meets with the boss) the objection must again be qualified. The boss could even be using the "... *take advantage of us ...*" statement to hide still another issue such as an inadequate budget, personal desire for the competitor's product, desire to negotiate, no real interest in the product, or the most probable meaning, "You haven't sold me yet!" Until the boss's true feelings are qualified, and the real meaning behind the boss's statement is understood, the salesperson's most persuasive and eloquent explanations will be futile.[1]

○ Incremental Value: If your price is higher, your perceived value must be greater

In this situation, once you have the true, hidden objection, you must show the customers the incremental benefit realized with your product. You must establish what it is they will get more of for the higher price. If the customers know they are not paying more than the value is worth, and if that is the real objection, then you are heading in the right direction. If they understand that they are getting an additional benefit for the price, you will change how the customer thinks about the fact and will not have to alter the price.

Remember, normally it is not the fact, but what is thought about it that troubles the customer. By focusing on the customer's belief system, irrational and illogical convictions can be changed and objections can be overcome.

○ New Belief: Replace objections with new beliefs

After you successfully overcome the objection, do not stop. It is not enough to simply free the customer from the illogical

[1]Alexander Hamilton Institute, *The Marketing Letter,* Vol. 4, No. 5, Aug. 1977, p. 1 and Vol. 2, No. 11, Feb 1976, p.5.

conviction; you should now set a new belief in its place. Not only must you overcome the objection, you must replace it with a new credible persuasion.

Not only must the customer now understand and trust that you were not trying to take an advantage, the customer must believe you were giving them something more for the price.

The customer must now believe that the "more" is important and must now want it. The customer's belief system should be set so that a product without this particular benefit, no matter what the price, will not be purchased.

S: *"... so in summary, as you can see from the financial section of the proposal, our unique on-line graphics capability will save you thousands of dollars a month when compared to using an outside service. This means you will start realizing an incremental return above the 15% price differential within a year. As for the budgetary issue, we do offer a lease purchase agreement. Shall I meet with Purchasing to work out the details of the purchase order?"*

C: *"Yes."*

The underlying objections were uncovered and overcome, the illogical belief was dispelled, the incremental value was explained, a positive unique benefit was installed and the salesperson asked for the order. Any competitor without on-line graphics capability will have trouble turning the situation around.

Dealing with the underlying objections is a three-step process:

- Determine what the customer believes about the objection.

- Convince the customer of the irrationality of that belief.

- Replace the illogical belief with a positive belief in a value of your product.[2]

By following these steps, you will both free the customer from irrational thinking and equip the customer with a positive belief about your product. This will also lock out the competitor.

[2]Ivey, *Counseling and Psychotherapy*, pp. 295-300.

CHAPTER

(34)

Turn objections
into benefits

It is impossible to anticipate objections if you do not know
your product. Product knowledge is a fundamental tool to
anticipate finding, understanding, and overcoming objections
related to price, time, credibility, technical issues, and competitive issues. If you know your product, company, customer, and
competitor, you can categorize the likely objections and prepare answers in advance.

○ *Anticipate and Categorize: Answer*
objections before they arise whenever
you can

A vital principle of sales is to anticipate every possible
objection a customer might make, then turn them into benefits.

Every product has some undesirable feature or shortcoming that your customer is most certain to identify. Worrying or hoping that the customer will forget to bring up major objections won't help. Don't wait for the customer to surface an objection. Instead, bring it up first, but as a benefit. Brag about it. Sounds strange, but it works. It also makes it difficult for the customer to bring it up later.

Converting objections into benefits is not as difficult as you might think. Review the objections you heard in the past, catalog them, and develop an answer for each. List all the technical issues about your product. Work with your engineering personnel, and develop answers for your apparent weaknesses and work-arounds for your deficiencies. Once you know how to handle them, turn the would-be objections into benefits.

Weave factual answers to anticipated objections through your presentation so that anticipated objections are answered before the customer verbalizes them. This requires a planned presentation delivered from the customer's viewpoint and focused on the end value.

If your competitor uses the latest model computer in their product, and you have an older version, focus on the fact that your company chose to stay with the older computer because it is field-proven and very reliable.

Your competitor's product may take less floor space but your company chose to make your product 15% larger for improved cooling, easier access, better reliability, and, most important, future option expansion to protect the customer's investment and lower the cost of ownership.

If your competitor offers a one-year warranty and you offer five years, this may not be perceived as a benefit if your price is higher. The competitor may have told the customer,

"Most failures occur in the first 90 days. We stand behind our quality and reliability. If it were necessary to offer a warranty beyond one year, which is incidentally nine months after infant mortality failures have been corrected, we would extend it. So why pay for something you do not need?"

To prepare for this tactic and stop the competitor, tell the customer early in the sales cycle and before the competitor attempts it,

"We have a higher entry price than most other systems because we put a lot of capability into the equipment to keep the

cost of ownership low. The real cost of owning the system is the cost to operate it. As you can see by these investment return figures, the cost of owning our system is significantly lower than most other conventional systems. One of the major reasons for the low ownership cost is high reliability. We are so confident in these figures that we warranty our system for 5 years. Should an anomaly occur you are protected through the depreciation period of the system."

The salesperson anticipated a price and reliability objection might be perpetrated by the competitor and answered them before the customer formulated them.

Exaggerate for Effect: Exaggerate the customer's objection to get the customer to see that it is not significant

When attempting to forestall an objection, observe the customer's reaction. If the customer's head moves up and down, or if he or she says, "I was wondering about that," you were probably successful. You did not have to respond directly to the objection. You simply presented data and staved off the objection before the customer verbalized it.

Obviously, you cannot know beforehand of every objection nor can you predetermine the customer's feelings or mood. Customers are bound to complain. When an objection breaks through, one way to disarm it immediately is to feed it back in terms more extreme than the customer is likely to use.

C: "The system you sold us last year is always down!"

S: "Always down! Well, I will have my audit team here tomorrow. We will spend the next two weeks running all the system diagnostics and fix the problems."

C: "Wait! We are using it two shifts a day, we can't afford to have it down two weeks. What we mean is the printer is always jamming."

S: "I will have a replacement printer shipped to you tomorrow. Our new system uses the new highly reliable and high speed laser printer. Not only will you not experience normal mechanical printer downtime but we can replace the printer on your existing system with the new laser *printer as well and I can give you a good trade-in on the old one."*

The salesperson's objective was to win the customer back to close on the new system order. Even though this objection was not anticipated it was turned into a benefit.

Often your greatest sales leverage will result from an objection. If you overcome it you can close quickly.

Care must be taken not to create objections. If you are selling a device test system to a semiconductor manufacturer who produces *standard* devices, and you focus your presentation on *custom* devices, you will generate incompatibility objections and could lose the sale.

Although objections may be anticipated and prevented, they should never be passed by. Some sales training courses will teach you that the first time a customer raises an objection, you should acknowledge it but not answer it, and go on with your presentation or meeting. If it is raised a second time, the point is really important to the customer, so you deal with it. This approach may work, but it risks generating a festering objection that may surface at the eleventh hour. It is best to uncover all real objections and deal with them upfront.

Objections should not be confused with lingering doubts which are minor concerns that nag a customer and are usually based on the customer's own insecurity or indecisiveness. Care must be taken not to focus on lingering doubts. Avoid them. Too much focus may turn them into objections. Lingering doubts should be suppressed through persuasion and assurances.

○ Buyer Quirks: Read between the lines, for some buyers won't say what they really mean

Some buyers will fabricate objectives because they simply are not going to tell you that you lost the order. It is up to you to find out on your own. Others will never notify you of competitive activity or of a potential buy, leaving it up to you to find out. Both may appear helpful and courteous but simply will not volunteer any information. These **concealors** are not to be confused with the professional closed mouth buyer who is discreet until a final decision is made and all potential suppliers are informed.

Concessionaires will use objections to play one supplier against the other to intensify the competitive struggle and increase supplier concessions. The more unscrupulous buyer will have already made up his or her mind concerning which product to buy and will still lead the unsuspecting, unwary, rejected supplier along as leverage against the unknowing, selected supplier to obtain even more concessions.

The *customizer* is the buyer who will object to the product or terms of purchase as a matter of course. No product is ever right for this buyer. No standard offering can ever meet this buyer's needs. This buyer will demand a tailoring to his or her specifications. Often this can be costly to the supplier especially if the engineering department underestimates the difficulty in making the "minor" change.

Finally, there is the *procrastinator* who uses objections to cover up her or his procrastination. This buyer is noted for the consistently long period of time necessary to process an order. Their intentions are usually honorable, they are just slow. You must speed them up through their management or peers.[1]

Objections come in many forms and must be evaluated carefully for what they are, otherwise control will pass from you to the buyer and you may end up trying to rationally deal with objections which border on the lunatic fringe of idiocy in rhetoric.

[1]Holden, *Vanguard,* (Referenced).

CHAPTER

Focus on detail

It is better to do something than to do nothing, even if the something proves not to be the best possible something. You are not perfect. Trade-offs will have to be made, but if you take action and cover every base, you have a better chance of winning. In fact, cultivate within yourself a sense of urgency. Don't allow lethargy to set in, especially when you are winning, because it is never ok to lose.

In the words of Winston Churchill, "Let us not delude ourselves by thinking that there is a substitute for victory." These words were echoed by Douglas MacArthur in his infamous and career-limiting letter to a congressman where he said, "... There is no substitute for victory."[1] This is certainly true for sales.

You can work on capturing an account day and night. You can plan and strategize, cover every technical and political

[1]Bradley and Blair, *A General's Life*, p. 627.

base, do everything you can think of, and then you relax one day and you lose everything.

Lyndon Johnson failed in his first attempt to become a senator because he relaxed. Since he thought he was so far ahead in the 1941 Texas senatorial race with O'Daniel he did not have his men on the scene at the ballot boxes and as a result, those who wanted O'Daniel in Washington stole the vote from Johnson. In his biography of Johnson Caro says, "He had planned and schemed and maneuvered for ten years—had worked for ten years, worked day and night, weekday and weekend—had done everything. And, for ten years, he had won. He had relaxed for one day. And he had lost."[2]

◯ *Do Not Relax: Sales must stay sold*

Believing you have won the order before you have the hard copy is a dangerous assumption to make in sales. You cannot afford to relax until the order is in your hand, and even then you can only relax a bit.

Develop a disposition for taking care of every detail, no matter how minor. Look at each issue; look at it from every aspect. Listen to everything the customer says; worry about it from every angle. If you ask enough questions to uncover every possible objection, you will be prepared with every possible answer.

When visiting an account, touch every base. Meet everybody you can. Don't neglect anyone. Stop and chat with peers, assistants, secretaries, and management. Be smiling and deferential. Agree with everyone. Soon they will be willing to help you when you need it. Impress the management, especially the influential people, with your responsiveness and competence so they feel secure in your hands. Never hint at any difficulties you might encounter when doing them a favor. Always hint of higher authority behind your efforts. Above all, be dependable. If you make a commitment or give your word, don't break it.

◯ *Focus on the Positive: Don't neglect the positive aspects of your product in answering objections*

If a customer focuses on the negative aspects of your product or company, give selective attention to the positive

[2]Caro, *The Path to Power,* pp. 737-740.

things the customer said. This is a nondefensive approach that focuses on the positive comments and beliefs about your product and creates an upbeat atmosphere in which to work on an objection.

> C: *"I know you have a good company and a good product, and the price is right, but I am very concerned with the ability of a small company like yours to support me when the going gets rough."*

It is important to avoid an overly optimistic response that does not reflect or draw on the positive dimension presented by the customer. Don't immediately give assurances.

> S: *"We will provide you with full support. We are committed to support you. Our company has invested heavily in service, is backed by a large financial group, and has a local service office."*

This response may appear to be satisfactory and may constitute the bulk of the assurances you will make, but it does not reinforce the positive dimensions highlighted by the customer. It may appear defensive, optimistic, or even demeaning, especially if the customer already knows this, but is still concerned.

> S: *"I can appreciate your concern. As you have just pointed out, the fact that we can produce a good product with an attractive investment return for you, is in itself an attribute of a good company. Support for the product is also an attribute of a good company and our very existence and success are not dependent on the product, since we both agree the product is successful, but on our ability to support it. Wouldn't you agree?"*

At this point get the customer to say "yes," then continue with assurances until he or she is convinced. Assurances build confidence and remove threats or pressure associated with a possible bad decision. The degree of assurance you must provide will often depend on the size and reputation of the company you represent. In high technology, big is not always good. A small company may have more credibility, especially when new technology is the issue. On the other hand, support and the question, "Will you exist next year?" are the major concerns a customer has with a small company.

Assurances must be directed toward the person or department that needs them: technology to the engineer, financial resources to the controller, service capability to the maintenance department, and product quality and reliability to the quality department.

Assurances directly validate a point or sale. Assurances include technical manuals, financial statements and investment data, actual performance data from past successes, tours at your company and demonstrations, specific analysis of the application and an example of exactly how you will address it, engineering reports, support capabilities and standard warranties, and guarantees or other commitments that may also necessitate a letter or visit from your upper management. Company strategic business plans, product plans, and growth projections are also useful tools of assurance, if confidentiality is not compromised.

If you still cannot overcome the objection, try references and testimonials. References and testimonials should be matched to the customer. Be careful with testimonials from the competitors of your customer, they could backfire.

○ Circumvent the Negative: Don't brush aside negative feelings or comments, but offer reassurance

When you move to close a sale, although the solution may be obvious or a decision may have been made, emotional or political factors can block implementation. Beware, be aware, be sensitive as the implementation of a crucial decision nears. If at the eleventh hour the competition attacks you negatively, respond in a way that will shame them. If the competition surfaces a reasonably valid issue related to you, your product or your company, rather than trying to hide it, deny it or answer it, emphasize it instead, and in a dramatic fashion. Make the issue work for you.

If the competitor says you have many unhappy customers, give your customer a *qualified* list of your customers' names and telephone numbers. The chances of the customer calling are slim, and if your product is moderately successful the user is unlikely to complain anyway. In fact, users will probably brag about your product because they will want others to follow their decision.

If the customer is concerned about the ten cents a share loss your company just experienced, say you are proud of it. It shows management's strength of character not to cut back R&D expenses to correct a short-term financial problem.

If he says your product is not field-proven, agree. A new state-of-the-art product cannot be field-proven although it has been field tested. Then overwhelm the customer with assurances.

S: *"We recognize that your application represents 'Leading Edge Sophistication' that will, from time to time, call upon system performance that in some cases has not yet been totally 'field proven.'"*

Let's review both the present and proposed alternatives and options available to you to ensure a full realization of your expectations.

"Our entire Senior Management group has personally committed themselves to ensure the success of the installation.

"In an effort to ensure prompt problem resolution, we will provide you with a direct access to our Product Manager. This is in addition to your utilization of our Customer Support Center.

"To ensure maximum communication, during the first 12 months of the installation, we will conduct bi-monthly system status reviews with you to ensure that we are constantly updated on the status of the installation and the application and to provide you with a first-hand understanding of our related development efforts."

In essence you are offering the customer a partnership. How can the competitor with older technology fight this?

Win Over the Nonsupporters: Once you have won the sale, consolidate it

When you win the order, thank your supporters but thank your enemies first. Send a personal letter of thanks to each individual who supported your competitor as well as those who supported you. Your objective now that you have the order is to cement your relationship with your supporters, and also to win the others over to your side. No effort was spared to defeat the non-supporters, so now no effort should be spared to gain their support.

A letter of assurance may also be appropriate. It need not be elaborate but must emphasize the commitment.

Dear Customer:

We would like to re-emphasize to you our total commitment to your company. We are fully aware of your specific application, and we have discussed it in detail among ourselves and our respective personnel.

We, therefore, jointly commit ourselves to ensure that your installation is fully supported, consistently meets and, where feasible, exceeds your expectations.

Yours truly,
(signed by the complete management staff)

But once they are won over or reconciled, take heed. Attend to every detail, no matter how minor. The competitor could still turn the order around. Be ever vigilant. Let the competitor sleep while you watch.

CHAPTER

(36)

When negotiating, make silence your ally

People negotiate to achieve satisfaction. What satisfies you may cost your opponent little and vice versa. But at some point in the negotiation, one of you is likely to gain at the expense of the other. As a salesperson, your objective is not to win it all but to get the order under conditions satisfactory to both you and your customer.

To reach this state of affairs in a negotiation, you sometimes must show the customer what to do. Like power in selling, power in negotiations is the ability of the salesperson to influence the behavior of the customer. When negotiating with the customer it is important not to get bogged down attempting to assert the right you know you can not exert.

○ Know Thyself: In negotiating, the first rule is to know yourself

To use your power to influence in a tough negotiation, the first rule is understand yourself. You will be a better negotiator if you have high self-esteem, naturally and quickly earn the respect of others, feel secure in both your life and job, and do not easily let others know what you are really thinking or feeling. If you are normally willing to take more risk than most concerning opportunities that enhance your career or finances, you will probably find negotiating easier than most. To a certain extent, you are already an experienced negotiator, unless the risks you took were foolhardy.

If people like you socially or if you have charisma, you will be in a good position to get others to follow your lead. Leadership ability is enhanced if you feel comfortable and natural when leading. Measure yourself on these qualities and use them to your advantage. Power in negotiations is often a matter of perception.

Although neither you nor the buyer normally enjoys absolute power, if you are in the preferred position, the buyer must perceive that you are willing to use the power of your position for your own advantage.

You need not expedite this awareness. Let the realization slowly and naturally dawn on your opponent. Skillful, experienced, and professional negotiators will follow their opponent with a keen watchfulness, alertness, and mental agility. As the master of strategy and tactics, they will bide their time.

They may even appear puzzled, muddled or wobbled until they see their chance, then with adroit energy they will bear down on the opponent and snatch a concession, after which they will quickly appear perplexed, characteristic of their recidivous ploy. This diversionary behavior will be repeated until the negotiation concludes.

○ Win—Win Is Best

If both you and the buyer are committed to a long-term relationship, then you will not exploit the buyer and the buyer will not intimidate you. The buyer is negotiating to gain something. You must let the buyer gain. For example, if price is an issue, do not concentrate solely on minimum cost or maximum price, but include the long-term rewards of repeat business in your calculations.

You will have to take some risk if you intend to use your power to reach a buy decision during the negotiation that meets your objectives. There are certain issues neither you nor the buyer are willing to give up. There are other issues which both of you deem expendable. These are the issues that should be negotiated. Your objective is an amicable contract. It is essential to clearly understand and agree to the areas of difference between you and the buyer, and to an objective criteria for decision making before you start negotiation.

○ ### *Ten Step Negotiation: There are ten key points in learning to negotiate*

To win in any negotiation, remember these ten key points:

1. Practice negotiating at every opportunity.

2. Prepare well for every negotiation.

3. List every issue before starting.

4. Listen well.

5. Ask probing questions.

6. Make the other party work for every concession.

7. Price every concession.

8. Use good business judgment and common sense.

9. Don't be afraid to say no.

10. Count to three before replying unless you are negotiating the price, then count to five.

Practice negotiating at every opportunity. When buying a house, car, furniture, appliance, or art object, negotiate the purchase. This includes price, payment terms, delivery, options, service, and other related items. Remember everything is negotiable. Negotiate with people in your own organization. Negotiate salary objectives, resources, priorities, sales quotas, and the like. Like anything else, the more you practice, the better you will be at it.

During these "practice" negotiations be persistent, be patient, and give in slowly if at all. Never threaten the other party. Make it a regular practice to make a low offer. If selling, make a high request. The more you do this, the more comfortable you will feel at it.

Also be sensitive to the personal issues of your opponent. Issues such as work load, job security, resources, and "What the boss might say" are important. The acid test of your negotiation ability is to ask the boss for a raise or sales commission twice the average for your group or department. You may not get it, but if you made a credible case and were not afraid to try it, you're ready to negotiate with the customer.

Prepare well for every negotiation. You must lead the negotiating team. Consult with experts and use them on the team as often as possible. Develop acceptable alternatives to probable options your opponent may wish to exercise. The Japanese go to negotiations with experts in every related discipline. Bring your experts to support your negotiating strategy and to provide immediate and credible responses to your customer.

During your preparation check out everything you were told by the customer or about the account. Accurate knowledge will give you an advantage. Encourage them to reveal all demands first while you keep your positions secret. You should go out of your way to get close to your customer. Get personally involved. Through this association you will be able to compile the data you need.

Before going into the negotiation, set difficult negotiating targets. If you aim high you will have a better chance of winning, even if the win is more modest than the goal.

Once you have set your objectives, *list every issue.* There should be three categories: known customer issues, possible additional customer issues, and your issues.

Do not assume the customer knows what he or she has to gain or lose, or that the customer knows your issues. Be prepared to discuss every issue on your list but do not permit any discussion of new issues for which you are not prepared. Retire, then institute another round after you have prepared your position on the new issues.

Be a good *listener.* Things are rarely all one way or another, so look for ambiguous situations. *Listen* with special attention if someone expresses ideas you do not agree with. Be sensitive to the customer's needs and motivations and body language.

Proper interpretation will give you insight into how far you can go.

Do not be intimidated by power, status, statistics, hearsay, principles, precedents, or irrationality. Do not dwell on the limits of your power. Study the limits of your opponent's power, then put yourself in a comfortable frame of mind when you are with them. You are their equal or they would not be negotiating with you.

Learn what counts and use *probing questions* to penetrate and get at the real issues of the negotiation. Remember as you probe that you are committed to customer satisfaction. You must ensure your customer does not get hurt. This does not mean you make unnecessary concessions. As you probe, do not hesitate to say as many times as necessary, "I don't understand that," even if the explanations were adequate. Negotiating is a psychological game.

Since you are negotiating, it is not too important to be liked. You cannot do a good job of negotiating if you are worried about what the customer is thinking about you. It will all come out in the end if your focus is on the problem rather than the customer. Use your negotiating power, based on your knowledge, wisely and moderately without any guilt feelings. You are the expert on your product. Be confident. Take a hard product line if necessary but go easy on the customer.

Concessions should not be made lightly. In fact, make your customer work for any concession you make. If you give in too easily, the customer will not think the gain is worth much or will not appreciate it. The rules of the concession game are: do not make the first concession, do not accept their first concession, do not counter-offer a ridiculous concession, get something for every concession, do not concede one for one unless your "one" is bigger than their "one," learn their concession pattern but do not reveal yours, make your concessions slowly and do not feel guilty about accepting a concession beyond your dreams.

Go for the best overall short- and long-term financial or business arrangement for your company. This does not just mean the list price of your equipment alone, but the cost to support it as well. If the customer pays list price but negotiates an expensive support package at a fraction of its real cost, you lose.

Know your true costs and *price every concession.* Everything has value. Price concessions at what they are worth to the customer even though they may have little value to you. Keep track of all concessions you make and those made by your customer. Calculate your concessions at cost yet present them at a value equivalent to their worth to the customer.

When you negotiate, integrity is important. You must ensure the customers get what they think they are getting. The customers in good faith should live up to their commitments, especially equipment acceptance conditions and payment terms. As you negotiate, your two best allies are **common sense** and **good business judgment.** Be open-minded but secretive about your business interests. Be skeptical about what you are told in the negotiation, and work to optimize your interests in all respects.

Do not be afraid to say no. Think like your company's financial controller and learn to say no. In fact, depending upon the customer's action, do not be afraid to take back a concession previously made. Be flexible, tactful, and discreet and enjoy the challenge of direct negotiations.

If you win big and the agreement turns out to be quite bad for the customer, you can always let them negotiate a better contract. Then you will be a hero. On the other hand, remember that a deadlock is unpleasant for both of you. An impasse will not necessarily result in a deadlock but if it does, emphasize the losses to both of you if you both cannot come to an agreement, be reasonable. If you made a mistake, don't be afraid to admit it.

When you negotiate, you will be under a lot of pressure. It is important that you think clearly under pressure. It is just as important to think clearly when the pressure is off so you do not inadvertently give something away.

If the negotiation peaks and the room becomes emotionally charged, stay calm. It might be difficult but do not show stress or excitement. During this final countdown you will have to be resourceful in coming up with creative solutions. At this point you will have to handle the toughest questions of the negotiation. Ensure you are under no time pressure. If your flight leaves in one hour, tell the customer you have all week. If the customer knows you're under a time pressure he or she will try to panic you into a final agreement by the time deadline or attempt to intimidate you with the "last and final" offer.

Every time the customer asks a question or makes a statement that requires a response, use silence to your advantage and slowly **count to three** before replying. Often the customer will speak again giving you more information or even answer his or her own question before you have finished counting. If not, when finished with the count reply with a positive or flattering introduction before answering the question or statement. If you are negotiating the price or something that may cost you money, slowly **count to five** before replying. If the customer asks another question, makes another statement or just speaks, before you have completed the count, be patient, reset the count to zero and start again.

C: *"We demand a 12% discount!"*

S: *(1 ... 2 ...)*

C: *"Well at least 10%, that is fair!"*

S: *(1 ... 2 ... 3 ...)*

C: *"Your competitors offered us 7%. We expect you to at least match it!"*

S: *(1 ... 2 ... 3 ... 4 ...)*

C: *"Okay, your offer was 3%, but we honestly cannot accept less than 6%."*

S: *(1 ... 2 ... 3 ... 4 ... 5) "That is reasonable and I appreciate your position but I cannot go above 3% on a single system purchase. If you can commit to purchasing additional systems in the future we do have a quantity purchase agreement contract—or if we modify the configuration somewhat the net effect will be equivalent to a 3% discount...."*

Try it; it works.

CHAPTER

$$\textbf{37}$$

Never ask the customers "if" they want your product

The action a salesperson takes to obtain a firm commitment on the part of the buyer to purchase the product is the close. Often the salespeople, caught up in their own enthusiasm during the euphoria following a successful presentation, forget to close or agree to send the customer a quotation or proposal, thinking they have closed. A close, final or conditional, requires a commitment on the part of the buyer, not the salesperson. In these instances, while the salesperson is preparing the proposal, the competitor is closing. The salesperson then wonders what happened.

Most sales courses concentrate on teaching how to get a customer to sign on the dotted line. They teach you to bring the contract out at the beginning of the meeting, place it in front of the customer, and have a pen handy for signature when the buyer flashes a buy signal. This is all well and good, but it is not the way it happens when you are selling high-priced, high technology products. The signature on the contract or purchase order is usually a formality that occurs well after the close.

○   *Early Commitment: Get the commitment to buy as early as possible*

Since a buy decision is usually made long before the hard copy order is placed, concentrate on making your most profound impression on the customer in the early stages of the sales cycle. Usually, a series of events will motivate an individual or a committee to commit to you and your product.

Generate questions until the customer is ready to buy, then close. If you are not sure of how and when to close, you may oversell and talk yourself right through the customer's ready period, ending back where you started. If your presentation is believable, and if the buyer is satisfied with your solution, close. Any further presenting is overselling. Overselling will either lead to disbelief in the validity of the solution or lose the sale through confusion or boredom.

If the customer isn't ready to close, maintain close contact. Make conditional closes and get as many commitments as possible. This means you must never leave the buyer's presence without linking to another meeting. Good two-way communication between you and the buyer is necessary to understand where you are in a sales process so you do not miss the buyer's ready state.

For you to close, the buyer must be interested and satisfied with the evaluation of your solution, be ready to make the decision, and have the funding.[1]

One sure way not to close the sale is to assume you will lose it. This will almost guarantee you will. Confidence in both yourself and your product along with a positive assumption that you will close the sale will be communicated to the customer through your discussions and demeanor. Confidence is a subtle but powerful psychological reassuring influence on the buyer. The events that lead to the final close include your one-on-one sales effort, the presentation, the proposal, the demonstration, a testimonial, and the efforts of your inside salesperson.

Once the customer has made a commitment to you, the order will follow. It is important to obtain this commitment

[1]Holden, *Vanguard,* (Referenced).

early. Therefore, use all the resources available to you to effect a close.

In addition to your resources, use the customer's resources. Request a conference room to use for your presentation. Ask for a slide projector or an overhead projector. Use theirs, not yours. You win by getting them to do favors for you. Help them write the purchase specification. Act as a counselor or consultant for the application and develop a partnership. A partnership means you and the customer will explore together means and alternatives to solve the problem.

◯ *Conditional Close: Make as many conditional agreements as you need to get a final agreement to buy*

It has been said that the time to close is now. In other words, the salesperson is always closing. For this reason, in addition to aligning with key people in the account and developing a partnership early, start closing early. This is accomplished by knowing how the purchase decision will be made, by qualifying every decision influence, by identifying the real issues, the things that excite the customer, and by closing on them one by one.

Closing does not necessarily mean you should ask for the order every time you meet the customer. Nor should you call the customer just to ask for the order. It does mean you should get some kind of agreement or commitment from the customer every time you call. Also, on each call, reaffirm previous commitments or agreements. These reaffirmations are important because the decisions and decision-makers can change, or the competitor's strategy can shift. These agreements and commitments are called interim, trial, indirect, or conditional closes. During the lengthy buying cycle, these closes are a reliable way to monitor your progress.

Continue asking and getting answers to questions such as, *"If I could deliver this system next month with the software packages specified, when could you place the order?"* If the response to the question is positive, you are on your way to a sale. If the response is noncommittal or negative, you know you are in trouble. In any event, you will know well before the hard copy purchase order is signed whether or not you have the sale.

○ Final Close: Get the final agreement to buy and get it in writing

The final close in high technology sales is usually a verbal commitment by the customer to give you the order. In this case, you should press for a purchase order number from purchasing. Failing this, request a letter of intent to purchase from the customer. Ensure that the customer understands the commitment you and your company will be making based on the verbal purchase order. Keep very close to the account and continue to obtain minor agreements that will strengthen the commitment they made to buy. Also, keep making reinsurances to overcome any buyer's remorse.

○ Closing Takes Practice: Practice closing and do not fear rejection

Fear of being rejected or waiting for the buyer to give you the order can both lead to a lost sale.

Your product cannot be wrong for the customer if it provides a solution and it does the basic job. So you should not fear rejection. Your attitude toward closing has as much to do, if not more to do, with closing than with your ability to sell. It is essential that you believe in your ability to close. Do not fear or avoid asking for the order. The worst thing that can happen is that you will uncover another objection, which you must eventually deal with anyway. If the order has already been lost, then when is a better time than now to find out?

As for waiting for the buyer to give the order, Jim Holden says, "High technology salespeople often massage the sales situation down until the order pops out. Had they asked for the order earlier in the sales process, they would have saved both themselves and the customer time, reduced the risk of a successful competitive thrust, and obtained the order earlier."

Some salespeople feel closing is uncomfortable or difficult. Closing, like any other skill, takes practice. The more you try to close, the more comfortable you will feel about closing and the more successful you will become at it.

When closing, try executing Jim Holden's ten-step closing algorithm.

First: Ask for the order.

Second: Be quiet.

Third: If you get a negative response, ask why.

Fourth: Answer the emotion behind the closing objection.

Fifth: Ask for the order.

Sixth: Be quiet.

Seventh: Repeat three, four, and five as often as necessary.

Eighth: Get a commitment.

Ninth: Thank the buyer.

Tenth: Advertise to solidify the commitment.[2]

Closing Objections: Answer closing objections by offering alternatives

Answering closing objections is different from answering selling-process objections. Focus on the emotion, not the content, and don't use the forbidden words *if* or *assume*.

Never offer the customer an alternative that gives the customer an out. Never ask the buyer *if* the buyer wants your product. Control or close by jumping objections.

C: *"We want a five percent discount."*

S: *"If we can solve the price problem, will you buy?"*

C: *"Yes."*

Then control the close by offering the customer alternatives that are both attractive.

S: *"Well, we can change the delivery of the product to meet your budget release date or offer you a lease-purchase agreement. Which do you prefer?"*

Or control the close by offering hypothetical reasons against the objection that make it difficult for the customer to stay with the objection.

S: *"I know you want to negotiate a discount, but like your company, we do not discount our product. We offered you*

[2]Ibid.

> *the software at no extra charge. As you know, suppliers normally charge for the software."*

Another response might be:

S: *"If you recall, in the efficiency analysis we did, you will realize a return with a net result well in excess of the dollars represented by a five percent discount. You in effect will have a significant cost savings, or discount, with our product."*

Anticipate the probable closing objections and be ready for them. The important point is not to answer the closing objections until you have the customer's commitment to purchase if you satisfactorily dispense with them. Once a commitment is made, if you have done your job earlier, you will be able to dismiss the closing objection quickly because the customer is already mentally committed to your product. You may have to make a minor or token concession, but the order is yours.

Once you have a commitment, be quiet and get out of there as soon as possible. The only discussion that should take place after a final close is a discussion on the mechanics of generating the hard copy purchase order.

CHAPTER

(38)

Ask for the order

Closing high technology sales is not a single event but a series of events over time, which ends in the customer's commitment to buy.

When you develop your sales tactics, set a series of goals or things to accomplish that link through the typically long selling cycle to the close. Have a specific time, place, and method of closing in your strategy. The closing tactics can always be modified depending upon the reality of the sales situation.

The specific point in your strategy when a close should take place is not important in and of itself. You can easily miss the mark. What is important is that you have thought it out and know what you must do to get the order.[1]

---

[1]Alexander Hamilton Institute, *The Marketing Letter*, Vol. 2, No. 1, Apr. 1975, p. 7.

◯ ## When to Close: Close when the customer is ready to buy

When you sense the customer is ready to buy, end your discussion or presentation immediately and ask for the order then and there. Perceiving when to ask for the order requires sensitivity and experience. If you do not have the experience, try anyway. If you try to close too soon, you will learn. If you attempt to close too often, you will learn. If you close too late, it is too late. It is better to close too often than not often enough. It is better to close too soon than too late. This may seem academic, but seasoned salespeople make this mistake. More sales are lost because the salesperson did not ask for the order than any other single reason.

The buyer knows you are there to get an order and expects to be asked to buy. The buyer would like to get it over with as quickly as possible. So ask for the order.

Asking for the order does not necessarily mean "Mr. Black, please give me the order," although this is what salespeople typically think when told to ask for the order. In fact, every time the customer makes a commitment in your favor, your position is improved. With each conditional close, you are closer to the order.

◯ ## Closing Techniques: The method of closing depends on many variables

There are various ways to close a sale. Sales folklore is filled with stories and anecdotes about closing. Many of the following closing techniques may be familiar to you by other names.

Closing with a direct question such as, *"May I have the order,"* is a common method used with the buyer who is effusive and outgoing and with whom the salesperson has developed a rapport. The **direct question close** is also used with the decisive buyer who is a professional, likes his or her job, and knows why the both of you are having this dialogue.

The **indirect question close** works better with the indecisive personalities since it is not challenging. Yet it is a hard close that facilitates a choice between two responses, both in the salesperson's favor.

S: *"Should I write the 64K RAM order for the 8K × 8 or the 4K × 16 CMOS version?"*

S: *"Shall I have the factory reserve the next 32-bit processor or the less expensive 16-bit version while you generate the paperwork?"*

The ***interrogation close*** is a variation of the question close and works well with the dominant buyer who sees the salesperson as a challenge. Usually this buyer is rather egocentric or a snob. The salesperson must be brisk, persistent, and decisive and never show weakness, yet cater to the buyer without being obsequious. When the salesperson thinks this buyer is ready to commit, a closing question is asked.

S: *"As I see it, Mr. Big, you need to decide on whether you want your system shipped in May or June. Is that correct?"*

If the buyer says yes, a close is in the making. If the buyer says no, an objection is uncovered. The next move is to interrogate the buyer and try to close on the objection once expressed.

With the egocentric buyer, persistence pays. The salesperson never stops closing until the order is granted. The interrogation close only works if the buyer is ready to buy, but has an objection, is being coy, or is just not motivated to give a direct answer. The interrogation close is a direct, formal, and systematic approach to closing that requires the skills of medieval inquisitors without the use of their tools.

In response to the *"...May or June shipment?"* attempt to close, a customer might say,

C: *"Not so fast. Your price is beyond my budget."*

After some discussion about the value and the budget, the salesperson might say,

S: *"Would you prefer a lease or extended payment terms?"*

C: *"But your competitor's 16-bit product is cheaper."*

After more discussion about what the customer is looking for or needs; that is, the value the salesperson is offering, the salesperson may go on to say,

> **S:**   *"Then it looks like our equivalent 16-bit version is what
> you need, or do you still prefer our new and unique 32-bit
> machine?"*
>
> **C:**   *"We had a bad experience with a new product in the past."*

After explaining why such an experience will not be repeated, the salesperson may go back full circle to the beginning.

> **S:**   *"So, shall I advise the factory to reserve a system for you
> for May or June delivery?"*

The salesperson keeps asking for the order after dealing with each objection. Although not absolutely necessary, in each case the salesperson ties each attempt to close to the objection in an attempt to ensure it was overcome and at the same time obtain the final close.

The **consolidated close** finds its application with the stereotypical detached *give me the facts* engineering type who will not allow a rapport with the salesperson to develop. This buyer is frequently found in high technology sales situations.

The consolidated close joins together in a series of one liners the product benefits and previous agreements chronologically and secures the buyer's consensus on each one as it is mentioned. This close is used to prompt the buyer to commit when indications are that attempts at personal selling are a waste of time. If the consolidation tends to be abstract and conceptual, it is more likely to elicit a favorable response.

A variation on a consolidated close is the **analytic close.** This close is most effective with a logician, especially when the sales motion is stymied. On a sheet of paper or the white board, the salesperson draws a line down the middle and writes "Yes" above the left column and "No" above the right column. The salesperson then asks the buyer for the reasons to buy the product and helps with the answers. Then the buyer is asked for the reasons not to buy and the salesperson remains quiet. No help with the "No" column is given.

If mathematically inclined, the salesperson will ensure the "Yes" column has more reasons to buy than the "No" column has reasons not to buy. The salesperson will deal with the "No" column by answering as many of the objections as possible and getting consensus on each.

At this point, there should be no significant objection left. If the customer is holding back for a minor point, the salesperson will appeal to the buyer's logical mind.

S: *"Mr. Dielectic, do you agree with me that the pros far outweigh the cons?"*

If the buyer is used to saying "yes" during the sales cycle and if the buyer says yes now, the salesperson is on the way to the close. Insuring the buyer says yes earlier will make it easier for the buyer to say yes now.

With the **speculative close** the salesperson assumes the sale is closed and suggests actions that substantiate this. The salesperson may start taking the action for the buyer.

S: *"Mr. Jolly, since we both agree this product will do your job and meet your budget, I will have the factory reserve the next system for you. Shall we now go see purchasing about generating the purchase order?"*

With tacit approval, the salesperson has reviewed the situation somewhat casually and made a speculative close. Other things that can substantiate the speculation is to arrange training for the people, have purchasing sign a letter of intent or a nondisclosure agreement, or some action that demonstrates confidence that the decision has been made in the salesperson's favor.

This close is ideal for the dependent or passive person who is warm, personal, and friendly.

Sometimes, the speculative close is replaced with a variation of the direct question close called the **unimportant close.** In attempting to use this close, the buyer is asked to decide on a relatively unimportant, insignificant point or aspect of the product.

S: *"Do you want your own people to conduct the installation or would you rather have us do it?"*

Instead of asking the customer to buy the product, the salesperson asks about the installation. What output voltage, what color, which payment terms, or some other issue that has a low threat potential changes a large buying decision into a small one.

The *dramatic close* starts when the salesperson takes the spotlight on center stage and brings to bear his or her acting talents. The salesperson begins doing something the customer will have to stop unless in agreement. This is especially effective if the salesperson is in the enviable position of holding all the cards and the customer must buy but is being a bore about it. The salesperson starts by picking up his or her things and begins to leave. The buyer will most likely stop the salesperson. If, for example, the buyer says further assurances are needed, the salesperson acts surprised and makes a spontaneous yet prearranged telephone call to another customer using a similar product. The call is prefaced to overcome the last objection between the salesperson and the customer.

> **S:**   *"Mr. Doubtful, I will call Mr. Happy right now, and you can talk to him. He had exactly the same reservations you have."*

Obviously, this close is a risky technique. It should only be used by the experienced salesperson when a stubborn buyer refuses to see what is best for his or her company.

Most buyers like to be associated with successful people. Some like to imitate successful people. This is especially true of the professional purchasing agent, who tends to be a conformist. The conformist is businesslike, conventional and conservative, and precise and proper. This buyer is difficult, if not impossible, to take to lunch, plans things carefully, and rarely misses any details. With this buyer, the ***influential close*** is best. This close aligns the buyer with a person or activity with which he or she would like to be associated. The buyer understands the principle of influence through association and will use what is offered to his or her advantage. The salesperson helps the buyer see himself or herself in terms of the successful person being discussed.

If you attempt this close, it is incumbent on you to ensure that the buyer respects the company or person you are describing. Talk also about the successes of your product at other similar acccounts or past successes of your product in his or her company if such is the case. This buyer tends to purchase name brands, won't take risks, and is concerned with dependability, reliability, cost savings, and guarantees. Your closing strategy should be conventional, low keyed, and detailed. It should include both facts and testimonials.

Prior to closing, always ask, or find out in some other way, if there are any unanswered objections. This buyer will deliberately hold back objections, then spring them on you after you think you have the order. Usually, it is not necessary to directly ask for the order. Through your actions, you, in effect, ask for the order. Unless the conformist still has a serious objection, he or she will give you the order without ever having said yes.

There are other closes that are effective with insecure or emotional buyers. One is the *freebie close,* which appears to give the buyer something for nothing. Freebies are normally held in reserve in case things get rough when you are negotiating a close. But freebies can also be used to induce a close since a buyer can go back to management with the no charge freebie such as extra service, additional capability, a software package, or an extended warranty.

A second inducement to effect purchase is the *crisis close,* which says, in effect, "If you don't buy it now, you will lose due to a price increase or product availability or the like." In the crisis close role, you are not executing a confidence trick but rather providing advanced information about discomforts or disadvantages the buyer can expect if the purchase is not made in a very short time frame. You do not want the buyer to come back to you later with an acrimonious, "Why didn't you tell me?"

The crisis close induces a customer to act now to avoid loss, especially if it is the loss of something he or she feels was already earned. This close should only be used if all others fail.

Closing does not happen spontaneously. Closes often must be induced. In summary, closes can be induced by asking for the order as often as necessary, by summarizing the benefits and agreements and obtaining the customer's concurrence, or by assuming that you already have the sale and acting accordingly. In assuming you have the sale, if you are adroit, the buyer will feel that an order is inevitable.

◯ Stay In the Present: Keep your eye on your objective, the close

Customers often talk about the past, the future, or the irrelevant present, but not the relevant present. An inexperienced salesperson may reinforce the avoidance of a close through excessive interest in trivia and company or personal details that have no bearing on getting the sale. This is also the sign of a poor closer, who will do anything to avoid popping the question.

A good salesperson deals with the here-and-now. A consistent pattern of avoiding the present on the part of the customer or salesperson is simply the avoidance of a decision to buy or a decision to ask for the order.

People do not like to give bad news, so the buyers, through trivia and other discussion, will avoid telling the salesperson that he or she is losing or has lost. On the other hand, salespeople often hear only what they want to hear. They will process all the customer's positive comments, even those unrelated to the purchase, as indications the customer wants to buy. Since salespeople do not want to hear they lost, they do not ask for the order.

Salespeople who fear closing demonstrate this fear by failing to examine issues between them and the customer. They avoid looking for objections, and grab at any positive word the customer may utter as a sign of progress. They will deal with the past or the future and avoid the present. A closer will focus considerable attention on the present, and deal directly with current issues. It is important to understand the tense in which you and the customer are conversing.

C: *"I don't think I am ready to decide yet."*

S: *"Well let's go over what we discussed to date so we can determine what needs to be done."* (past)

S: *"What do we still have to do so you can make a decision?"* (future)

S: *"I think we covered everything, why not decide today?"* (present)

The past approach may resurrect old objections and revisit decisions already made. The future approach could result in a number of tasks to be done, which may or may not be relevant. The present tense is the most powerful approach. It is immediate and focuses the customer on the here and now. It solicits a decision to buy, or uncovers another objection. Staying in the present keeps the chance of closing open. Reverting to the past or heading into the future will result in a delay in the decision.

Since closing takes practice, some closing techniques may at first be uncomfortable for beginners. Although all these closes are surprisingly effective if properly executed, it is important to remember that most buyers and purchasing agents have seen hundreds of presentations, proposals, and closing techniques. In fact, professional buyers know more about closing than most salespeople. Consequently, tricks are unlikely to work.

If you properly qualified the customers and if you can convince the buyers your product provides the value that meets their business and personal needs, you will be providing a real service to the customers. You are there to sell to the customers, nothing more, nothing less. In the final analysis, you will undoubtedly have to make commitments to the customers to effect a close, but it is their commitment to you that constitutes a close.

CHAPTER

(39)

Close—then advertise

Once a buy decision is made in your favor, tell people; advertise the decision initially to the appropriate people in the account, and later to the world, if the customer agrees. Never advertise outside the account without the customer's permission. Holden says, "The reason to advertise is to have as many people as possible aware that a decision has been made in your favor. This makes it difficult for decision-makers to change their minds without damaging their credibility. It also solidifies the commitment."[1]

◯ *Exceptions to Advertising: Don't advertise the sale without the customer's permission*

There are exceptions to the advertising rule. There may be circumstances or times when it is essential to keep the decision

[1]Holden, *Vanguard,* (Referenced), (Advertising after the close is a Holden tactic.)

a secret for a finite time period, especially if the competition is strong in the account, or has a good relationship with upper management. Another reason for secrecy is if your inside salesperson or fox is still quietly pushing the decision that resulted in the close through the political structure. Advertising is a tactic that should be planned as part of your strategy, but only used in the right circumstances.

In high technology selling, the key decision-maker is usually not the purchasing agent, but rather an engineer or manager who may or may not be head of a buying committee or group. If they tell you you have the order and if Purchasing is not present, it is best to have them arrange an immediate meeting with Purchasing so you can secure their commitment in the form of a verbal purchase order number, or a letter of intent to purchase, or the actual hard copy purchase order.

If the decision was a technical one, you may have to negotiate the terms and conditions of sale, which could be a lengthy process and involve technical, financial, purchasing, and legal personnel. Often it is a face-to-face negotiation between your contracts department and theirs. As these negotiations take place, it is best to have as many other people as possible in the account endorse the decision.

○ Who to Contact: Advertise the sale to the customer first

Contact top management and thank them for the order. Tell them the contract negotiations may take a little time, but you will start your factory working on their order immediately. Make sure they understand you trust their word.

Do not make this statement if in fact your company will do nothing until the hard copy order is received and approved. Usually you can reserve a specific system or product delivery for the customer, based on a verbal purchase order number.

Contact all the people that worked with you in arriving at the decision. Thank them and tell them what you told the management. Avoid any specifics concerning prior commitments or issues. If they wish to discuss any details, tell them you will be addressing these issues individually with them or in a group meeting after the hard copy order is placed. You do not want to chance bringing up an issue that could interfere or delay the order or would reopen negotiations. You do not want to deal with any new or old questions or objections until you have obtained the hard copy order. Countless sales have been lost because the salesperson stayed too long, talked too much, or addressed a new issue.

Contact other individuals who may not have been directly involved but were either influential in the decision or will be affected by it. This might include facilities, training, maintenance, operations, and other peripheral personnel. Tell them you will be contacting them in the future to discuss their interface with your product or system and your support for them.

Prior to the decision being made, work with the customer's public relations department to approve a press release by your company, a joint release, or separate releases, depending on the druthers of the customer. Some customers will not permit a press release and in fact will not permit you to divulge the information at all. Others welcome the publicity, especially if it is the purchase of high-ticket capital equipment which, if known, will enhance their position in the market place. In any event, it is good policy to obtain authorization before publicly announcing the sale.

After advertising keep selling your contacts on the correctness of their decision. Be alert for competitive attempts to recover the order and nip them in the bud with the implementation plan.

○ ## The Implementation Plan: Publicize and obtain agreement to your implementation plan

President Truman made a courageous political decision to fire MacArthur, yet failed to mobilize the country behind him. He did not have the unanimous unshakable backing of the top civilian and military leaders nor of the press or populist. As a result, MacArthur was able to make a triumphant return. The U.S. government failed again to garner the necessary support in the case of the Vietnam war.

Obviously, you have cultivated some support or you would not have the order, but to obtain total support within the account, the first step is to reinforce the customers' feelings that they made the right decision, to strengthen your position. The company, especially in a hard-fought competitive battle from which you rise supreme, is unlikely to commit all necessary resources to make the installation successful unless there is solid support for the decision to invest in your product, a carefully delineated set of objectives, and agreement to execution of the implementation plan recommended in your proposal. All concerned must be committed to the success of your product. The purchase order alone is not a total commitment.

After receiving the hard copy purchase order and advertising, effect a planned cultivation of activities to cement the customers commitment. Send a letter of thanks to the key decision makers, influencers, and other involved people in the account.

In the letter sent to the person who will actually use your equipment or who has responsibility for the user group, include confirmations that the purchase order has been formally entered, and the most probable delivery date. Request an appointment to decide how the implementation program will be monitored and modified as required by the actual situation. The activity associated with modifying and monitoring the implementation plan will convert it from a recommendation to a mutually accepted and developed program.

Upper management should be included because their involvement will help engender cooperation and commitment to the goals at the lower levels. Both target dates and individuals responsible by name, along with exactly what has to be done, should be established. If necessary, help your customer select the right people for the job.

O   *Progress Review Sessions: Review implementation progress frequently*

Review sessions should be arranged. These sessions must be frequent enough that delinquent activities are spotted before they become serious problems. Your objective is to conduct these customer-supplier meetings with your technical people in attendance. Your management should also be in attendance at the first meeting and at subsequent meetings if there is a potentially serious problem. Never delegate this responsibility. It is your account. You are responsible for ensuring a successful installation and generating repeat business. Your objective is to develop a long-term continuing relationship that will benefit both you and your customer.

Prior to the delivery of your product, follow up the order acceptance by your factory and resolve any issues. Follow up on the delivery commitment and warn the customer of any potential slips before they occur so the customer has time to compensate. Establish appropriate dates and enroll the customer's people in your training course if training is required. Attend, with your customer, the acceptance of their product at your factory. Visit your customer during the installation. Help ensure your customer is up and running as soon as possible after delivery. Repeat business is often proportional to the success of a fruitful implementation program that was mutually established and mutually executed.

○ Maintain a Log: Document the program review meetings

It is essential to keep notes of each review meeting, and confirm specific commitments, schedules, and responsibilities in writing. In high technology sales, these meetings often take place only after there is trouble. If you wish to generate lucrative repeat business, avoid trouble and keep the competition out as well as keep the customer committed, have these periodic review meetings. Through this forum you will stimulate additional purchases before they would otherwise be made. Consequently you will obtain the business quicker and ensure that the customer has the required equipment or product when it is needed.

Since your product will affect other departments, you have legitimate reasons to visit them. During these visits, qualify them for additional business. This legitimacy extends to other divisions, subsidiaries, and executives. If you are clever, you will secure unescorted visitor privileges and have the run of the company.

During these visits, ask a lot of questions of a lot of people to get a lot of information that will help you find and book a lot of incremental business. You will quickly become well known and sought after to discuss issues related to your area of expertise. Through these relationships you can determine new application areas and new projects for your products. By qualifying the associated departments and divisions, you will identify other decision-makers, determine their needs, and find out when they will be ready to buy. Incremental and repeat business will flourish.

CHAPTER

$$\textbf{40}$$

After six calls, forget it

The list of things that can go wrong in a sales situation is awe-inspiring and fear-provoking to both new and seasoned sales people.

If an account is properly qualified, a lost sale means you were outsold. If you do not admit you were outsold and try to find reasons beyond your control for losing, there is no point attempting to recover the order. Only if you admit you were outsold will you be in the right frame of mind to successfully implement the loss-recovery technique.[1]

The sale is lost when you sense it is lost. If your perceptions are good you will know well before a purchase order is placed. If you allow yourself to be deluded into thinking you can't lose, if you are complacent about the account and entertain a false sense of security, or if you are unwary concerning the competi-

[1]Holden, *Vanguard*, (Referenced), (Loss-Recovery is a Holden Tactic).

tion, you will be in a disastrous position by the time you realize you're in trouble.

◯ *Loss Recovery Questions: If you lose a sale, find out why*

As soon as you know or sense you have lost the sale, set up a meeting with the key decision makers. Before the meeting Holden suggests you obtain three important pieces of information.

What are the issues? If you know why the competitor won or why you lost, you can intelligently address the issues at the meeting.

How much time do you have? Find out the nature of the commitment to the competitor. Did the customer place a hard copy purchase order, a letter of intent, or a verbal commitment, or is this information a result of a meeting or hallway chat?

Who knows? If the competitor was smart, they started advertising to the appropriate people in the account that a decision had been made in their favor immediately after securing a commitment.

When the meeting you set up takes place, request as much information concerning the decision as possible for purposes of accurately advising your management why you lost the sale. As you obtain this information, look for a way of providing a mechanism whereby the decision-makers can gracefully and credibly change their decision.

Addressing the issue alone will not turn the order around. If the decision-makers change their minds without good reason, it will reflect negatively on earlier judgments. They want no one to imply that a poor decision was made or to accuse them of vacillating. What you need to do is provide them with a way out, an escape vehicle. An escape vehicle is a new piece of information that might have prompted the decision-makers to decide in your favor if they had had access to it earlier. It is a face-saver.

◯ *The Face-Saver: Don't make the customer admit to a mistake in not buying from you*

A face-saver or escape vehicle need not be complex, or represent some major strength that you have held back. It is not designed to do your selling for you. Addressing the issues will do that. It is merely a way out for the decision-maker, a way that gives you an opportunity to readdress the issues.

Sometimes this can be accomplished by simply taking responsibility for not properly covering a particular objection or benefit. One approach is the **phoenix close.** Like the phoenix, you were consumed by the fires of a lost order; the result of your own action. Also like the phoenix, you have an opportunity to rise from those ashes, reborn, if you act quickly. After being told you lost, as you start to leave, be humble, acknowledge that you made a mistake, it is not the customer's fault. You might say something like, *"… If I could make you feel like I do about my product, you would invest in it. Would you mind telling me where I went wrong?"*

Now be quiet and let the customer respond. When he or she expresses the issue or objection, you express surprise and enthusiastically say, *"Oh, you mean I didn't cover that?"* Then address the issue and attempt to close on the final objection. The escape vehicle for the customer was your failure to cover a particular point.

Other escape vehicles include new information such as an enhanced implementation plan, new product or option, a revised management commitment, or a new financial proposal. Sometimes a new demonstration of your product or the testimonial of a major user will suffice. This all assumes that you have credibility, a good reputation, and rapport with your customer. In other words, they would actually "like to buy from you, but …"

With the key decision-makers armed with an escape vehicle, you are now ready to involve other participants in the decision process to help secure the order for you. If, as is often the case, one or two key decision-makers are adamant, standing by their earlier decision, you will have to involve the rest of the group. Work on them individually and as a group. Get those in favor of the change to apply peer pressure on the hold-outs to motivate them to also change.

Failing this, upper management support may have to be solicited. Going around the decision-makers is dangerous unless done with their blessing, or with the help of others supporting you and involved in the decision.

If unsuccessful, do not give up too quickly. Stay close to the situation. Something may happen that will reopen formal discussions. The competitor could slip. This is not uncommon in high technology sales. Stay close to your inside salesperson and keep him or her chipping away at the decision. During this process, do nothing to compromise your credibility. You want to be remembered as a person whose visits were valuable and worthwhile, and whom the customer will want to buy from in the future, even though your competitor's product was chosen this time.

If successful, stay even closer to the account and advertise. High technology sales are volatile. If you turned it around once, it can be turned around again by your competitor.

○ ### Buyers' Fears: Be aware that buyers may be afraid

Buyers will tell you that salespeople may be impressive, but they will not allow their winning personalities to affect their buying judgment. They will say salespeople who think they must sell themselves before they sell their product are wasting time. All a buyer wants is a quality product or service at a fair price.

In reality, the buyers' behavior is governed by emotions more than they may care to admit. Facts and figures are only part of their decision criteria. Often a buyer is motivated not to buy by fear. this is especially true if the salesperson is offering a new product or technology.[2]

In high technology sales where a committee or team normally makes the buying decision, risk-taking is tempered by the group. Judgments are more rigid. Evaluations are more rigorous. The long buying cycle along with the long approval chains exacerbate the possibility of rejection. Emotional factors will govern the final decision even though it is a group making the decision. The common factor motivating a group not to buy in high technology is the fear of buying a one-of-a-kind white elephant if the product is new and your company or division is just starting out. This fear is linked with the fear of being first and blazing the trail into the unknown. These fears can be countered with the fear of purchasing old technology or with the positive motivation of having done or recommended what is new and right for the company.

Other group fears include a reluctance to change as long as the status quo is acceptable, fear of being criticized for making

[2]Alexander Hamilton Institute, *The Marketing Letter*, Vol. 3, No. 4, July 1976, p. 1, Vol. 3, No. 5, Aug. 1976, p. 5., and Vol. 4, No. 6, Sept. 1977, p. 1.

a mistake, or fear of being turned down by top management. Counteracting fears that can be brought to bear are the fear of being left behind, the fear of being criticized for not acting, and the fear of losing credit or allowing a more venturesome colleague to garner the credit for a courageous decision. On the positive side, the desire to be a leader and innovator will counter these fears.

The customer may agree to buy and give you the order, but if you have not adequately addressed underlying fears, you may be in trouble. The competition is in a position to use scare tactics or a negative sell, to turn the situation in their favor and stop the order or facilitate a cancellation.

In high technology selling, the real selling sometimes starts after the order is signed. If your product requires installation, training, extended delivery schedules, special application hardware, software, or interfacing, the chance of the sale being cancelled is real.

The competition will not give up just because you have the order. As long as there is any doubt in the minds of the group that purchased your product, you are vulnerable to a competitive thrust.

Difficult Buyers: Don't spend too much time with difficult buyers

If you are repeatedly unsuccessful in attempting to sell to an account, do not say, "I'll never take no for an answer!" This is nonsense. Beating your head against a brick wall, hoping the wall breaks, is not persistence but stupidity. You just can't win some accounts. Some people just won't buy from you. If you are a good salesperson and know how to sell, it must be the buyer's problem for not buying rather than yours for not selling.

The buyers who are most difficult to sell are the ones who are indifferent. These buyers will use you as a means to an end. With a cold attitude, they will seek to manipulate you. They care nothing about you, your company, your product, long-term relationships, or their company's long-term needs. They are in business to put you out of business. They want something for nothing.

Do not confuse the indifferent buyer with the buyer who has no interest. The buyer without interest will pay little attention to you, will remain passive, or sometimes become caustic or even antagonistic. Instead of prolonging the sales process, cut it off. Don't ask but tell the buyer you will keep in touch, then move on to bigger horizons.

○ Errors Salespeople Make: Be aware of your own problems

Unfortunately more often than not buyers are justified in their treatment of salespeople. Lack of selling knowledge about delivery dates, shipping data, and billing procedures, inadequate product knowledge, inadequate preparation for the sales call or sales presentation, and lack of authority to negotiate the purchase will annoy buyers and lead to a lost sale.

Improper handling of objections is another common error salespeople make. A satisfactory answer to a valid objection will obliterate it. Treating illegitimate objections, made by the buyer to delay a decision, lightly will cause them to fade away. Defensiveness, assuming your product is unsurpassable, criticizing the competitor, or excessive and continual flattery will irritate the buyers and challenge their judgment rather than overcoming their objections.

Inability to communicate clearly or to ensure that the customer understands you will result in uncertainty. You may clearly understand your technological marvel, its mysteries and advantages, but unless your customers clearly understand its benefits, they will not buy.

Other ways you may lose the sale are by idle talk that wastes the buyer's time; by not making enough quality sales calls on the customer, which due to the demand on the salespersons time is quite common with high technology products. A lack of follow-up service or making promises that can't be fulfilled, which may secure the order initially but can very easily cause you to lose it later through a cancellation, also lose sales.

Other mistakes include the desire to be too careful. If you treat the customers as fragile beings and communicate this feeling through your actions, you will lose their respect. If on the other hand you are dynamic but lack sensitivity to the customers, you will also lose their respect. It is important to sense where the customers are. Treat the customers in a normal manner and try not to undersell or oversell.

Things that are not under your control but that could also cost you the sale, or at least delay it, include loss of budget, change in management, acquisition of the customer's company by another company, a down market, change in technology, change in product, and the like.

○ ### Stop Calling Strategy: Stopping sales calls can be a sales strategy

In any of the aforementioned situations, the big question in most salespeoples' minds is when to cut it off. The unquantified answer is easy: after a predetermined number of calls. Since most sales are made by the fifth call, the most likely number is six. But independent of the exact number, a good salesperson knows when to strategically withdraw and how to follow up the withdrawal.

Following up a strategic withdrawal requires planning. Once you have decided enough is enough with a particular account, do three things. Drop the buyer a personal line on a regular basis with something of interest and with some information on your products. Maintain close contact with someone of influence in the account by telephone and with an occasional lunch. When you know you will be in the area, arrange a visit. Ultimately you will win, and the cost of the win will be low since you planned a minimal but effective follow-up coverage strategy.

This follow-up method also works well with accounts that are friendly but have no need to buy immediately. Of course, with no-need accounts you should be working to create a need.

Poor salespeople give up too early. They mistake the busy buying executive for the no-need, no-interest, or indifferent buyer. A salesperson must learn to differentiate the appearance of hostility or unapproachability from the real thing. If the buyer is just busy and you are persistent, you will eventually be successful. A good rule of the thumb is that once you think you have called enough, when you've just about had it, call once more.

○ ### Sales Ability: Analyze the situation and plan your strategy

If you have sales ability it is doubtful you will ever have to execute a stop-calling strategy. Figure 6 summarizes Parts I and

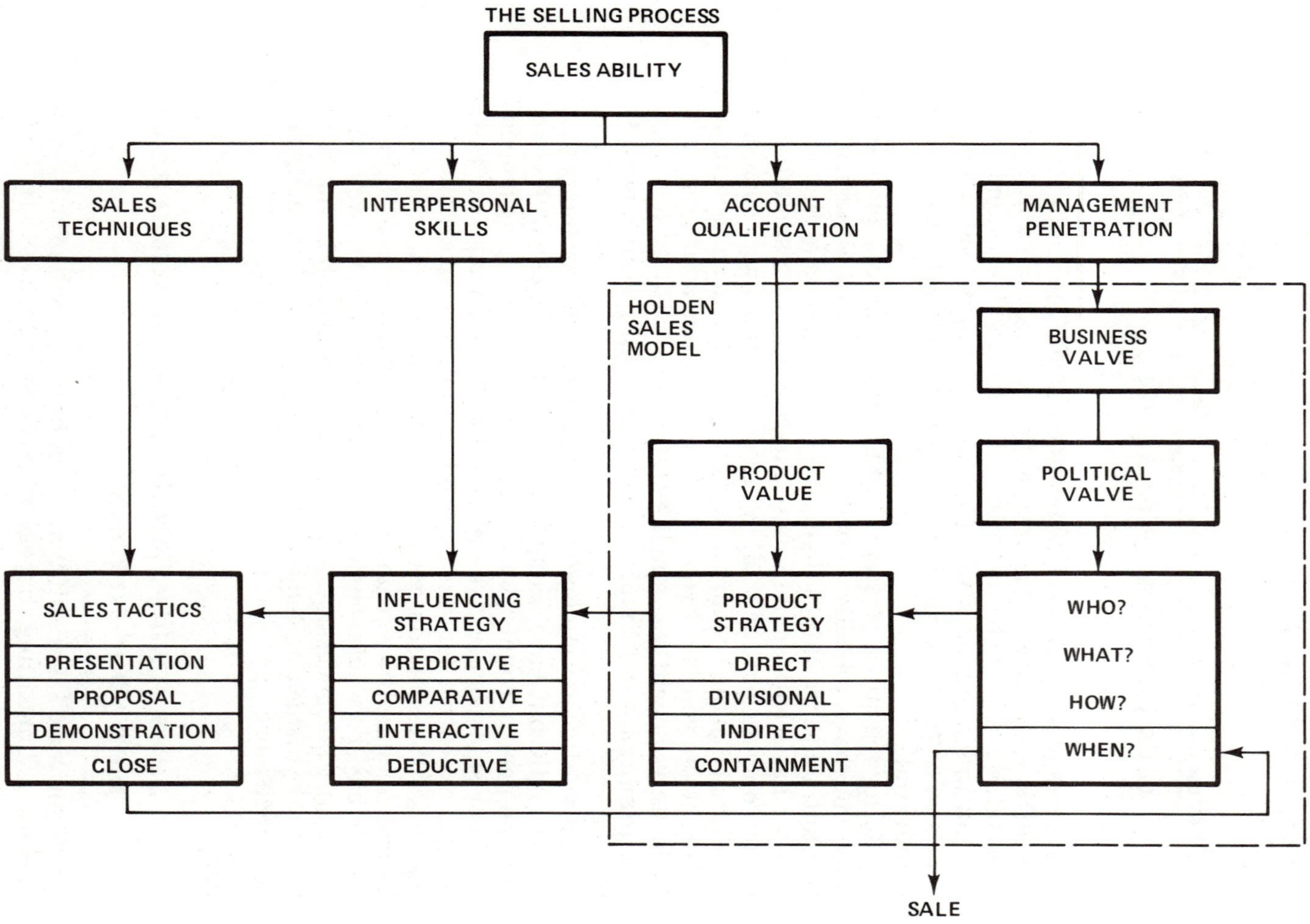

THE SELLING PROCESS

SALES ABILITY

| SALES TECHNIQUES | INTERPERSONAL SKILLS | ACCOUNT QUALIFICATION | MANAGEMENT PENETRATION |

HOLDEN SALES MODEL

| | | PRODUCT VALUE | BUSINESS VALVE |
| | | | POLITICAL VALVE |

WHO?
WHAT?
HOW?
WHEN?

SALE

PRODUCT STRATEGY
DIRECT
DIVISIONAL
INDIRECT
CONTAINMENT

INFLUENCING STRATEGY
PREDICTIVE
COMPARATIVE
INTERACTIVE
DEDUCTIVE

SALES TACTICS
PRESENTATION
PROPOSAL
DEMONSTRATION
CLOSE

Figure 6: The Selling Process

268

II of this book. Sales are a direct result of sales ability. Sales ability encompasses the power to efficiently penetrate the management structure and power base of the account. This must be done to determine the business value for the company in general and the political value to key individuals in particular that you can provide. The sales plan results once you have clearly identified *who* must be sold, *what* value you offer, and *how* you will sell the value you offer.[3]

A second parameter of sales ability is the competency and efficiency of account qualification. Time is not wasted on an account that does not qualify. For a qualified account the product value must be ascertained and a product strategy selected to sell your solution while frustrating the competition.

Skill in interpreting interpersonal relationships is the third parameter of sales ability. Through this interaction the influencing strategy needed to model the situation and develop arguments for decisions is selected.

Influence is then exerted through the organization of the sales motion. Sales techniques and tactics are employed to develop the sales strategy and substantiate the values proffered. The sales strategy, consisting of both a product and political component, unfolds in concert with the influencing strategy as executed by the sales tactics to close the loop, orchestrating *when* the order is placed.

As illustrated in Figure 6, the result of this process is control:

- Control of the company through business value.
- Control of the people through political value.
- Control of the application through product value.
- Control of the competition through product strategy.
- Control of the dynamics through influencing strategy.
- Control of the purchase order timing through tactics.

Part III also focuses on control, control of the sales force and the sales territory.

---

[3]Holden, *Vanguard*, (Referenced).

PART

3

The Manager and
the Territory

CHAPTER

41

Sales managers make things happen

Managing is the process of organizing, leading, and supervising. Organizing requires staffing, leading requires motivating, and supervising requires planning, measuring, and resolving conflict.

○ *Organizing: A sales force needs structure*

A sales organization is built around aggressive, dedicated, success-oriented people. These people function as a team. They do not work for the organization, they are the organization. The sales manager's objective in terms of the organization is to recruit qualified people, then facilitate co-operation. To facilitate co-operation means the sales manager must talk to them then listen, listen, and listen.

○ *Leading: The sales manager must lead the sales force*

In terms of leading, the sales manager says, "This is the objective." The manager then sells the objective, "That is where we want to go, it is a good place to go, and here is what you get once we get there." Then the manager establishes his or her leadership, "I am the person who can get you there."

To lead does not mean to do. The biggest single mistake made by sales managers is bypassing the salesperson on the account and in effect taking over the sales motion and with it the responsibility for the sale. Another common error is for the sales manager to allow another top manager in the company to bypass the salesperson. This is the surest way to lose sales. If the sales is not lost then often money is left on the table or costly follow-up support is given away.

The salespeople with integrity and pride will resign if management regularly bypasses them, regularly visits their accounts without them, especially when they are closing, or otherwise act in a way not consistent with the salesperson's strategy. Experienced and successful salespeople will tell you that the best time for management to visit their account is early in the sales process or after the close. The worst time is during the close.

Inexperienced salespeople will want to bring management in to close the sale for them. Poor salespeople will orchestrate the sales motion to allow management to take over. If the sale is lost, it is not their fault, for after all their management couldn't close. Of course, if they win, it was because of their foresight in bringing management in to close.

Unscrupulous salespeople will set up unsuspecting management to effect a big giveaway such as a significant discount, special support, or unfavorable purchasing terms.

Sometimes experienced salespeople will involve management to negotiate the close. In this case, everything has been predetermined and rehearsed. Management knows the rules and defers to the salesperson at any unexpected turn in the negotiation. The salesperson stays in control.

Company management in general and sales managers in particular should not compete with their salespeople. They must act as a support system, but stay in the background. Sales managers should nurture their salespeople and get their own thrills by vicarious means, that is, through the accomplishments of their salespeople.

○ Motivating: Providing motivation is part of leading

Leading also includes motivating. Motivation can be accomplished through goading, spurring, inducing, or by the more common method in sales, incentive. Ideally the sales manager does not motivate the salespeople but rather develops an environment in which the salespeople will desire to achieve their objectives and not fear to take responsibility for their actions.

Ideally the sales manager says, "Do what you think is best... use your own judgment. I will support you. You have my complete confidence."

In the fast-changing high technology environment, the sales manager earns the respect of the salespeople by taking action and being decisive. Inaction leads to disrespect; indecisiveness results in failure. Action-oriented, decisive managers will prevail because almost everyone else is not.

A motivational environment is one where communications are open. A sales manager understands how to communicate. A manager who understands communicates with the salespeople to effect behavioral change much the same way the salesperson communicates with the customer. Communications can be one- or two-way. Instructions and information may be communicated one way, manager to salesperson, but all other matters should involve feedback. Good two-way communication will lead to a healthy environment. One thing a sales manager must remember is that understanding the message being sent is the responsibility of the sender, not the receiver. The military dictum, "I have not been told is no excuse," does not apply in sales management.

○ Supervising: Supervision can tell you when you are not working toward your goals

Supervising is the process of ensuring that daily operations are taking place in accordance with the planned actions. The first step in planning is to define the objectives and list them along with the tasks required to achieve them. Next, quantify and prioritize the objectives, and, finally, assign the salespeople to implement the strategy to achieve them. Additionally, check-points are defined to measure progress and a process is set in place to resolve issues.

Progress is measured by determining the degree of agreement between actual and planned results, which is then reconciled with the forecast. Resolving conflict involves problem solving. If the sales organization operates as a team and if each person takes 100% responsibility for the success of the team, then problem solving becomes a welcome challenge rather than a stressful, onerous task.

Another important task of a sales manager is to ensure the salespeople are properly trained. A regular training program should be established for both new and experienced salespeople.

In summary, a good sales manager is one who understands the protean or versatile nature of the salesperson, and is able to find and attract successful salespeople, then train and motivate them. The good sales managers are masters at organizing the territory as well as deploying the salespeople in a methodical way. They also know how to sell their factory as they once sold their customers. Finally, they maintain at all times both sales ethics and a quality sales force. In the final analysis, they do not, as another famous person must have said, watch things happen or wonder what happened, they make things happen. They are professionals.

CHAPTER

Your first duty is to get the sale

High technology companies often experience phenomenally high growth. If your company grows fast, is commanding a leading worldwide market share, has sold to virtually every targeted account, is the technological leader in your market segment, and is profitable, beware. You are vulnerable. There may be nowhere to go but down. You are the target of every major competitor in your market place. You may be suffering from the "King of the Mountain" syndrome.

○ **_Keep Your Best Salespeople in Your Best Territory: Take care of your best customers and your best people_**

This syndrome is present when salespeople start to spend most of their time on nonproductive work, when they say their customers are locked in, when they do not pay as much attention to detail as they should, when they take their customers for granted, when they disdain the competitors or write them off, when they become vain, and when deep inside they start to fear they will fail.

Soon sales start to drop off, especially new accounts. Competitors capture some of their key accounts, for which their is always a good excuse. The salespeople start to sell undesigned future products. Price becomes a major issue so that sales are made at a discount, and the big deals that are about to break increase in number but seldom break. The "king" starts to fall off the mountain.

Customers are not loyal. The word customer, simply stated, means those who are accustomed to buying from you, the customary purchaser. In fact a buyer will buy from the most convenient source for the best overall price. Therefore, it is dangerous to assume follow-up business.

Once you capture an account it is important to stay on guard at all times. Do not take your customer for granted. Do not depend upon "friends" in the account. Keep your finger at all times on the pulse of the account. Watch out for new employees in positions of authority who could influence a change in suppliers for a variety of reasons. Above all, don't ever write off the competition. Be prepared to counteract competitive threats. Your competitors are lying in the bushes waiting for the opportunity to attack. Keep your most productive salespeople in your most lucrative territory. Go after the easy sales first. Put new or junior salespeople in new or difficult territories. Keep your best salespeople on your best accounts and reward them for repeat business. Never make a key account a house account by providing sales coverage from the factory with factory personnel. This is an open invitation for the competition to move in.

Ensure your customer continues to perceive the value of your product. Make price concessions for multiple purchases and justify clearly any price increases. Be prepared with credit terms and leasing arrangements (third-party) if required. Keep your service and other support up to standard. Ensure you continuously keep your customer educated about what is happening in your company, especially advance information on new products and options. Maintain good application support and stay on top of the customer's future requirements. If your product fails to perform to the customer's expectations for any reason, resolve the issue immediately.

For key accounts, you may have to ask the factory to provide custom products, options, or software. The customer is naturally willing to pay a premium for special or custom products, and it will behoove you to meet the customer's real needs.

Finally, keep close contact with top management and watch for shifts in company policy, objectives, changes in their products, or changes in their market. If you let your guard down, even for a moment, your competition will move in and you will lose.

○ *Cold Calls: Cold calls are absolutely necessary to building a customer base*

To establish new accounts, cold calls are often necessary. Cold calls are calls on an account by telephone or in person without a reference or an appointment. It is the prospecting function of selling that is avoided by many poor salespeople. In fact, reluctance to make cold calls is their nemesis. They do not like to call on an account unless previous contact has been made.

Many salespeople will tell you they are not drummers selling brushes door-to-door, but sales engineers selling sophisticated high technology products. This may be true, but cold calls or prospecting is a necessary part of the salesperson's job.

If you find your salespeople shuffling papers, only calling on friendly prospects, or just too busy to call on new prospects, they may be suffering from cold call reluctance.

Cold call reluctance does not mean they are lazy. It may mean they are overly concerned about a perhaps unconsciously perceived threat.[1] "What will they think of me?" They have a certain self-perception, and a model of how they would like others to perceive them. They want people to see them that way. If making cold calls does not fit their model, they will develop a reluctance to make them. Unfortunately, we all live in our own reality. Others do not see the world the way we see it. They don't see you the way you think they see you. They are acting too.

[1]Leavitt, *Managerial Psychology*, p. 346.

To overcome this reluctance, teach the salespeople to feel at ease about knocking on doors or in using a more modern method, the telephone. To feel more comfortable, tell them to learn all about the company they are cold calling, whether the call is based on a lead or referral or neither. Also, have them first find out the name of the person they are calling. Tell them not to just call and ask for the engineering manager; the customer will think they are head hunters, recruiting. Finally, have them jot down exactly what they are going to say, and have them practice saying it. Also make certain it contains a value statement.

Their objective is to make an initial account qualification, and obtain an appointment. They should not be afraid to ask questions. There is no such thing as a stupid question. If the person they telephoned is impolite, berates them, or hangs up, tell them not to be discouraged. It's the prospect's loss. The prospect could have been helped with the product. There is almost always a need for a new product.

Sometimes there is also a reluctance to call on unfriendly customers. "He won't return my calls." "I can't get her to see me." "He told me he doesn't need our product; he is perfectly happy with the competitor." All are excuses not to make the sales call. If they use them, they are defaulting to the competitor.

Selling is a process that encompasses cold calls, unfriendly calls, and friendly calls. If they are reluctant to make the first two, and think of them as obstacles rather than simply part of a process, they will be subconsciously prepared for defeat. You'll know exactly why the call will fail, and you'll be 100% correct.

To overcome the reluctance to make cold or unfriendly calls requires discipline through habit. Make firm plans concerning who will be called and when. Make it a point to have the salesperson call at least one unfriendly customer and make at least one cold call a week. Have it done automatically, as programmed work, each week.

Before each call, they should call a satisfied customer. This will boost their morale and make the next call easier. If the "satisfied" customer isn't satisfied when called, they may nip a problem in the bud. This is a secondary benefit of the call. If they get through to their cold or unfriendly target, have them make a firm appointment. Get their foot in the door. They may be selling a sophisticated high technology product but—like the brush salesperson—they still have to get in the door.

○ Incessant Change: Dealing with incessant change is the challenge in high technology sales

The high technology salesperson is also confronted with a myriad of problems to be solved, not the least of which is incessant change. Everything changes over time, but in high technology the change is extremely rapid. In fact, one thing all high technology products and services have in common is rapid evolution. The customer's application may be modified, people may move into different positions, the political situation may shift, the technology may evolve, the salesperson's product may become obsolete even before the sale is made, competitive pressures and dirty tricks may intensify, and the buying terms, conditions, or budgets may be altered. The challenge to the high technology salesperson is to deal effectively with such change.

A salesperson's objective is to manage this change and to change the customer's behavior by motivating the customer to buy. This involves persuasion, influence, and sometimes manipulation, which raise ethical considerations. Ethical considerations include both what a person ought to do and the way it ought to be done. When is it right and when is it wrong for a salesperson to change the customer's behavior to convince them to buy? The core of ethical responsibility consists in doing nothing to *harm* the customer. The bulk of ethical responsibility lies with the salesperson.

A customer who has a problem is vulnerable and open to embarrassment, or even professional destruction, by an unscrupulous salesperson.

○ Integrity: A salesperson must be consistent in speech and action

An ethical salesperson has integrity. Integrity means there will be consistency between what the salesperson says and what the salesperson does.

Integrity is the most valuable attribute a person can possess if he or she is to succeed in a sales career. Integrity is a wholeness, a soundness, rightness, and honesty. Integrity is not easy to measure. To a great extent it is intangible because it implies people are wholes, but made of parts seeking completeness.

Salespeople with integrity are able to take control of their lives. With integrity, a person finds it easier to step forward and commit publicly to personal risk and then take responsibility for the results. The key to success in any endeavor, but especially in the complex, ever-changing high technology sales environment, is to have the inner strength to accept responsibility for your actions.

The customer believes that what the salesperson is selling to solve the problem is what he or she will actually get. In other words, the value is real. Consequently the salesperson must be careful in explaining what the product will actually do. If there is a misunderstanding, it should be corrected prior to accepting the order. Customer satisfaction is a test of the salesperson's integrity.

Of course customers are sometimes unreasonable, or the product does not perform as the salesperson was led to believe it would. In these cases, the salesperson is not directly at fault, but is still faced with a problem he or she must work to solve.

A salesperson's first duty is to get the sale. In high technology, the sale is a long-term relationship with the customer which will result in repeat sales. With an established account relationship, the salesperson will have a significant advantage. The salesperson must nurture this relationship both by stressing the long-term benefits to the customer and by developing trust and credibility.

An ethical, trusting, and credible relationship occurs when integrity is present during the selling process. If the salesperson and the customer are intellectually honest with each other, and if they respect one another, their relationship will be authentic and reliable. Sham, pretense, and deceit will be eliminated. A healthy and synergistic association will result.

The sales manager's first duty is to foster this association. The sales manager ensures that the sales forces' concern for making the sale does not supersede concern for the customer. The sales manager instills integrity in the sales force.

CHAPTER

(43)

Do not base decisions on hope or fear

Although almost anyone willing and determined can develop into a salesperson, high technology salespeople must be professionals to survive. They must act and think like professionals and look upon sales as the honored profession it really is. They view themselves not as hucksters, but as professional problem solvers dedicated to legitimately trying to help their customers.

○ Types of Salespeople: Avoid these salesperson stereotypes

There are other types of salespeople. The trite, vulgar, commonplace, or hackneyed salesperson is called a **hack**. The hack is obtuse—the proverbial "Kit Kitych." The hack chases all warm bodies capable of purchasing the product without first qualifying the account, is heedless of company policy and philosophy, and is uncaring about the customer's true needs.

The hack, although uncomprehending of the big picture, and obtuse in terms of long-term objectives, is often sly. Sometimes, the hack wins, but often at the expense of both his or her company and the customer.

Superficial hacks hope to win and charge forward *totus procus* without regard or understanding of the consequences. They are hard sellers who overstate their product's merits, criticize the competitors, and make almost any concession necessary to get the sale. Hard sellers have little concern for the customer because they believe the customer will only buy under pressure, and won't regret buying the product. If the customer does regret it, "so what?" is often the hard seller's attitude. Outwardly, these hacks may appear confident, but, if probed, the depth of conviction is shallow, careless, and unconcerned. These insouciant salespeople use brute force as their tactic.

The **hesitant hacks** also hope to win, but due to indecisiveness and hesitation, are often too late. These demurrers seeing the correct course of action, instead of taking it, will object, study, delay, or look for approval. They are order takers with little or no sense of urgency. They have little concern for the customer because they assume the customer knows what he or she wants and can't be influenced anyway. By the time these hacks act, any advantage has diminished or disappeared.

Insecure hacks don't listen to the customer, are unable to face the fact that they may lose, and jump on insignificant sympathetic statements as indications that they are winning. These eviscerate salespeople interpret the customer's compassion as a sign they will get the order. They think they're winning when in reality they are losing. They find that the customers sometimes love them, but buy from their competitors. Such salespeople lack the vital force, the concupiscence necessary to win.

Superficial, hesitant, and insecure salespeople make decisions based on hope. They lose.

Reactive hacks react to their own fears. Fear that they will lose drives them to try too hard. Fear that customers will not believe them drives them to oversell. If the customer responds with an objection, they will often overreact or, worse yet, become defensive or excited and argue or challenge the customer.

Whereas the reactive hacks fear is directed inward, the **weeper-wailer's** fears are focused outward. The weeper-wailers always see disaster and are always sure they are losing because nothing is ever right at the home office. Prior to a customer visit the weeper-wailers hover over the factory like mother hens.

When the customer says jump, they ask how high. They are out of control or, worse yet, under the customer's control. The weeper-wailers' fear of losing impells them to make unnecessary commitments. In fact, they give away the store. They're intimidated by the customer's many "last and final offers." They panic when putting together proposals or going to a negotiation. They back off into an ostrich stance if the issues appear overwhelming. They are also intimidated by status or power.

Affected hacks are also motivated by fear. The most important issue for these salespeople is their personal reputation. A false sense of honor prevails. and they pay little regard to anything else. They are often insincere and hypocritical. From the customer's perspective, their fear is perceived as a lack of faith in their product, company, or themselves. From the employer-company perspective, this poseur appears intractable and intransigent.

Reactive, weeper-wailer, and affected salespeople make decisions based on fear. They also lose.

There are other hacks who operate furtively from both hope and fear. These people are more difficult to detect. They are the **dichotomistic hacks.** They worry about the needs of the customer out of proportion to the customer's expectations. If they are managing a field sales force, they constantly worry about losing their people and often drive the factory to provide support beyond what is required.

Dichotomists allow humanitarianism and compassion to supersede good business judgment. They hope to make everyone happy. They fear adversity from customers, peers, or subordinates, yet, paradoxically, they engender displeasure from the home office.

Their dichotomy manifests itself when they deal with the factory. They are often reproached for their biased concern for customers. They think the customer is always right—and they lack empathy for their own company. The dichotomists have difficulty controlling short term situations to realize long-term gain. They feel the home office owes the customer even before the customer has purchased. They feel the home office should not take hard positions in negotiations.

Their loyalties are confused by their fear of incurring a customer's displeasure and their hope of bringing in the order by being obliging. Dichotomistic hacks usually have influential benefactors within the company so they are difficult to dislodge. They are costly, and once discovered, should be removed. Confused or contradictory loyalties result in expensive or lost sales.

○   ## The Problem Solver: Salespeople should consider themselves problem solvers

The salespeople with a more compatible image for selling high technology products are the **problem solvers.** These salespeople are concerned about making the sale but also have genuine concern for the customer. Problem solvers look for opportunities by prospecting for customers with problems or needs who will appreciate a good solution or suggestion. They analyze the data they collect by studying what has gone before, by developing a willingness to question everything learned, and by not being overly dependent on the way it was done before. In other words, they are innovative and at times even creative. They are professional strategic planners.

Problem solvers also have the customers' long term interests at heart. They know a customer will not benefit from the wrong product, so they qualify their accounts. Although they sell for the love of selling, they also sell to make a contribution to both the customer and their own company. If an attempt is made to coerce them into misleading the customer they will resign; yet they will always work to advance their company to its legitimate objectives. Above all they care.

Although they may be called by a variety of names such as account executive, product specialist, consultant, field representative, manufacturers representative, sales engineer, sales agent, marketing representative or sales counselor, they are proud to say they are salesmen or saleswomen.[1]

In terms of the sales force, it is the sales manager's duty to find, train, and support the professional problem solvers while ferreting out the hacks who make decisions based on hope or fear.

[1]Alexander Hamilton Institute, *The Marketing Letter,* Vol. 3, No. 4, Jul. 1976, p. 6, and Vol. 3, No. 6, Sept. 1976, p. 3.

CHAPTER

Don't hire the sales candidate who says, "The customer is always right!"

There are three steps to follow when you select a sales candidate: review the resume in detail, interview the candidate, and check the references. Take your time and find the right person. In high technology sales, a sales manager is often looking for a person with a technical background from design engineering, field service, applications, or software engineering.

A person who understands capital equipment selling but is not highly technical should not be overlooked for a high technology sales position. Business issues such as investment return, cost of ownership, and other financial considerations are growing in importance as a deciding factor in the purchase of high technology, high-ticket capital equipment.

○ ## Review the Resume: Does the resume sell the candidate?

When you review the resume, look for the ones that sell. This is the candidate's advertisement. It should be action-oriented and bulletized. In this context, bullets mean a series of one-liners or brief, vigorous, direct, simple sentences. The resume should be double-spaced between categories, neatly typed, one page, two at most, and personalized.

Look for an accompanying cover letter that lists the candidate's objectives. Both the letter and the resume should be free of errors and be interesting, catching your attention. The resume will tell you a lot about the candidate and help you screen out those not qualified. It will give you data on the candidate's schooling, work experience, accomplishments and sales knowledge, but it is a two-dimensional piece of paper, not the candidate.

○ ## Interviewing: Make candidates sell themselves.

Once you have screened the candidates based on their resumes, or the recommendations of others, they must be interviewed. At least four people should interview the candidates: the sales manager, a person not directly involved, such as the purchasing agent, an upper management person, and the personnel manager. These interviews are the most important element in the entire hiring process.

In interviewing, do not depend upon the individual's past responsibilities, but review in depth their past accomplishments. Analyze the results of their current and previous jobs. Look for a results-oriented person rather than a hard worker.

Tests may be administered by the personnel department—especially aptitude and psychological tests—but the results are only useful as supplementary data. Their worth is usually to confirm what the interviewing process has already told you.

In interviewing, select the characteristics or traits important to you and weigh them with factors of 10, 5, and 2. Then rate each candidate on a scale of 4 to 1, with 4 equal to excellence, 3, good, 2, passable, and 1, unacceptable. The sum of the weighing factors multiplied by the rating for each trait gives you the candidate's score.

These scores result in a comparison of how the interviewers rated the candidates. This is not a scientific method, and a hire or not to hire decision should not be based on these scores alone. If a candidate scored high in everything except integrity, you might be taking a significant risk in hiring the person. The value of the scoring is in the common base among interviewers. In discussing the candidate, the scores point out differences in the interviewers' perceptions, even though subjective.

Category I, with a weight of 10 for each trait, includes sales experience, empathy, enthusiasm, ego-drive (ambition), and integrity. Category II, with a weight of 5, includes persuasiveness, persistence, and perception. Category III, with a weight of 2, includes control, thoroughness, compatibility, dedication, stress handling ability, creativity, and organizational ability.

Other important qualities are: loyalty, technical skills, appearance, sociability, verbal skills, ability to listen, ability to follow instructions, and competitiveness. Independent of the rating, the recommendations or references of others and your own intuition are important decision-making criteria. No matter how the candidate fares in tests or even some parts of the interview, if you feel the person will make it, if other interviewers feel the same, and if analysis of the previous job substantiates this, you may want to take a chance and hire the person anyway.

Fifteen typical interviewing questions for a sales candidate follow. The interviewers look for and rate specific traits. For the questions to reveal the trait mentioned, skill on the part of the interviewer is required.

"Tell me about yourself."

Your objective is to relax the interviewee and obtain some general information about his personal or business background. Observe how he presents himself and if he tries to take control of the interview. Grade on control.

"What do you know about our company?"

See if the interviewee has researched your company. The more she knows about your company, the better. It shows she does her homework and would probably research a potential customer before trying to sell the product. Grade on thoroughness.

"Why do you want to work for us?"
Find about his objectives. See how specific he is. Find out about his career plans, where he wants to be in five years, and his compensation expectations. Look for his motivations and ambition. Grade on ego-drive.

"How does your spouse or significant other feel about your coming to work for us?"
Find out about her family life. Find out more about her personal life. Grade on compatibility.

"Are you willing to travel? What percentage of your time?"
In a sales position, extensive travel may be required. It is important to get this issue on the table early. Find out if there are any blocking issues. Grade on dedication.

"Why do you think you are qualified for this job?"
Find out what qualities he thinks he possesses. How much emphasis does he put on experience? Look for empathy and persuasion. See how convincing he is. Grade on persuasiveness.

"What is your major weakness? What is the worst thing you have ever done, or the worst mistake you ever made in your business life?"
See how candid she is. Look for indications of stress or pessimism. See if she holds herself or others responsible. See if she appears honest and candid. Grade on ability to handle stress.

"What is your major strength? What is the thing you are most proud of having accomplished in your business life?"
Look for optimism, pride, modesty, humility, and straightforwardness. Grade on enthusiasm.

"Sell me this pen." or, for experienced salespeople, "Sell me on buying the product you are currently selling."
See how she goes about presenting the pen. Grade on creativity.

"Are you a team player or an individualist?" "Explain."
Watch the body language. See if it supports the verbal response. No matter what the response, respond with a negative

non-verbal message. Ham it up a little if necessary. Observe the reaction. Grade on perception.

"What factors do you think result in upward mobility in a company like this?"
See if he understands the importance of politics in an organization. Regardless of his response, continuously challenge it. See if he sticks by his guns. See how much conviction he has. Grade on persistence.

"How do you relate to me?" "How do you 'feel' what is important to me?"
Observe how she responds. Does she draw you out then self-disclose? Grade on empathy.

"How much sales experience have you had?"
Find out how, where, and what he has sold. Find out what he has accomplished. Grade on sales experience.

"How do you manage your time?" "How would you manage a sales force?"
See what her personal and business philosophy is. See if she thinks like your company thinks. Grade on organizational ability.

"What do you think about the statement 'The customer is always right'?"
If he agrees with it, do not hire him. He will be expensive, overcommit resources, expect too much of the company, and have confused loyalties. He may also be reactionary, especially under pressure from the customer. His first inclination will be to give the customer anything the customer requests. He will also be a poor negotiator because his sympathies will be with the customer. Through judicious questioning about buyer and seller rights, you can gauge honesty, integrity, and sincerity. Grade on integrity.

Check References: Some things do not come out in the interview

For each candidate who successfully passes the interviewing process, thoroughly check references. Although the salespeople may do an excellent job selling you on their qualifications for the job and their compatibility with you and your company, they could also end up being a problem. Good salespeople will try a trial close somewhere in the interview, usually toward the end. Don't make it easy for them, and don't offer an opening to close.

Conduct a telephone reference check with the employer or employers of the candidates for the previous three years. If it is not possible to contact their immediate employer, contact others who know the candidates and can speak about them professionally. Also meet their families. See if their family life is success-oriented and conducive to a successful career.

By taking this systematic and precise approach you are likely to avoid costly mistakes when you hire salespeople.[1]

○ *Sales Attributes: Things to look for in a salesperson*

The following list of attributes should be considered when selecting a sales candidate or evaluating the performance of a salesperson. Certain attributes such as integrity, attitude, and ego-drive, if lacking, are clear reasons not to hire a candidate or even to dismiss an existing salesperson.

- Sales experience, track record and accomplishments
- Customer and product knowledge
- Ego-drive, enthusiasm and motivation
- Empathy, persuasiveness, ability to listen and communicate nonverbally
- Honesty and integrity, (once agreed stays committed)
- Articulation, appearance and sense of presence
- Problem solver, creative, or innovative
- Nonreactionary, ability to handle stress, assertiveness, and control
- Attitude and compatibility of philosophy

---

[1]Alexander Hamilton Institute, *The Marketing Letter*, Vol. 2, No. 7, Oct. 1975, p. 8.; Vol. 3, No. 2, May 1976, p. 1; and Vol. 3, No. 3, Jun. 1976, p. 1.

- Persistent, responsive, thorough, and follows through
- Benefit, value and concept oriented, rather than a seller of features
- Proposal, presentation and demonstration ability
- Strategic thinker, tactical implementer through planning
- Politically astute and able to penetrate management
- Exercises good account control and knows how to influence others
- Forecast ability and knowledgeable about the competition
- Organized, has control over the factory, and makes good use of resources
- Ability to overcome objections and negotiate
- Recognizes buying signals and can close
- Team player, dedicated and loyal.

CHAPTER

Just about anybody can learn to sell

From reading this book, it should now be apparent why salespeople must have ego-drive, the desire to win, and the persistence to pursue a sale to its conclusion; why they must possess empathy, the ability to perceive things not obvious, a sensitivity to subtleties of expression, and the skill to think and feel as the customer thinks and feels; and product knowledge, the knowledge necessary to understand and innovatively solve customer problems, and to persuasively present the product. But salespeople must also be positively motivated with confidence in themselves and able to broadcast this with enthusiasm to others. Finally, salespeople must understand the business.

○   *Learning the Skills: Know what can and cannot be taught*

The controversy over whether selling skills are innate unacquirable talents, or learnable skills, has raged since the advent of the psychology discipline. Although it may be difficult, if not impossible, to increase a person's intelligence or change a person's personality, it is not impossible to teach a person to be goal-oriented, to be empathetic, and to understand the market, customer, and product.

A person can be taught to pursue an objective to its conclusion, which will suffice in many sales situations for ego-drive. Training abounds on how to learn to be empathetic and sensitive, read body language, and improve perceptions. The product can be mastered through personal application and study. To learn how to develop innovative or creative solutions to customer problems, a person can enroll in creativity training. Creativity is not a mystical process, reserved for the subconscious, but a method or way of thinking that can be learned.

Enthusiasm is a function of motivation. Motivational training and seminars are plentiful. Training in both generic selling skills and streetwise strategy applications is also available. Therefore, anyone should be able to learn to sell.

Bernie Cornfeld once employed 16,000 salespeople. When asked what kind of people he looked for to sell his product, he said, "... just about anybody will do." With the proper training and motivation, almost anyone can be turned into a first-class salesperson.

○   *Sales Experience: Good business sense is essential to becoming a high technology salesperson*

Another factor that must be considered when hiring a salesperson, especially in high technology sales, is sales experience in a business sense. In the customer's eyes, the salesperson is the company's representative. From the company's perspective, the salesperson is ultimately responsible for the profits of the business. Therefore, the salesperson must not only be businesslike, but must understand the business, as he or she develops the customer's trust.

Poor salespeople believe the customer is always right, and reject new ideas. They believe nothing will help because up until now, nothing has. Gunther Klaus says, "You can tell a bad salesperson because he always sells what you ain't got in inventory, always talks about the big deal that is about to break but never does, always sells cheaper than the competition, and has bad taste in clothes."[1]

Salespeople may possess good selling skills but lack business knowledge about the product, market, and the customer. This knowledge is as important as the selling skills.

A good, businesslike salesperson knows how to analyze the customer's business, how to relate to the customer's objectives, and how to question to qualify, and can then tailor the sales strategy in terms of the customer's business rather than the salesperson's product.

Experienced professional salespeople know how to go about knowing their customers. Knowledge about the customer's business and application differentiates the top performers from the mediocre salespeople. Salespeople may know their products inside and out, but if they do not understand the customer's application and cannot translate the product features into business benefits, they will lose. Product knowledge is necessary, but knowledge about the product application and business is essential.

Yet, although salespeople can certainly learn and benefit from experience, experience is not necessarily the best teacher for playing the sales game. When Francisco Pizarro was surrounded by 50,000 Incas, he invited one hundred of their leaders to a banquet, then pounced upon them, killing or imprisoning them. Leaderless, the other 49,900 Incas surrendered. General Custer at Little Big Horn had not benefitted from the knowledge of Pizarro's experience.

Admiral Togo began the Russo-Japanese war with a surprise attack on the Imperial Russian Pacific fleet that lay at anchor in Port Arthur. With speed and surprise helped by the laxness and unpreparedness of the Russians, he put their ships out of action. Thirty-eight years later, the Japanese did it again at Pearl Harbor, and the Americans mirrored the Russian's shocking command failure.

Awareness of history, as with experience in sales, does not automatically spell success. Experience alone does not neces-

[1]Klaus, *Marketing by Objective,* (Referenced).

sarily result in the correct action. Success is a result of looking at each situation as a unique set of circumstances and making no assumptions about it. The successful salesperson draws upon his or her experiences and learns from them, but does not rely upon them.

Selling is not autodidactic. It is difficult if not impossible for people without natural sales ability to teach themselves how to sell. Yet those without natural sales ability can be trained to sell.

Management consultant Edward B. Reynolds told the Alexander Hamilton Institute's Marketing Letter; "Success in sales is a function of self-discipline, sound work habits, effective time utilization, and recognition of customer needs and their unique problems." He went on to say, "Key ingredients for successful selling can be taught and learned, provided that the sales management understands the nature of those ingredients."[2]

Sales ability is not a rare gift, but a learnable skill.

[2]Alexander Hamilton Institute, *The Marketing Letter,* (Referenced).

CHAPTER

46

Most sales training is disastrous

There is no right or wrong way to sell. There is only your way. If it works, it is right. If it does not work, you have a problem. Everyone has his or her own style, methods, and ideas.

○ *Control in Sales: Remaining in control of the selling process is the key to successful sales*

What works for one salesperson or was successful for one sales trainer may not work or result in success for you. The best sales training provides you with information on how to manage yourself, your customer, your company, your competitor, and, most important, your time.

Control of the sales process is the key to successful selling. Sales trainers can show you techniques, help you improve your sales abilities, show you how to better read and understand people, or put you in the right frame of mind through motivational hype. But unless you know how to think strategically, unless you *are* in control, all may be for naught.

Therefore, learn what you can from the various sales training courses your company may put you through, but, more important, learn how to gain and maintain account control. Jim Holden, president of The Holden Corporation, which specializes in high technology sales and sales management training programs, says, "Achieving success in any process is a function of control. And that's certainly the case in selling where the salesperson must set the pace for the competition. He must lead, not follow, to get and maintain a competitive advantage and stay on top in the buyer's mind."[1]

◯ On The Job Training: The most expensive training is by critique of actual selling

Good sales managers who help and guide their salespeople may not be qualified to train them. The managers may be well versed in selling fundamentals and may have good selling techniques, but it doesn't necessarily follow that they have the ability to impart their knowledge effectively to others. They can provide counsel, point out weak selling methods, and motivate. The best way sales managers train salespeople is on the job.

This training is accomplished through joint calls on accounts, and critiques of the meetings immediately afterward. During the customer visit, the sales manager can do the selling while the salesperson observes, or they can sell jointly.

If the sales manager acts as an observer and lets the salesperson sell, it will be difficult (if not impossible) for the manager not to jump in if the salesperson gets in trouble. Ideally, the sales manager should remain an uninvolved observer, even if it means losing the sale. If the sales manager is charged with training the sales force, the manager must sit on the sidelines and train through coaching, and never play on the field of direct physical action. This training can be expensive. It

[1] Holden, *Vanguard*, (Referenced).

may also be a waste of the manager's time since the desired improvement in the salesperson could be more quickly realized through a more formal training method.

○ *Streetwise Selling: How to control the competition*

The major objective of a Holden Training Program is to improve productivity. Sub-objectives include steepening the salesperson's learning curve, shortening the sales cycle, and extending management's capacity. If the objective and sub-objectives are achieved, the result will be increased profits, decreased cost of sales, reduced turnover, and an increase in bookings per salesperson.

The elements of a productivity-oriented sales training program were developed to increment sales. The program is streetwise rather than academic or esoteric. The streetwise approach focuses on the competition and addresses competitive issues. It teaches how to control the competition. It is independent of style. It does not tell you how to sell but arms you with techniques to put you in control in the selling situation and to help you manage your time.

It is not tutorial but interactive and team-oriented. It ensures that everybody is involved so they can exchange ideas, pool experience, share existing skills, and try new techniques. It is customized to real-life sales situations you are facing today. This makes it both meaningful and pragmatic. Finally, it covers the political component of selling. The objective is to arm you with the ability to develop political insight that will enhance your control of the selling situation.

This program should not be confused with a generic verbal or nonverbal training course that focuses on how to sell and is designed for people who have not sold before. Productivity training is geared for people who have actively sold or are actively selling. It emphasizes methods that concentrate time and energy to gain the best sales advantage. It provides practical solutions.

○ *Training Is On-Going*

Training, like selling, effects behavioral change. Change is not binary, but a continuous process that must be continually reinforced. Therefore, training is on-going. One training session will not do it for you. You must have follow-up activity. Follow-up training will enhance your investment from the initial training. Follow-up seminars or workshops will reinforce the techniques previously learned.

The best workshops are competitive counter-strategy sessions focused on specific accounts or current sales situations. These are powerful training methods that can facilitate immediate results. In these workshops, opposing teams test sales strategies through competitive counter-analysis. You will relate sales concepts and techniques in a spirit of camaraderie.

One advantage of this training program is compatibility with almost any existing in-house course or other generic, theoretical- or psychological-based program or course that attempts to teach you how to sell. In essence, it enhances the benefits of these other courses.

To implement this training plan, first discuss feasibility with the trainer and develop a pilot plan. This results in a proposal. If acceptable, the program is then tailored to your specific needs. The trainer must develop insight into your product and market objectives. The program should complement any in-house training or previous training as well as the experience and philosophy of your sales team and company.

Next comes field preparation, where the trainer talks with key field sales personnel, concentrating on field problems and competitive issues for enhanced tailoring. The training program is then implemented and followed up three to six months later with workshops for tracking results, and reinforcing past training.

A program developed along the lines presented here will result in control in the selling process, a clear understanding of the political component of selling, the skill to implement what was learned, and the ability to analyze the outcome. The net result will be an increase in productivity and incremental sales.

Jan Marini of Janayne Consulting, San Jose, California, a training organization, says:

"There is *no such thing* as one approach to fit every need or purpose. To ensure success and be cost effective, the following must be included in any training program:

"A thorough needs analysis to assess training requirements and recommend programs.

"Indepth contact with key individuals and organizational procedures prior to training in order to tailor all instruction to meet specific needs.

"Follow-up procedures to monitor results for continued impact and productivity.

"Facilitators that are chosen to instruct only those classes for which they have expert qualifications and credibility.

"Special 'train the trainer' packages that enable companies to implement classes in internal training programs.

"A personal relationship that encourages mutual trust and expert advice."[2]

For a sales training program to be cost effective, it must be focused on a specific subject, tailored for a specific company, and reinforced with follow-up workshops.

---

[2]Jan Marini, Janadyne Consulting, 1150 N. First St., No. 150, San Jose, CA 95112. Excerpt from her sales letter.

CHAPTER

Superstars can help the average performers

A sales organization consists of salespeople. Some are strong, some are average, and some are weak. In a typical sales organization, 80 percent of the sales will come from 20 percent of the salespeople. The superstars, those 20 percent who continually bring in the orders, should be nurtured, protected, well-paid, and recognized as key contributors. Most important, they should be left alone to do what they do best—close orders.

The weak salespeople should be given other jobs.

This leaves the average performers. A progressive sales-manager will use the talents of the superstars in group sessions to help the average performers work at their best level of achievement.

○ ## *Role-Playing: Role-playing is an especially effective training method*

Salespeople, especially experienced salespeople, frequently express negative opinions about role-playing. In fact, they question sales training in general. They may openly challenge the methods and ideas being advocated, and if they participate in role-playing, do so passively or react defensively.

They claim role-playing is childish. In fact they may simply be upset because their personal egotistical needs for status and self-esteem are challenged. They fear they may be embarrassed during the role-playing, hence hesitate to take part. Conversely, others may ham it up, emphasizing acting instead of concentrating on the problem at hand.

Role-playing is a laboratory method. It is the spontaneous acting out of a realistic situation. Dialogue involuntarily grows out of the situation as it develops. In some respects, it is better than the real thing or a true experience because it permits techniques of observation, discussion, and emphasis. Participants are often videotaped, then a critique is made during a replay. The value of such a critique is in question. If the videotape creates tension and embarrassment, why use it? People can certainly describe what went on by taking notes.

On the other hand, in going back over the tape, people not only hear what they said but can watch how they said it. They can observe their nonverbal language. If having others see the tape is the person's concern, it could be viewed in private.

Role-playing has some drawbacks. It is time-consuming and requires experienced trainers or "actors" playing the customer. The role of the customer is critical to the success of the role-playing.

An advantage of role-playing is that it speeds up experiences. What happens in a day of role-playing might take months or years to experience in real life situations. Also, many different approaches to a problem may be tried.[1]

People role-play every day, sometimes without knowing it. All it takes to role-play a sales situation is a little imagination and a little courage. Once into the *role,* the *playing* often becomes *real.* Role-playing can be a powerful tool for training salespeople, but it must be introduced carefully.

[1]Keith Davis, Ph.D., *Human Behavior at Work,* Organizational Behavior, (New York, NY: McGraw-Hill, Inc., 1977) pp. 181-182.

○ *Role-Play Example*

The following scenario typifies a role play situation:

Your product: Automatic Tester

Customer: Kongsware

Organizational Chart: Larry President
           Bill   Department Manager
           John Test Manager
           Jerry Program Manager

Competition: Company A
         Company B

SALES SITUATION (TO THOSE ROLE-PLAYING THE SALESPEOPLE)

General Comments:

Kongsware has been using competitor A and sending more complex products to a test laboratory that has competitor B testers. John is the head of the Test Group. He is an old-line hardware guy, very powerful within the company, and outspoken. He believes if you can't touch it, it ain't real. Jerry was just hired into the organization from IBM®. Jerry was recommended by the president of Kongsware, and hired by John's boss. Jerry is John's peer but his exact job is unclear. Kongsware is considering a new tester from Company A, and your company. Competitor B is a dark horse. John feels that competitor A has the hardware covered and software will naturally follow. He feels competitor B is too dependent on software. He likes your tester architecture but feels competitor A is ahead of your product in demonstrated hardware.

You have arranged a meeting with Jerry to talk about your software. Jerry has informed you that John made his decision for competitor A but that he will still attend the meeting. Jerry indicates he feels software is important but, since he is new, must respect John's decision. As you enter the meeting, John's boss, Bill, is present. Bill's major concern is getting on-line fast, hence he likes competitor B. You quickly scope the situation and ascertain: Bill—competitor B, John—competitor A, Jerry—unknown.

John says that you have 20 minutes of their time to discuss the issues. Bill's hot button is return on investment, John's is hardware, and Jerry's is software. You know your product has some hardware deficiencies compared to competitor A, but is clearly superior to both in terms of software, which means a better return on investment.

CUSTOMER SITUATION (TO THOSE ROLE-PLAYING THE CUSTOMER)

Bill was informed by his boss that the company must focus on software in all areas if they are to succeed, but he is unwilling to make any substantial investments to do so. Larry recommended Bill hire Jerry, who is a software expert from a computer company. Jerry is new but also knows he must make his mark quickly if he is to be successful in Kongsware. John resents Jerry since he is not sure why he was hired. He is concerned that Jerry has arranged this meeting and that Bill is present to override John's well-publicized decision to buy from competitor A.

John is politically astute and will change his decision if he sees personal benefit in doing so. If the salesman can convince Bill of his return on investment benefits, and Jerry of the software benefits, John will change his decision—but not easily. The salesperson's argument must be convincing but not challenging. John must not lose face. The salesperson must create doubt and in doing so, give John an escape vehicle so that he can gracefully change his decision.

This can be done by focusing on software via Jerry with new data not previously shared with John, and taking responsibility for not sharing this data. If coupled with the return on investment advantages, the thrust will be more powerful.

The participants now act out their assigned roles, then critique the activity learning from the experience.

○ *Creativity: Encourage creativity by holding group training sessions*

Group sessions can be very effective in developing innovative or creative ideas. In a group session, individuals familiar with the problem are teamed with individuals familiar with the accounts, product, and selling strategy. Together the group members will often produce ideas in rapid succession.

Innovation is the ability to take a given set of facts or conditions and from them reach a conclusion, or generate an idea, that is a variation or departure from the obvious. Innovation gives way to creativity when the idea is original.

Innovation or creativity requires the interaction of the rational, analytical, and organized portion of the mind with the irrational, instinctive, emotional, and illogical portion. Consequently, creative people are often imaginative, intuitive, manipulative, and somewhat rebellious.

Contrary to popular belief, innovative thinking is a learned skill. Generating new responses and new ideas based on old or existing data takes practice. Innovation requires some imagination, spontaneity, and an openness unhindered by routine. An impediment to innovative thinking is the inability to see alternative methods to the methods entrenched in your mind.

Innovation and creativity may well be a function of unconscious thinking. Creative people, after gathering and assimilating the facts, consciously forget the issues for a time. Often after a sort of incubation period, the solution to the problem, or a unique strategy, comes to mind.

On the other hand, innovation and creativity may have nothing to do with unconscious thinking, and simply result from relaxing the mind after strenuous attention to the problem. Creativity and innovation are enhanced by looking at the problem from different, sometimes irrational points of view. Illogic often illuminates the solution.[2]

○ *Counter-Strategy Workshop: A counter-strategy workshop uses top salespeople to help average salespeople*

The "counter-strategy session" is a forum for innovation that can also effectively tap the superstar's talent. These sessions will allow management, top salespeople, and the average salespeople to share information and gain insight about competitive activity. If the session is focused on a specific account,

[2]Ivey, *Counseling and Psychotherapy*, pp. 25-29.

it becomes a powerful sales training method that can facilitate immediate results.[3]

In a counter-strategy session focused on a specific account, the account situation is analyzed by the group and a strategic sales plan is developed to counter the competition. An intensive analysis of the plan follows. The top salespeople then work with the average performers on how best to tactically execute the plan. The session should take place at least quarterly, and may be expanded to include sales forecasting. Sessions can also be localized to specific sales territories.

Once a strategy is developed and tested, the group should break up into three teams. One team portrays the customer, one the competitor, and one your company's sales team. The sales team tries to execute the counter-strategy, the competitor's team tries to stop them, and the customer team acts as the unbiased judge.

This is not a role-play per se, where any person or team is being tested, but a method of testing the plan. Interaction should not last more than fifteen minutes without a critique. The customer team keeps notes on the effectiveness of the strategy. The competitive team has an advantage over the real competitor since they know the sales team counter-strategy. If the sales team's counter-strategy can hold up under these conditions, they have a good chance to win in the real situation.

After this interaction, the counter-strategy is modified to reflect the changes resulting from the group strategy session. Through counter-strategy sessions, the complete sales team benefits from the collective knowledge of the group.

A general strategy session is a variation on the counter-strategy session, where the sales team focuses on each competitor in succession, outlines their strengths and weaknesses, and develops overall global tactics to counteract the competitor's strengths and exploit their weaknesses. Care must be taken when analyzing the competitor's strategy not to be too profound for often the competitor's strategy, if there is one, is quite superficial.

Another variation is to analyze a specific account and develop a group strategy to capture it. Often it is both helpful and wise to bring a sales trainer or consultant to these sessions. To get the most from these sessions no idea should be judged or

[3]Holden, *"Building A Selling Machine,"* The Holden ATE Newsletter, (Schaumberg, IL: Holden Corporation, Winter, 1983.)

suppressed. Wild and free thinking is appropriate for this process. By relinquishing criticism, fresh light may be shed on the solution. Illogical thinking often provides logical results. Especially when the obvious is obviously not obvious.

CHAPTER

(48)

Participation is the panacea for a sales conference

The sales manager is responsible for the sales conference. Whether it is a small local area sales meeting or a large national or international conference, it must be properly planned. Effective planning at least 12 to 18 weeks in advance will invariably ensure success.

○ ### Set the Objective: A sales meeting should have an objective

Once a program is suggested, the objective must be established and it must be determined what the salespeople are supposed to get out of the meeting. Management's objective may be confidence in the sales force, a believable sales forecast, presentation of a new product, or a better trained sales force. You might arrange the meeting so the sales force can obtain training in selling or new products, have a chance to communicate with management, have a forum to air their concerns and problems, or an opportunity to discuss their successes and suggest what the company might do to increase its growth.

○ Set an Agenda: The agenda should address the needs for achieving the objective

Once the objectives are clear, a sales force needs assessment is made. A random sample of salespeople and all the sales managers should be interviewed. From this data, the attendees are determined from field and factory, and the agenda is established. The questions to be answered at the meeting are tabulated and the selected attendees are assigned specific questions they are responsible to answer. If sales training is on the agenda, a sales training company should be chosen and their requirements incorporated into the meeting plan.

If this is a company-wide public meeting, emotions will be charged. Anxiety will be evident, especially if role-playing is on the agenda. Some will feel challenged or threatened. Consequently, the participants should be involved early. Information should be solicited. Sending a questionnaire to each salesperson concerning the agenda and requesting their input is not unwarranted. Make it their sales conference—after all, it is.

One last point is if someone had the foresight to request critiques of the last sales meeting and saved them, review them prior to finalizing the agenda. Refer to these critiques as the conference is planned.

○ Draft a Theme: Develop a theme and get everyone to contribute

With the agenda in hand, draft a theme. Make sure it is catchy, motivational, humorous, or relevant.

"I got my THRILL at TRILLium." "I saw the light in Crete." "I survived the Bermuda Triangle." or "We test your parts."

Purchase hats or t-shirts embossed with it. Include it on all literature. Build the conference around it. This can make the difference between a dull meeting and a fun conference. Hype everything. Get a motivational speaker, the local high school band, Tom Selleck, or the Dallas Cowgirls. Whatever you do, do it with style. If the conference results in a well-motivated hyped-up salesforce, it will pay for itself tenfold in incremental sales.

○ *Coordinator Role: Use one effective coordinator to plan the meeting*

Now select a sales meeting coordinator. One person should be in charge of planning the meeting. As you would not divide account responsibilities for the same product in the same territory, you must not divide conference arrangement responsibilities. The coordinator must be competent. This is not a part-time job. Hire or contract a professional. Remember there are many mundane issues like location (is there an airport nearby?), group rates, transportation, hotel accommodations, meeting rooms, equipment, furniture, dinners, lunches, breakfasts, coffee, soft drinks, snacks, air conditioning or heat, electrical outlets, AC plugs, A/V equipment, extension cords, lights, pencils, paper, ashtrays, matches, recreational activities, and activities to keep the spouse or significant other busy, if they accompany the conference attendee. This is not a task for an amateur.

Once the location is established, hopefully someplace like Lake Tahoe, the Philippines, or a cruise ship on the Mediterranean, determine if it meets the budget. The budget is in two parts: direct conference costs and delayed sales. If your sales force is in control, you may delay sales but you will not lose any. If what you expect to accomplish with the conference will result in benefits in excess of the cost, continue. If the budget is short, sell your management like you sell your customer and obtain additional funding.

Do not confuse real issues with trivial matters at the meeting. Treat it like a sales situation and get to the point. Address the issues and focus on the theme. Do not miss the expectations of the sales force.

○ ## *Preparing the Meeting: Structure variety into the meeting*

Vary the format and avoid excessive lecturing. Consider discussion groups, peer groups, and role-playing.

In discussion groups, three to eight people talk over the lecture with a specific objective in mind. A spokesperson is identified to respond to the lecturer.

Peer groups are established to discuss problems encountered in the field. Their objective is to suggest solutions to management. It is not uncommon for management to participate in a peer group.

Any suggestions made must be addressed by management, preferably at the conference but certainly later. Failure to honestly evaluate and consider the solutions or respond to them will compromise management's credibility with the sales force.

Role-playing is the bane of many salespeople because they know that after a few minutes they are no longer playing. Sometimes by labeling role-plays as sales skits the anxiety level among salespeople decreases. Even though role-playing is a powerful sales training tool, no salesperson should be forced to participate. In role-playing, normally one subgroup of salespeople act as the customer, while another subgroup portrays the sales team. A variation on this method is for a third subgroup to impersonate the competitor. The results can be very enlightening.

If required by the agenda, workbooks or other handout materials should be prepared in advance and mailed to all attendees. This will save conference time and the salespeople will have a basic understanding of what will transpire as well as incremental knowledge about the subject at hand.

In lieu of, or in addition to, reading material, audio cassettes or video tapes could be sent. They are more effective than reading material if the objective is to stimulate the participants.

Audio-visual requirements must be carefully planned. Murphy attacks A/V equipment with glee, everything from AC plugs that do not match and AC cords that are too short to burned-out overhead-projector bulbs and screeching audio feedback. In spite of all these drawbacks, A/V equipment and flip charts are vital to the success of the conference.

To ensure effective use of A/V equipment, inspect the room prior to the meeting and make sure everything is in order. In addition to currently operating A/V equipment, check the air conditioning or heat, and the arrangement of tables and chairs. What is appropriate for encouraging group or cross discussion may not be suitable for A/V extravaganzas.

○ Conducting the Meeting: Make sure the serious part does not destroy the fun

The conference should begin in some wild, creative way, but eventually someone will start presenting serious information. If the engineer presenting product information is a droner or mumbler and puts even the most charged salesperson to sleep, as in the case of the customer demonstration, have a marketer give the presentation and have the engineer answer questions. If the marketer is a droner, make the marketer an engineer.

Lecturers often beget restlessness, even with visuals or question and answer sessions, because people's minds absorb data three times faster than most people can talk. This creates dead time and allows listeners' minds to wander. Therefore, lectures must be interspersed with participation or demonstrations.

Participation, especially discussion groups, must be part of the agenda. Role-playing and open forums also perk interest and stimulate the participants.

Demonstrations delight salespeople, especially if they go awry. If the product is portable, bring it to the conference and demonstrate it. If it doesn't do anything, show it. If it is a large system controlled by a computer, bring a terminal and modem and demonstrate the software. Demonstrations are stimulating.

In addition to all this activity, allow unstructured and free time. Even though people will get acquainted at cocktail parties or dinners, they also need time to think over and absorb what has been said by swimming or playing golf. Divide the conference day into two of the following three parts: lecture, participation, and free time. Lectures are always in the morning, free time is always in the afternoon, and participation is either after a lecture or before free time. Any other combination is ineffective. Special morning outings such as a fishing trip are an exception.

○ *The End: End the conference memorably*

End the conference with a fireworks display or a food fight and a critique sheet. Always develop a method to evaluate the meeting. Use a questionnaire or survey and allow time during the conference to complete it. If you expect the attendees to mail it back to you, good luck.

Two points to remember during sales conferences: first, at the start, introduce the coordinator and his or her assistants; don't assume everybody knows them. Second, during the sales conference, observe the sales force. This is a sales manager's opportunity to gain insight. Who is in control, who is participating or vacationing, helpful or disruptive, hiding or power seeking, team playing or individualistic, creative or catatonic, goal-oriented or lackadaisical, who has management potential or is a superstar (not necessarily mutually exclusive!), who is pessimistic or optimistic, complaining or supporting? Then ask yourself one question: "Was it all worth it?"[1]

[1]Alexander Hamilton Institute, *The Marketing Letter*, Vol. 2, No. 1, Apr. 1975, p. 6, and Vol. 4, No. 10, Jan. 1978, p. 6.

CHAPTER

(49)

Discontented salespeople get the job done

Some of the more successful salespeople think they dislike selling. Most people think salespeople are outgoing, persuasive, and energetic, but a good number appear introverted, mild-mannered, and less than energetic. One thing most salespeople have in common is the desire to win. But to be positioned to win, they often must do things they do not want to do. They are motivated by an all-consuming need for results, and sometimes the only way they can achieve the desired results is by doing things they do not like to do.

◯ Content vs. Discontent: Discontent inspires achievement

If salespeople are contented with their current selling style and results, they may not avail themselves of the opportunity to learn. Conversely, a discontented neophyte may be discontented because he or she is not a top performer. Consequently a concerted effort is made to learn at every opportunity. Motivation stems from discontent.

The salesperson's attitudes and values will not be easily changed by argument or debate if the emotional factors and rationale that support the behavior are strong. The only way to alter these attitudes and values is to change the behavior. Behavior is want-driven. If you want something bad enough, if necessary, you will change your behavior to get it. If you want something, it follows that you need it for some reason. It may be personal satisfaction, to keep a spouse happy, or for self-actualization in business. Therefore, a want is an unsatisfied need.

Motivation is a result of an unsatisfied need. Motivation causes you to act. If you are motivated to so something, it means you are not satisfied with the way things are, so you do something about them. This results in learning. With learning comes behavioral change. With behavioral change comes a change in attitudes and values.

On the other hand, mediocre salespeople often sell because they like the interpersonal activity and freedom of movement. These salespeople are normally satisfied with whatever results they get. Exposure or experience does not necessarily make a salesperson better. Unless properly motivated, they might learn nothing from repeating an experience such as selling.

If a salesperson does not believe in the job or the product, or if there is a conflict between what is being sold and what is believed right, proper, and dignified, then motivational methods have short-term benefits at best.

If not inspired to believe in the social importance of selling, or if selling to someone perceived to have no need or whose need could be better served with another product, or if the salesperson does not feel dignified putting his or her "foot in the door," then the salesperson will feel guilty or depressed once the motivation wears off.[1]

⭘ *Conflict vs. Perception: Resolve inner conflict by changing perception*

These salespeople may hate themselves. The sales manager can continue to fire them up by motivational means, but eventually the salespeople will quit.

---

[1]Leavitt, *Managerial Psychology*, p. 70.

There are three solutions to this problem: help the sales-people find another job, rationalize the issues to them so that they can reconcile their belief systems with what they are doing, or deal directly with the issues and resolve them, at least in their minds.

If the issue is one of psychological conflict between the need to do the job and the need to satisfy beliefs, then the conflict must be dealt with first. Conflict is a matter of percep-tion. It is not tangible; it exists because salespeople say it exists. Salespeople may have the necessary sales skills and know how to do everything right, but feel uncomfortable or undignified asking for the order. If they can be convinced that the customer not only expects but wants them to ask, they may see the situation in a new light. Now both needs are satisfied. Asking for the order solves the job need and knowing that the customer both wants and expects them to ask for the order will help them feel more comfortable. Their self-respect and dignity are compromised only if the customer resents the question.

Salespeople who feel society is condescending to salespeo-ple will never refer to themselves as salespeople but as cus-tomer engineers, marketing executives, or some other cover. If they learn to feel differently about being a salesperson or learn not to worry about what they think society thinks, they can overcome the conflict. This can be accomplished if they under-stand the importance of selling to society and that every suc-cessful person is a salesperson in one respect or another.

A conflict that exists between what the salesperson is selling and the competitor's product which is perceived as "better" can be resolved by discovering where the salesperson's product is better. It could be reliability, cost versus perform-ance, or a specific feature that provides a unique benefit. By focusing on what differentiates the product, he or she can overcome the feeling that the customer might be better served by the competitor.[2]

If he or she feels the customer does not actually need the product being sold, the conflict between doing what is "right" and making the sale can be resolved through rationalization. By rationalizing the actual need versus the selling benefit, conflict in terms of the value the customer receives can be eliminated. The value received may be coverage of future or anticipated needs. Not actually knowing why customers buy but assuming the customers know what they are doing is a plausible ra-

[2]Ibid., p. 48.

tionalization. The prestige of owning the product, assuming the product is prestigious, is another value received.

Motivational methods are powerful influences on salespeople only if job conflict is not an issue. Yet sometimes motivation is a result of a discomfort. Results can also be driven by discontent. Consequently discontented salespeople get things done.

○ ## Discontent vs. Motivation: Discontent can be a temporary motivation

For example, if you believe it is not whether you win or lose but how you play the game that matters, and someone tells you that winning is really all that matters, you will not necessarily change your attitudes or values because of this revelation. You may win a few sales and lose a few, but be satisfied with the overall results. One day you may see a house in an expensive area of town that your spouse decides you want. To get it you will need to increase your income by earning more sales commissions. To earn the additional sales commissions you have to win more sales. You are now discontented because you want something. Your discontent is driven by your personal need, the satisfaction of owning the new, more expensive house.

Therefore you are motivated to act. You change your behavior and fight for every sale. Your lackadaisical attitude toward winning changes. Your value system changes. You learn to sell differently. You buy the house and then go right back to your old ways so you can find the time to enjoy the new house. Unfortunately for your company, your discontent is now driven by the desire to spend time in your new house. Your motivation to win in every sales situation is now replaced by a motivation to get more free time.

The novices in the meantime have passed you by in terms of sales ability because their primary motivation is to win the sale. They kept taking advantage of every opportunity to learn because of their discontent. Their state of mind was such that they saw each objection, resistance, and obstacle as a challenge or rival to be conquered. Once on top, they are no longer novices and are driven by the discomfort that would result if they were not on top. They want to stay there.

Motivation by monetary reward has short-term benefits but is not the primary reason salespeople are successful. Successful salespeople are victorious because they are discontented. Discontent in this context does not equal frustration and assumes the person is secure.

Salespeople do not have to get into emotional uproars to sell. If they are comfortable and confident about their basic needs, they will be objective in their approach to selling. They will concentrate their energies on the job of selling and do so objectively. If they are dissatisfied with their sales skills or a particular selling situation they will be motivated.

The best motivation for a salesperson is self-motivation driven by discontent. A good sales manager will help the salespeople develop their own dissatisfaction about making the sale, since discontented salespeople get sales.[3]

[3]Ibid., p. 53.

CHAPTER

50

Create sales and customers

Although 80 percent of your company's business may come from 20 percent of your customers, the other 80 percent are also important. Although volume purchases from key accounts is mandatory if you hope to control the market, they are not necessarily the only route to satisfactory profits. Your company may make major concessions to penetrate key volume accounts, yet smaller accounts often represent lucrative and profitable business. Smaller companies and foreign accounts may carry you through a business slump when the majors are not buying.

Smaller accounts may be influential with larger accounts, and may eventually become bigger accounts. A small account may be just what you need to make your sales forecast. A company that concentrates only on major accounts and avoids small accounts may be successful in the short term but is vulnerable over the long term.

○ ***Account Classification: Classify your accounts and concentrate on the important ones***

A good territorial strategy is to classify your accounts and develop a sales strategy for each classification. The first class of accounts are those customers who have already purchased your product. These accounts must be nurtured, expanded, maintained, and loved. If you lose one of these accounts you may well lose your job.

The second class of accounts is everybody else. "Everybody else" may be further subdivided into four categories. Key accounts are the first category and are normally prestigious Fortune 500 companies, singled out by your management for penetration. These accounts will represent heavy repeat business for your company.

The second category comprises flagship accounts. These are accounts you have targeted for penetration due to their reputation, or because they are influential with other accounts. For example, a scientific laboratory may have a need for just one of your products but, by virtue of that purchase and their prestige within the industry, may facilitate other sales for you in other companies. A flagship account may also represent a showcase for your product, especially if it affords a place for the industry to see and hear about it and become familiar with it.

The third category is a test site. This account will test a new product for you and give you feedback concerning its performance. These sites often develop into key accounts. The last category is whoever is left.

○ ***Account Qualification: Assess your accounts to determine the time to spend on each***

Once you have classified and categorized your accounts, you must qualify them to determine which should become sales targets and how much time you should devote to each. Account qualification is a dynamic process. First, establish the qualification criteria and apply it to all accounts equally. Then periodically check each account against the criteria to re-qualify them.

There are three qualification groups. Group A represents any account that will purchase products within a reasonable time, usually one time period. Group B are accounts that will not purchase for a longer time, but within two time periods. Group C represents accounts with low priority emphasis.

Once you have grouped the accounts for efficient and effective use of your time, address the accounts that represent real business. You have only so much time available and can only focus on a finite number of sales situations in one time period. Obviously you should focus on short-term business, but not to the exclusion of maintaining the pulse of other accounts.

To determine which accounts represent real business, you must establish the group qualification criteria. This step is the foundation of your sales campaign because it will establish where you will be expending a good deal of your time and effort. Each account in each group should be tested with this criteria and be regrouped accordingly.

Each salesperson will have his own qualification criteria and each territory may dictate its own. Some gross elements of judgment are: location, your chances of capturing the account, their budget, funding, and chances of being able to buy, their overall financial condition, and the short and long term business potential. Also consider the compatibility of your product and their application, the compatibility of philosophy between your two companies, and their competency in using the product. Finally, determine the timing of the sale or delivery and why that timing is important.

Each criterion may then be weighted to reflect its relative importance. Once you establish the weighted criteria, they must not change. For this qualification process to work, both the criteria and weighting must remain constant as you test each account. If an element is added to or removed from the list, or a weight is changed, all customers must be retested.

◯ *Account Activity: Maintain contact with your accounts*

A good rule of thumb is to visit current customers at least once a month unless they are in Group A. Group A accounts should be visited weekly or daily if necessary. Group B accounts should be visited monthly. Contact should be maintained with Group C accounts by telephone or an occasional quarterly visit.

When you deal with your current customers, you are in a maintenance or hand holding mode. You will be building additional business based on favorable attitudes that already exist. When a current customer becomes a Group A account, you will be especially vulnerable to attack from your competition. Strong support and personal attention will be necessary to keep the customer content and happy with the relationship. Your objective is to preserve and deepen their satisfaction with the status quo.

With everybody except current customers in Group A, you are not maintaining a relationship but developing one. This selling is more difficult than selling to an established account. These new accounts may not view you or your product favorably. They will probably resist change, especially if they are buying from your competitor. The atmosphere may be unfriendly. You may be rebuffed repeatedly, and common courtesy may be lacking. You will need time, talent, resourcefulness, and ingenuity to win. For this reason it is important to ensure you do not spend all your time with the current or friendly accounts. It is the incremental business from *everybody else* that ultimately results in growth for your company.

By classifying and qualifying your customers and potential customers in the manner suggested in Figure 7, you will be better able to manage your territory efficiently, and less likely to miss out on new sales opportunities.

ACCOUNT CLASSIFICATIONS

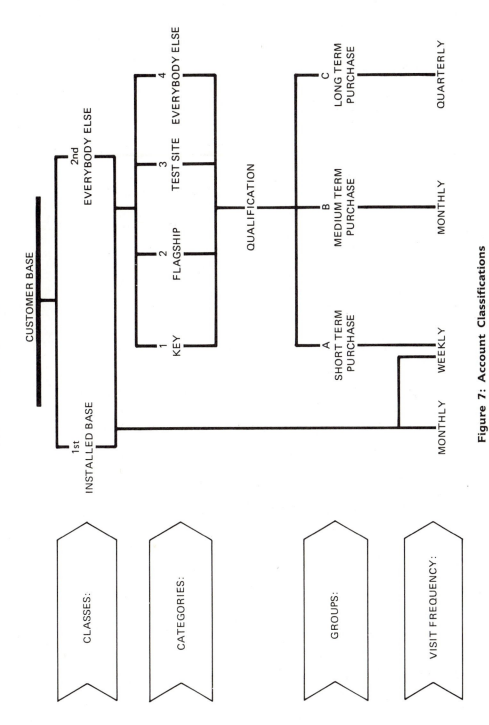

Figure 7: Account Classifications

CHAPTER

(51)

One person must be in charge

The Russians believe in dual command. Each army unit has a military officer and a political commissar who work in tandem and share the authority. This is true for each echelon of the organization. A dual command structure of this nature in sales can lead to disaster. Only one person can be responsible to execute the sales strategy. Unity of command is essential for success.

○ Dynamic Organization: Adapt your sales organization to changing sales situations

A high technology company may start out with a sales force that sells the product to target accounts or whoever will buy it. As new products are introduced, the sales force initially sells multiple products, but sales eventually may be structured along independent product lines.

As the product lines grow, since different industries have different demands, the sales force that was specialized by territory, respecializes by customer or industrial group. Each focused industrial sales group sells all products to a specific industry such as automotive, computer, telecommunication, and other specialized market segments. Eventually, certain customers will have a desire for all products and require a single point of contact to cater to their needs. This results in a national accounts program where designated individuals are responsible for planning and organizing the sales effort for a particular account. This is the natural evolution or development of a high technology sales force. The transitions are never made without confusion, difficulty, and super human effort.

○ ### New vs. Old Accounts: Be aware of the differences between selling to old accounts and new accounts

Another problem high technology companies face is selling to existing customers versus selling to new accounts. The skills required are different. The new account salesperson must exercise creativity while the existing or maintenance account salesperson must keep the customer happy. The maintenance salesperson focuses on reasons not to change; the new account salesperson focuses on reasons to change. When these individual sales focuses are mixed with product and industry specialization and national accounts, a complex situation exists. The solution to control the situation is not always obvious.

The solution, although not obvious for all the involvements, has one *sine qua non* of success: account sales responsibilities should not be divided. *One person must be in charge.*

Division of the sales force along product or industry lines is immaterial to the sales process and is a function of the company's business or marketing strategy. What is material is that the local salesperson responsible for a given account is—in actual fact—totally responsible with full authority. Any third party involved, such as a national accounts person or a strategic account person, must complement the local salesperson's efforts, and the salesperson must perceive the value in it. This does not happen automatically.

If your objective is to develop new accounts, whether you organize by any of the organizational parameters is irrelevant as long as you focus on change for creating customers. People do not like to change. If the customer is happy with your competitor, you will have to create discontent.

If your objective is to keep and foster existing accounts, organize by customer or industry in different territories, but with one salesperson selling all generically similar products to an account. You will be dealing with people who are buying your product and whose habits are conducive to such activity. The focus is on fear of change, and reluctance to find new suppliers. Your objective is to keep the customer happy in his relationship with your company. To do this, keep abreast of the customer's application in detail, and develop tactics capable of warding off competitive thrusts. Your focus is constancy.

The job of selling to existing accounts is different from finding and selling to new accounts. The basic selling skills are unchanged but the new accounts require special emphasis on strategy. It requires a creative strategist capable of developing original approaches to unseat entrenched competitors and capture new accounts.

Creative new account strategists are often mavericks whose beguiling, brilliant, conniving selling genius may make them loners rather than team players. In the case of repeat business from existing accounts, the focus is more on teamwork. Sales creativity may be tempered by the achievement of common goals. Performance is balanced with stability. This involves a combination of people working toward a common objective. The customers are not only buying your product; they are buying into your company. They are buying your experience, expertise, reputation, and support. These are important factors for existing customers, and the maintenance salesperson must understand them well.

○ *Strategic Account Management: Develop a strategy for new account sales*

Since people with the qualities sought for new account sales are scarce, many companies institute major new account selling programs with strategic focus to coordinate multiple facilities of target new accounts through the local salespeople.

Communication between the strategic account manager and the local sales organization is vital to the success of such a program.

The strategic accounts manager has different goals than the local salesperson. The local salesperson's responsibility is to get the order. The strategic account manager's objective is to strategize the account, planning and organizing the sales effort on a national or international scale. Emphasis is on developing new accounts by supporting the local sales force with strategies and tactics.

The strategic accounts manager identifies target new accounts, contacts the influencers in the account, analyzes the account, and develops a sales strategy in terms of the customer rather than the product or products. He or she integrates management into the sales process early. A relationship with the top executives is developed so that they see value in doing business together. If not already involved, the local salesperson is brought into the picture at each facility, after qualifying the account but before developing the strategy.

After joint development of the strategy, the local salesperson executes the strategy tactically with the help of the strategic accounts manager. By strategizing the account on a national or worldwide basis, the local sales people will have a better overall understanding of a complex corporation and the assistance of a strategist in developing and executing a sales strategy. This will enhance the local salespeoples' ability to book orders, capture new accounts, and defeat the competitors. They will perceive the value in this approach and support the strategic account manager. The local salespeople will still be 100 percent responsible for and receive 100 percent credit for the sale.

The advantage of the strategic accounts manager approach to developing new accounts is reduced conflict and less confusion about responsibilities. The strategic accounts manager is not responsible for the sale and is in a staff position to assist the local salesperson. This person is not on a commission or incentive program directly related to a particular sale but is paid a salary and measured on his or her ability to facilitate new account penetration. A bonus may be paid but it will be based on overall account performance.

Through a strategic new account program, as defined, the problems associated with twin sales forces are minimized.

The support to local salespeople to enhance their ability to create customers is realized and the transition from new account development to maintenance account selling is smooth and does not disturb the customer.

The local salespeople and managers will support rather than sabotage the program because it provides real value and is not threatening. Finally, it fixes the incremental cost of new account penetration, and does not divert the efforts of the local salespeople from the mainstream business. The objective of the strategic account manager is to create new customers.

○ National Account Management: Facilitate old accounts management

For maintenance accounts, a national account program may be established. The national account program differs from the strategic account program in that the focus is evaluation of the effectiveness of account support, repeat business generation, and the quality of communication among the customer's facilities, the customer's corporate headquarters, and the national account manager's company. National account managers represent their company in the account. They give guidance and direction. They maintain contacts throughout the corporation, and manage relationships and prospects for new applications for the products. In times of trouble they may head up a focused customer service task force. Their objective is not to make sales, which is the local salesperson's job, but to build relationships that lead to orders.

They pay pragmatic attention to service, quality, and reliability issues around their products. They find ways to get the customer involved in their company because constant customer contact leads to product improvements and competitive data acquisition. The relationship develops naturally and informally.

The job, like the strategic account manager's job, is a staff position that provides value to both the customer and the local salesperson. The objective of the national account manager is to keep customers.

○ Account Consultants: Account consultants counsel accounts

A variation on the strategic and national account programs is the account consultant. If a group of customers are geographically scattered, have annual sales in the millions of dollars, and purchase different products from the same supplier, account consultants may be assigned to each customer.

Account consultants do not have sales quotas. They are primarily concerned with enhancing the customer's profits by counseling them in improving operations through their business and the purchase and application of the most profitable mix of products and services. They enhance the profits of their own company by finding new areas in the customer's company to facilitate the sale of their product or service. Essentially account consultants are problem solvers whose methods foster heavy repeat business.

They may conduct executive education programs and technology-oriented seminars. They will work with finance on return on investment and cost of ownership calculations. They offer the local sales force headquarters intelligence, leads, and early warnings of potential problems. Account consultants focus on the day to day operations and are operational rather than strategic in the nature of their efforts.

The effectiveness of account programs, strategic, national, or consultive, depend on attitude and teamwork. Selling to large accounts with buying influences at more than one location usually demands the efforts of more than one person. Yet only one, the local salesperson, should be in charge. The key account program managers sell horizontally, across, or through the total account, while the local salesperson sells vertically by product to satisfy specific needs. The key account managers have the *savoir-faire* necessary to act as a catalyst for new business. The local salespeople use this resource to obtain the incremental business.[1]

[1]The following were referenced in developing this chapter:
*George N. Kahn and Abraham Schuckman, *"Specialize Your Salesmen!"*, (Harvard Business Review) January-February 1961.
*Alexander Hamilton Institute, *The Marketig Letter*, Vol. 3, No. 11, April 1976, p. 4, Vol. 4, No. 2, May 1977, p. 3 and Vol. 4, No. 11, Oct. 1977, p. 3.
*Jim Holden, *"Building a Selling Machine"*, The Holden ATE News Letter, (Schaumberg, IL: Holden Corporation, Winter 1983).

(52)

Let salespeople break the bank

A sales quota is a standard for measuring achievement in a sales organization. Companies set sales quotas to specify what a salesperson is expected to book during a specific period. Incentive or compensation is at least partially related to the salesperson's degree of quota fulfillment. The quota is usually set higher than the product build and booking plan. This is done in an effort to ensure the bookings plan is met and to develop backlog.

○ Quotas: Sales quotas can be beneficial or otherwise

Sales quota incentive plans look a lot simpler than they are. Often they generate game playing where salespeople complain that managers raise their quotas or move their territories if they are successful. The managers then accuse the salespeople of "sandbagging" or forecasting less business than is achievable in an attempt to realize a low quota.

Salespeople complain because quotas are inaccurate, do not reflect the actual business in the territory, are set too high, or are set without the involvement of the sales force. Quotas sometimes engender rivalry instead of cooperation within the sales force. Salespeople intrude on one another's territory or make incentive claims for equipment purchased in one territory but shipped to another. Finally, quotas may result in shipping too much product to a customer to realize short-term sales goals, at the expense of long-term customer relations.

If the quota system is simple it has the most positive effect. If the quota plan is so complicated that neither middle management nor the salespeople can manage or easily understand it, salespeople resign or sales managers ignore it and use their own simplified systems.

Different people respond to sales quotas in different ways. Some are stimulated to their highest efficiency; others are discouraged. If the quota is devised intelligently and compensation is fairly adjusted to performance, most salespeople will accept it. An intelligent quota combines top management sales estimates as goals, with sales territory or "grass root" estimates to help arrive at a sales plan, which is then translated into a quota.

The quota is not imposed on the sales force, but neither is it negotiated. Management should sell it to the sales force. Once convinced they can personally gain and that the quota is fair, the salespeople will be satisfied and will drive to meet or exceed it.

○ *Incentive Plans: Incentive plans should provide real incentive*

The incentive amount must be properly set. If the incentive is such that the salespeople reach their comfort level before they attain the quota, they may not work as hard as they should or they may appear to be working hard yet not achieve the desired booking results. One solution is to cut the territory. After the appropriate histrionics they will go out and meet the quota, as long as the quota incentive plan is competitive. If they still reach their comfort level before reaching their quota, cut the territory again.

Territories should also be split if optimum account coverage cannot be achieved by a single salesperson. The territory should not be cut just because the salesperson's earnings are high. If earnings are too high, rethink the incentive plan in terms of changing the incentive multiplier as a percent of volume, or effort required to reach the quota.

There are reasons, other than economic or product difficulties, that result in quotas being missed. Failure to meet quotas may be due to poor salespeople, in which case they should be reassigned. Some salespeople may not understand their objectives or know exactly what to do, in which case their manager should be reassigned. They may not know how to do it, in which case they should be trained. They may not want to do it, in which case they must be motivated or otherwise convinced they want to do it.

On the other hand, if the compensation plan is wrong, the salespeople will not work as their most productive selves or they will go to the competition. The marketplace for high technology salespeople is highly competitive.

Since the sales incentive is normally based on dollar volume, salespeople will try to increase the dollar volume at existing accounts. It is generally easier to obtain repeat business from friendly accounts than it is to fight for the competitor's accounts or prospect for new accounts. Everything else being equal, salespeople selling multiple products will tend to push the higher ticket items because their net compensation for the effort will usually be greater.

Additionally, salespeople who are not particularly motivated to push profitable products or increase the company's profits will sell the products the buyers see as good buys, and will petition the factory for discounts as the only way to get the order for the others.

Quota-incentive schemes drive salespeople to sell, but they sometimes ignore administrative duties, service to the customer, or follow-up activities, which are all so important in high technology sales.

One way of solving this problem is to devise incentive plans that drive salespeople to accomplish the company's objectives as well as meet the quota. These incentive plan and compensation packages are based on both volume and specific objectives such as profitability, new accounts, administrative work, market intelligence, and other management objectives.

The objective of these quota-incentive plans is to motivate salespeople to work more intelligently rather than harder. The theory is that through these objective-oriented plans, dollar-volume sales increase, the salespeople earn more, selling costs as a percentage of sales go down, and profits increase. Unfortunately, it doesn't always work that way. Poor salespeople who do a good administrative job often increment their income while selling superstars lose income. The net result is often dissonance and an overall reduction in sales volume.

Some incentive plans are based on units rather than dollars, others have weighted quotas depending on the territory and customers, while still others reward repeat business at a lower incentive percentage than new business.

◯ *Effective Sales Compensation Plan: Include salary, incentive, and bonus*

The most effective sales compensation plan includes salary, incentive, and bonus payouts depending on the various objectives to be accomplished. The salary is set at the salespeoples' basic needs. The incentive plan is based solely on sales volume where the dollar incentive increases at a faster rate than the dollar sales volume increases.

The incentive is not capped or cut back just because a particular salesperson breaks the bank. That is exactly what the objective was. When the word gets out that a salesperson has broken the bank, every salesperson will be motivated to match his or her performance.

Such things as "bluebird" or "windfall" clauses written to reduce or eliminate the incentive for unexpected or unforecasted orders have no place in the sales incentive contract. If the earning potential must be capped or controlled then a reduced incentive multiplier should be employed.

To motivate salespeople to meet certain objectives set by management, a bonus plan based upon achieving them may be added to the incentive plan. A bonus may be paid for every new account booked to solve the new account penetration problem. A bonus may also be paid for low or no discounts. In this case, include in the discount calculation the actual discount from list price plus "freebies" such as free spare parts, application support, software packages, extended warranty, extra training, and the like. All these items have a cost that must be considered when calculating the actual discount. Special bonuses for selling particular products to particular accounts will solve the multiproduct problem or the target account penetration problem.

In the case of contested incentive between salespeople where multiple territories are involved in a single sales order, the incentive should be split 33 percent to the territory where the purchase order was negotiated, 33 percent to the territory to which the factory ships the product, and 34 percent at the discretion of the sales manager, to be awarded in full or part to the appropriate territory or territories. Another method is to pay 125 percent incentive for multiple territory orders where 75 percent is paid to the territory where the order is negotiated and 50 percent to the territory to which the equipment is shipped. Both these schemes reduce inter-territory squabbles.

Administrative issues such as timely reports and market intelligence are considered during the salary review. If unsatisfactory, the base pay increase or lack thereof should reflect this. This type of plan is fair, easy to understand, motivational, and manageable. It accomplishes the management objectives and should result in the desired sales volume.

By paying a portion of the incentive when the order books and the balance after the customer has taken title to the equipment, the salesperson is motivated to follow up and assist the factory in obtaining customer acceptance of the product or system.

○ *Recognize Salespeople: Give public as well as financial acknowledgment*

The salesperson is a manager of the company's customers, the company's lifeblood. The salesperson is not a great expense but a key resource to the company. This resource should be developed and nurtured but it should not be coddled. Lack of results in terms of sales volume is just cause for dismissal.

Once a plan similar to this one is implemented, prepare other rewards associated with recognition. Since a salesperson is an important company asset, make them feel influential and help them understand they are a valuable resource to the company.

Top performers should be recognized company-wide. This recognition will prompt increased efforts by the people recognized and by those who failed to meet the goals but want future recognition. If the salesperson is to feel he or she belongs to the company, consider stock options. These can lock good salespeople in and ensure their loyalty. More important, the salesperson starts thinking like an owner and becomes concerned with profits. Salespeople may share a common thinking but needs and aspirations will vary according to circumstances.

Above all, top management must not isolate itself but be visible and available, and communicate with the sales force.

In high technology, the success of a company is a function of the sales force. You do not have to have the best product to win. You do have to have the best sales force.[1]

[1]Alexander Hamilton Institute, *The Marketing Letter,* Vol. 2, No. 2, May 1975, p. 3, Vol. 3, No. 8, Nov. 1976, p. 3, Vol. 4, No. 6, Sept. 1977, p. 7 and Vol. 4, No. 7, Oct. 1977, p. 4.

CHAPTER

(53)

A sales forecast
is never wrong

Accurate sales forecasting from the sales force is a myth. No salesperson can accurately predict sales. There are too many variables and other factors affecting the outcome.

○ The Sales Forecast: Predict who will buy what and when

Salespeople can provide a list of prospects and categorize them in terms of their probability of buying during specific time frames. By integrating this data with a set of assumptions about the market, the economy, the company's marketing plan, and the competition, a bookings plan of anticipated business over a specific time period can be made. The quantification of the expected results of this plan is the sales forecast.

The purpose of the sales forecast is to test the adequacy of the assumptions made and actions planned against the expected results, and direct attention to the need for changes. Therefore the sales forecast can never be wrong. The actions or database assumptions can be wrong. If the forecast is not being met and the assumptions are thought to be valid, then the actions taken to achieve the forecast must be wrong.

Constantly readjusting the forecast will not solve the problem. If a company is not meeting their forecast they have four choices: change the price, change the product, increase the selling effort (people, promotion or territory), or change the forecast. If the last choice is implemented it does not indicate an error in the sales forecast; it confirms poor planning. Rather than changing the forecast, find out where you are going wrong and correct it. If you are exceeding the forecast, by all means change it, but also find out why it was low in the first place.[1]

⃝   *The Prospect List: Customers likely to buy what and when*

The field sales prospect list, which supports the field sales forecast, is normally required monthly or quarterly. The prospect list records the products, different configurations, dollar amounts, customers, locations, and the month or period in which the booking is likely to take place.

A sample confidence key of high, medium, and low is listed with each prospect. High means the order will be placed this period. Medium indicates the order is possible this period but definite next period. Low implies the order will not be placed for at least two more periods. More elaborate keys may be used if desired. Competitors may be listed and a remarks section may be included.

The prospect list should be updated at the agreed interval. Once a prospect is listed it should remain on the report for the full business period or year as a means of tracking activity. If this is the case, two more categories may be added to the key: booked and lost.

The more complex the key, the less useful it will be. Often, percent confidence figures are used, but each salesperson and manager will interpret them differently. What is 60 percent confidence to one person may be 80 percent to another.

[1]Klaus, *Marketing by Objective,* (Referenced).

Sometimes budgeting or funding information is also added to the list. The essence of the prospect list is its quality. The less complicated or ambiguous it is, the better quality it will have. The prospect list should be discussed with the salesperson before being submitted to the factory. As sales manager, you may have to negotiate a revision of the figures up or down with the salespeople. Often this is a function of their past record, whether they were overly optimistic or pessimistic.

○ *Forecast Reviews: Review and adjust sales forecasts, but find out why the adjustments are necessary*

Many companies have quarterly sales forecasting reviews where the field prospect list, assumptions, and actual results are reviewed by the sales managers, financial executives, or division managers and marketing. Sometimes the salespeople also attend the quarterly forecast review. The result is an updated build plan and sales bookings forecast that represents the best thinking of the sales force and involved executives.

Forecast reviews and all meetings as well as paperwork should be short, infrequent and meaningful. Excessive paperwork or too many meetings can demoralize a sales force, become self-serving and waste valuable time.

When possible, meetings should be planned in advance or scheduled regularly at specific times so salespeople are aware of them and can schedule their sales activities around them. Frequent surprise meetings result in missed customer commitments. All meetings should have a specific purpose, an agenda, a time limit, and in the case of large groups a facilitator to keep things on track and discourage digression. During the presentation all questions (except for points of clarification) should be noted but held until the end of the presentation.

The following are four types of meetings common in sales:

MEETING	PURPOSE	PROCEDURE
• *Forecast review*	• *Assess progress* • *Set future direction*	• *Reconcile forecast and bookings* • *Review competition* • *Identify issues*

MEETING	PURPOSE	PROCEDURE
		• *Propose strategy* • *Define follow-up*
• *Support session*	• *Provide support and direction* • *Enhance accountability*	• *Review historical issues* • *Review performance* • *Reconcile objectives* • *Discuss new issues* • *Resolve problems*
• *Decision meeting*	• *Problem solving* • *Proposal or issue presentation and clarification* • *Decision or resolution*	• *Present proposal on issue* • *Review alternatives* • *Present recommendations* • *Clarify as necessary* • *Discuss concerns and inputs* • *Agree on: follow-up* *—Implementation* *—Rejection*
• *Staff meeting*	• *General information dissemination* • *Generic issue identification and resolution*	• *Review open issues from last meeting* • *Discuss new issues* • *Make decisions* • *Assign accountability for issue resolution*

Sometimes a strategy session is held after a forecast review to identify the necessary actions and resources required to meet the sales forecast.

The important thing to remember is that for a given set of assumptions the forecast should not change substantially. What should change is the action required to achieve it.

The salesperson's job is to provide a well-thought-out field prospect list by asking the customer the right question at the right time. The quality of the prospect list is affected by customer funding issues, by calibrating the inputs from the account, by the likelihood of multiple orders, and by gut feelings. The manager's job is to qualify the prospect list to meet the company's bookings forecast.

CHAPTER

$$\textbf{(54)}$$

Sell the factory like you sell the customer

"If salespeople are well organized, they will spend 20 percent of their time selling and 80 percent on the things that don't matter. If a company could relieve the sales force of 20 percent of the non-productive work and the sales force used that time to sell, it would be like doubling the sales force," or so says Gunther Klaus.[1]

Unfortunately, this is difficult to do. Often the sales force is concerned with customers after-sales support, which is important because support from the factory is not always forthcoming. One of the biggest problems in communicating with the factory is getting them to understand what sales really needs, and then getting the data back to the salespeople in a timely manner.

[1]Klaus, *Marketing by Objective*, (Referenced).

○ ### The Forgotten Sell: Often salespeople forget to sell the factory on the customer's order

Factory people do not understand what it takes to be a salesperson. Gunther goes on to say, "Anyone can produce the product or count the beans. The trick is to sell the product. A similar statement was once made by a young advertising executive in Victorian England, who said, "Any fool can make soap; it takes a clever man to sell it."

Factory support people often do not understand the difficulty in selling. Their support is often less than enthusiastic.

Yet in any sales organization there are those salespeople who get almost unbelievable support from the factory. Their proposals arrive on time and cover in detail those product benefits that will spell success. They are able to get special quotes quickly. Their promises to customers are always kept because the data they get from the factory is accurate.

Others almost never get cooperation. Their proposals are often late and incomplete; their promises to customers are often broken, and instead of looking like a professional, they and the company develop a poor image in the eye of the customer. These salespeople will always appear mediocre because they forget to sell the factory like they sell the customer … the forgotten sell.[2]

These salespeople, when dealing with the factory, will tell when they should sell, talk when they should listen, fail to get a commitment, and not follow up on their commitments. They have total control of the customer situation and little control of the factory. This is a success-limiting situation.

○ ### Factory Communications: Give the factory as much documentation as you give the customer

If it weren't for you:
"If my quota weren't so unrealistic, I'd be top salesman."
"If the factory would follow up, we wouldn't have this problem."

[2]Burge, *Sales Training News Letter,* (Referenced).

"If they would answer my telexes, we wouldn't be in this mess."

"It's all marketing support's fault ..."

"If it weren't for me ..." would be a much better focus.

Poor me the loser:
"What a lousy day. Lost my suitcase, the plane was delayed at Kennedy 5 hours, and with the boss's busy schedule I *know* you'll say he is *too* busy to see me!"

Poor me the winner:
"Talk about a bad day. Lost my suitcase and my flight was delayed 5 hours. I know our boss is very busy but you sure would make my day if you could get me in, even for 5 minutes.

The factory says:
"The shipment will be delayed 12 weeks."

Bad news reaction:
"Can't you *ever* do anything right?"
"If they cancel the order it's all the factory's fault."

Bad news action:
"Thanks for letting me know, I'll alert my customer immediately. I am sure we can find a solution to the problem this late delivery may cause. So I can better communicate with the customer, what are the reasons for the slip?"

The factory makes the statement, "I understand we lost the sale."

"They did it" response:
"Yeah, our competitor dropped their bid by 10 percent and the factory wouldn't discount. That's the reason we lost."

"I did it" response:
"I learned a lot on this one. I should have justified the price variance instead of trying to match the competitor's price."

The salesperson calls the factory. "I must have a 5 percent discount." The factory asks why. "To get the business. This is good business. Apparently you don't want the order!" The factory fails to approve the discount. Would this salesperson have said to the customer, "You have to buy my product."? When the customer asked why, would he or she have said, "To have the best system. If you don't want the best, then go to the competitor."

What should the salesperson do in this situation? First, get the factory involved early. Then create a desire in the factory to get the business. Give clear, concise justifications for the discount and give an honest assessment of what will happen if the sale is lost.

Get management involved with the account early and work closely with the product support person. This should result in no surprises and a very possible factory approval of the discount.

The customer is told the system will be shipped in 12 weeks, but the system is shipped late. When the salesperson tried to contact the marketing support person at the factory, he was out of the office. The salesperson needed delivery information immediately, so he transferred to the production manager and was told that the system would be out of Production in 12 weeks. He tells the customer 12 weeks delivery. What he failed to consider is that after the system leaves Production, it has to go through a two-week burn-in and acceptance test conducted by Quality Control.

The salesperson did not effectively communicate with the factory. He asked the wrong person the wrong question and, as a result, another broken promise resulted. This could have easily been avoided.

The customer asks for a proposal in three weeks and for a summary on the benefits of the product application. The proposal arrives two weeks late, without any discussion of the application. The customer sees another broken promise, but what really happened? When the salesperson called the factory, she told her support person that the customer would need a quote and a proposal in a few weeks and that she would get back with more details. Then she did nothing ... got busy on another account.

Three weeks later she got a call from the customer asking for her proposal; she then called the factory and found that nothing had been done. She exploded! What did she expect? The broken promise was really her fault.

How simple it could have been. First of all, some selling to get the support person enthused about her opportunity, then a clear definition of what was required, and the date for completion. Confirming the details of the commitment in writing, with effective follow up later, would have resulted in the commitment being kept.[3]

Professional salespeople generate enthusiasm in the factory, clearly explain what is to be done and are specific about commitments to the customer. They tie down the factory and get a commitment, then follow up. They sell the factory just the way they sell the customer.

Additionally, if management supports factory people going into the field and participating in selling situations, these people will quickly find out what selling is all about. They will develop a healthy respect for the salesperson, and this respect will result in agreeable relationships. Genuine and honest respect among the salesperson, the factory person, and the customer facilitates an atmosphere of harmony—the state of mind the Japanese call "wa."

[3]Ibid.

CHAPTER

(55)

"Got" business reports are important

A "got" business report tells the world why the order was won. The lost business report tells how the salesperson was outsold. Lost business reports are not onerous degrading self-criticisms but professional reports on how and why the business was lost. They give the factory important information on customer perceptions and product deficiencies, and help management comprehend the political component at work in the account.

Jim Holden says, "... The lost order report can be an opportunity for the salesperson to show diagnostic brilliance, identify competitors' strategies and tactics, and point the way to successful selling in the future."[1]

[1]Holden, *Building a Selling Machine*, (Referenced).

○ ***Effective Reports: Reports should analyze results, not merely announce them***

As for "got" business reports, it is the salesperson's opportunity to explain how the sale was won, to congratulate those who helped him secure the order, to help the factory better understand what wins orders, and to help the salesperson's peers in their sales efforts. These lost and got reports should not be lengthy dissertations, but one or two pages of concise statements, or bullets, concerning the issues. Ideally people will read them and then take action.

The simplest report lists the customer, the four or five major reasons why the order was won or lost, both the competitor's and salesperson's strategies, and the political intrigues at work. Most importantly, it recommends action to either reduce the chance of similar losses in the future or enhance the possibility of additional wins at the same or other accounts.

L'ideé fixeé among most company executives that salespeople avoid paperwork is unfounded. Salespeople avoid useless reports that result in no action, or have an ill-defined purpose. Salespeople have no time for exercises in futility. If the sales force is to respond with reports deemed important to management, then management must explain why they are important, acknowledge them, take action based on what they recommend, and disseminate the information. If management does this, the report will have validity, represent value to the salesperson, and become both popular and expected within the sales force.

○ ***Field Sales Support: Assign one factory person to each sales territory***

Communication between the factory and the field sales force often leaves much to be desired. The best method of dealing with communication issues is to assign people full time in the factory to support each sales territory. These people visit the territory regularly and have responsibility to facilitate clear communications between the factory and the field. He or she is asked to resolve management ambiguities as well as technical, contractual, and support issues. This person should have responsibility for the following items:

To ensure that requests between the territory and the factory are responded to in a timely manner by following up each communication and maintaining a communications log.

To review each sales quotation and provide guidance or feedback to the field.

To resolve issues for the salesperson that are blocking a booking due to credit, technical, contractual, or other purchase order items.

To follow up on all deliveries and act as an early warning system to the field for any problems.

To arrange customer visits, demonstrations, and presentations at the factory.

To "own" the customer when he or she visits the factory.

To assemble mobile factory task forces to audit existing problem accounts or help save or close an order. This task force must be capable of being assembled and dispatched on a moment's notice.

To ensure that the necessary reports (bookings, forecast, prospect lists, financial, marketing, service, and other information) are forthcoming from both sides.

To respond to the needs of the territory in all aspects of the business (management, service, sales, applications, marketing) within the framework of the factory's capabilities.

To help develop sales strategies multilaterally.

To assist in the development of good sales disciplines.

To motivate the field by ensuring that field feedback is utilized by the factory in evolving product strategies.

To interact with the territory in selecting and training new personnel where appropriate.

To conduct regular formal meetings between the territory and the factory. These meetings have the following purposes:

To review and assist in current sales situations.

To develop meaningful competitive and market analysis data and feedback.

To provide product or sales training.

To analyze performance versus goals.

To enhance allocation and utilization of both field and factory resources.

To follow up on incentive, quota, or bookings disputes.

Chris Sheldon of Genrad Europe says, "All these activities have value. When a company is winning and growing fast, if things look good it is easy to convince yourself that these niceties, which take much valuable time to produce, have very little value. But when things go bad or sales are lost, the tendency is to react."

Communications managed along the lines mentioned above will result in better factory-field communications and minimize the level of reactionary responses.

CHAPTER

(56)

If you can't perceive things that you can't see or hear, you don't belong in sales

Sam Rayburn had an indefinable knack for sensing the mood of the House of Representatives. He knew how far he could push, and what the vote would be if taken immediately. He never discussed or admitted he had the knack but once when asked about it he said, "If you can't feel things that you can't see or hear, you don't belong here."[1] This is also true for sales.

○ *Instinct and Intuition: Instinct and intuition are necessary to successful sales*

Never underestimate the value of your instinct or intuition. Instinct is a natural aptitude, tendency, or knack. Instinct,

[1]Caro, *The Path to Power*, p. 319.

whether innate or learned, stems from the interplay of maturation and the environment. Some people seem to have an instinct or knack for sales while others must work at it. Yet there is no limitation to the possibilities of instinct.

Intuition is decision-making without conscious reasoning. It is your gut feeling. Intuition is the unconscious processing of large amounts of data that your body senses. Intuition works around the conscious mind and is not prejudiced by it. Coupling this *sensed* and *processed* data with your experience base causes insight. You will suddenly arrive at a decision about something, someone, some place, or some circumstance. At this time your intuition is at work and is pure.

We've all heard that "initial impressions are important," and "rely on your first impression." Had Golda Meir relied on her first impressions, her intuition, and her instincts, instead of her advisors' observations and logic, her course of action would have been to mobilize her troops 24 hours earlier. Had she taken this course the Yom Kippur war casualty list would have been significantly abridged.

Hitler's Germany, along with the other Axis powers, must have appeared a formidable force to the declining British Empire. Logic dictated defeat for Britain.

Fortunately Winston Churchill was what C.G. Jung termed an extroverted intuitive, a man ruled by instinct. His thinking and feelings took a back seat to his intuition. Churchill used insight, not judgment, to take the course of action that united his country, inspired courage, and kindled enthusiasm against great odds.

Churchill's Chief of Imperial General Staff, Field Marshal Allenbrooke, the little-known yet principal architect of British war strategy, said, "He had a method of suddenly arriving at some decision as it were by intuition, without any kind of logical examination of the problem. ... He preferred to work by intuition and by impulse."[2]

First impressions are often reliable because the conscious mind has not yet had a chance to process other factors that may bias or distort the initial perception. The intuitive feeling is based on data. Customers may say all the right things so that you trust them, but their non-verbal activity or tone of voice may be sending a contradictory message. This dissonance will be processed by your unconscious if not your conscious self.

[2]Manchester, *The Last Lion*, pp. 18-19.

In essence, intuition and instinct are a function of perceptions, observations, experiences, and environment. Often the force of intuition and instinct will result in flashes of insight, but insight alone will not get you the sale.

○   ## Sensing the Environment: Pay attention to your feelings about a sale, even when you aren't sure why you have the feeling

Whether you sell based on logic or intuition, you must make a conscious decision on a course of action.

How many times have you been in a sales situation where logic said you were winning, everything was being done right, the buying signs you were taught to observe were present, yet you had this nagging feeling that something was wrong. Then suddenly the competitor got the order.

You thought you had done everything right yet you lost the sale, and what is more you knew you would lose the order all along, but you did not know why or how you knew.

Then as you wrote the lost business report, listing the logical reasons you lost, you suddenly remembered a look, a word, a feeling, a perception that told you you were losing or had lost. If you had stayed with it at that time, if you had pursued it, if you had consciously attempted to perceive what was happening, you might have saved the order. Instead you pursued a logical course. Yet logic is not always the best guide to a course of action in a sales situation.

Logic failed the Germans during World War II. When the Allied Forces executed the invasion of Normandy, an elaborate deception code named "Fortitude" did not fool Hitler, who predicted the Allies would land at Normandy, but, fortunately, it did fool his generals. They reasoned it was only logical that the Allies would land on the channel coast near Calais. As a result, only one German general, the prescient, one-legged Erich Marcks was at his post the night of the invasion. He had sensed that the time had come.[3]

Have you ever walked into a room full of people and sensed who supported you and who did not? Do you know when to ask

---

[3]Irving, *The Trail of the Fox*, pp. 341-347.

for the order, when not to ask, when to attack and when to withdraw, when to take "no" for an answer and when to feint? If your mind is in tune with your body, if you have mastered the ability to perceive things that are not obvious or apparent to the senses, if you've learned, as Sam Rayburn said, to "feel" things, you will significantly enhance your chances of success in a sales situation.

The reality of this *feeling*, this somewhat spiritual or mystical perception is unquestioned. Only through knowledge and training of the working of both mind and body can these perceptions surface.

○ ## Concentration: Concentrate on the whole of the sales process, not just the next step

In the words of Parmenides, "Thought and being belong together in their unity." Sam Rayburn probably had the ability to observe without consciously thinking about it. He had most likely mastered the art of concentration.

Instead of thinking of himself, his mind, and the environment as distinct and separate entities, he perceived unity. By perceiving yourself, mind and body, as unity and one with the environment, rather than as separate and antithetical, you will be able to concentrate on what is happening without rationalizing. You will sense moods, know where people stand, and feel the emotional tones. The gut feel will intensify.

When we think of ourselves, we think of our physical selves, our bodies. Since the mind has neither form nor substance, we do not think of our mind as our self. We normally train our bodies but rarely train our minds.

Common sense may tell you that Sam Rayburn's knack is mystical nonsense, but the trouble with common sense is that it bypasses the workings of the mind and focuses solely on the body. Since your body is only half of you, common sense is often only half true. Common sense once dictated a flat world in the center of the universe. We now know the world is round and at the edge of the universe. We can create life, but we have not even begun to understand, or accept for that matter, the power of the mind. We assume the primary function of the mind is to reason, when in fact it is to perceive.

If you concentrate, if you *look,* you will see much more than you ever *reasoned* possible. You can train your mind to concentrate by relaxing. Psychologist Eugene Gendlin teaches relaxation by focusing on *felt meaning,* which is not a pure emotion but the experiencing of what the emotional tones are about. If you are experiencing a certain emotion, find out where it is in your body and focus on it, experience it, understand it, and it will start to dissipate and you will relax.

Relaxation is also a function of bodily care. Eat and drink lightly when tense or in the heat of a sales battle. Exercise regularly, and don't sleep too much. It leads to lethargy.

Don't complain about all the things that go wrong. Think positively. Reinforce this positive thinking through rote. Look in the mirror each day and say, "I will master my emotions, I will be happy. I will persist until I succeed. I will be the greatest salesperson the world has ever known."

Once you are in a positive frame of mind and relaxed, practice concentration. The enemy of concentration is distraction. Distractions may be dealt with in several ways. The Aikidoists avoid distraction by concentrating their strength, what they call KI, two fingers below the navel. Mystics concentrate by consistently repeating a word or short phrase, what the Indians call a mantra. Through the use of a mantra the wandering mind can be disciplined to concentrate.

By contemplating an object, distraction may be ignored. If the distractions persist, then by yielding to them totally, the humiliation of defeat may stir the mind to new heights of concentration.

Concentration is the key to success in almost any endeavor. Imagine the concentration required of the receiver in American football, who is running at full speed along the sidelines pursued by would-be interceptors and tacklers. The receiver must not interfere with the pursuers, must find the football hurtling through the air, must catch it, must control it, must stay in bounds, and must continue to hold on to the ball during the inevitable bone-crushing tackle. All of this happens in the space of a few seconds through the din made by the tens of thousands screaming on-lookers. He must sense what to do. His senses have been tuned through countless practice sessions and intense concentration. At the moment of truth as his fingertips touch the ball there is no time for logical analysis.

The martial arts don, the mystic, the politician, the athlete, and the business person who masters the ability to concentrate will succeed. As a high technology salesperson, if you learn to relax your body and concentrate your mind, you will enhance your power of perception in a sales situation and become cognizant of what others do not perceive, or only sense unconsciously. This will give you a decided advantage.

If you are uncertain of the truth in this, remember Samuel Butler's famous dictum: "There is only one thing certain, namely that we have nothing certain; and therefore it is not certain that we can have nothing certain."

Topic Index

A

B

C

D

E

F

Financial justification, 82
Fox, influencing the, 206
Fox, profile of the, 204
Fox, the, 198
Freudian slips, 122

G

Ground rules, 147
Group communications, 48
Group sessions, 305

H

High technology products, 6
Holden training program, 301
Honesty, 23

I

Implementation plan, 257
Impression, bad first, 46
Incentive plans, 338
Individual relationships, 46
Influence, 97, 175, 197
Influence, coercive, 176
Influence, collaboration, 178
Influence, manipulation, 177
Influencing strategies, 180

P

Q

R

S

T

V

W

Y